DRIVE BUSINESS PERFORMANCE

DRIVE BUSINESS PERFORMANCE

Enabling a Culture of Intelligent Execution

BRUNO AZIZA & JOEY FITTS

WILEY

John Wiley & Sons, Inc.

Library of Congress Cataloging-in-Publication Data:

Aziza, Bruno, 1975-
   Drive business performance: enabling a culture of intelligent execution/Bruno Aziza, Joey Fitts.
       p.   cm. — (Microsoft executive leadership series)
   Includes index.
   ISBN 978-0-470-25955-9 (cloth)
   1. Management. 2. Performance. 3. Organizational effectiveness. 4. Industrial efficiency. I. Fitts, Joey, 1972-   II. Title.

   HD31.A984 2008
   658.4'013—dc22

                                                                    2008001411

Printed in the United States of America

10 9 8 7 6 5 4 3 2 1

This book is dedicated to our families, without whose support, dedication and love we would have never been able to write it.

Juliana and Sophia, "Eu amo vocês do fundo do meu coração. Obrigado pela paciência e pelo carinho, vocês não imaginam como isso é importante para mim." – Joey

Jenny, "Je n'y serais jamais arrivé sans ta patience et ton soutien – à travers les longues nuits passées sur ce livre—merci." Sophie and Sam, "Je vous dis souvent que je suis très fier de vous – j'espère, qu'un jour, lorsque vous lirez ce livre, vous serez fier de moi aussi – je vous aime tous les trois très très fort." – Bruno

Microsoft Executive Leadership Series: Series Foreword

The Microsoft Executive Leadership Series provides leaders with inspiration and examples to consider when forming business strategies to stand the test of time. As the pace of change quickens and the influence of social demographics, the impact of educational reform, and the impetus of national interests evolve, organizations that understand and embrace these underlying forces can build strategy on solid ground. Increasingly, information technology is bridging social, educational, and international distances, and empowering people to perform at their fullest potential. Organizations that succeed in the enlightened use of technology will increasingly differentiate themselves in the marketplace for talent, raw materials, and customers.

I talk nearly every day to executives and policy makers grappling with issues like globalization, workforce evolution, and the impact of technology on people and processes. The idea for this series came from those conversations—we see it as a way to distill what we've learned as a company into actionable intelligence. The authors bring independent perspectives, expertise, and experience. We hope their insights will spark dialogues within organizations, among communities, and between partners about the critical relationship between people and technology in the workplace of the future.

I hope you enjoy this title in the Microsoft Executive Leadership Series and find it useful as you plan for the expected and unexpected developments ahead for your organization. It's our privilege and our commitment to be part of that conversation.

Daniel W. Rasmus

General Editor, Microsoft Executive Leadership Series

Titles in the Executive Leadership Series:

Drive Business Performance by Bruno Aziza & Joey Fitts, 2008.

Rules to Break and Laws to Follow by Don Peppers & Martha Rogers, 2008.

Generation Blend by Rob Salkowitz, 2008.

Uniting the Virtual Workforce by Karen Sobel Lojeski & Richard Reilly, 2008.

Contents

Foreword

by
Robert Kaplan and David P. Norton

"The key reason people care about performance management is because they want to execute their strategies. Strategy execution and results are the primary benefit of managing performance." With these words, Aziza and Fitts define their common ground with our (Kaplan-Norton) strategy management work. They and we recognize that strategic decisions must be translated into tactical decisions that, in turn, become operational decisions. To successfully execute strategy, companies must link strategy to operations so that the thousands of decisions made by front-line employees align well with the strategy that has been formulated at the top. But accomplishing this alignment is truly where the devil is in the details. Aziza and Fitts have articulated a feasible and proven path to achieve this alignment.

One of our key strategy management principles is to "make strategy everyone's job." This requires that the work force understands the strategy and, further, understands how their local, everyday decisions can contribute to successful strategy implementation. Aziza and Fitts take this idea a step further by introducing a "Culture of Performance." They show how organizations like Energizer, the U.S. Department of Veteran's Affairs, and Fortis engage more employees in strategy execution by giving them the information, tools, and processes they need to support their decision making. Engaging informed and empowered employees creates successful results and sustainable competitive advantage.

The authors present a pragmatic methodology that builds capabilities around three key processes: monitor, analyze, and plan. They understand that a monolithic "cookie-cutter" approach can not succeed. The authors introduce a six stage framework to help organizations tailor an approach to their unique needs.

We appreciate the contribution Aziza and Fitts have made to build upon existing tested and proven approaches, like the Balanced Scorecard, to move the field of performance management forward in important new directions.

Boston, MA (USA)

January 2008

Dr. Kaplan is Baker Foundation Professor, Harvard Business School, and Chairman of Professional Practice at Palladium Group, Inc. Dr. Norton is Founder and Director, Palladium Group, Inc.

Preface

IMPROVING PERFORMANCE IS CENTRAL TO SUCCESS

Organizations seeking to drive business performance and lead in their markets must develop a culture of intelligent execution. The act of execution is decision making, and better execution comes from better decision-making abilities. Organizations that can improve these capabilities across their organization will outperform those that don't.

In the first decade of the twenty-first century, the business landscape is evolving at an unprecedented pace. We find ourselves in an increasingly global economy, facing a steady stream of new competitors, new fields of play, and emerging markets. Customers are continuously offered new products and services, compelling value propositions, and creative business models by the competition. The scope of opportunity and competition are both increasing, as is the scrutiny of the stock markets in assessing performance quarter to quarter. Companies are under constant pressure to do more with less and to deliver better returns than the competition. Public sector organizations face similar constraints as growing populations and increasing needs from the citizenship demand more from constrained budgets. Whether the goal is sustainable growth, entering new markets, or just to operate more efficiently, the key to achievement is in learning how to drive performance throughout an enterprise.

Performance management is a top priority for organizations of all types and sizes. Organizations are learning that you can cut costs only so much or acquire new business only so often. Eventually, the core of business productivity and shareholder value is the organization's ability to execute more effectively, with each person inside the company.

In order to execute more effectively with what they have, companies must develop capabilities to drive business performance. The ability to effectively manage performance can deliver the percentage points of increased margin, cost savings, customer satisfaction, growth, or market share, which can make the difference in outperforming the competition and increasing their stock price.

Developing performance management capabilities means changing the way people are empowered to make better decisions. It requires a transition from a restrictive, command-and-control approach to a management style that includes more participants in the performance management process. Involving more employees in the management discussion allows them to take greater ownership for their individual contributions, and empowers them to take responsibility for their performance, to be accountable for results, and thus deliver greater impact.

Just as telecommunications and Internet technologies have expanded from the executive suites to become powerful tools utilized across the organization, so have performance management capabilities become tools of competitive advantage across the enterprise. Just as it seems unfathomable for employees to communicate without a phone or for information workers to work without the Internet, so shall it seem unusual for people across the enterprise to be unable to manage their performance and understand their impact and strategic contribution.

ORGANIZATIONAL CHALLENGES

Many organizations are limited in their ability to compete because they lack the requisite capabilities for driving performance. These organizations report the following common symptoms:

- *Uninformed and uncertain.* Few companies have sufficient visibility into their operations to actually understand the verifiable factors that are impacting the business. As they operate without reliable information, they often propose the wrong solutions to the wrong problems.

- *Uncoordinated and underperforming.* Acting on gut feel and poor information, organizations disable both their strategies and their ability to execute. They operate in an uncoordinated fashion with multiple theories and missions, and with misaligned actions. Without alignment and accountability, they trip over themselves in the marketplace—with customers, partners, and even within their own teams. Unable to execute in a coordinated fashion, they underutilize their most strategic assets—their people and information.

- *Slow and inflexible.* Many companies are not effectively monitoring their business performance to know the factors that are impacting the business, and by the time they do recognize problems, they are inflexible and slothful in their response. They are unable to respond to changing conditions rapidly enough to capture opportunities, exploit competitive advantages, and identify and resolve issues that are limiting their ability to compete.

- *Unreliable planning and execution.* Some organizations are managing performance today by looking in the past. They are driving while looking out their rearview mirrors—on a foggy night, with shades on—because they haven't developed the capabilities to effectively manage information nor empowered their people to drive organizational performance proactively. Few can reliably make informed decisions on what changes to make to their organization and effectively forecast what the impact will be. When they do forecast, they often lack the confidence that the plan will be executed to deliver the anticipated results.

COMPETITIVE ADVANTAGE

For those who can manage performance, the benefits are tremendous. These organizations recognize distinct competitive advantage. Throughout this book, we cite several stories of exceptional results being realized by organizations which empower people and enable intelligent execution:

- *Clalit*: The world's second largest health maintenance organization (HMO) successfully brings information and people together to continue to set the standard for quality of service even as both the community of patients and quantity of competitors increase.

- *Energizer Holdings, Inc.*: The consumer goods leader's success is reflected in their stock price, "We're up over fivefold in the last five years. People have made that happen."[1] The company has changed its approach to empowering people to make "the majority of the organization's decisions ... thousands of day-to-day, week-to-week decisions that ultimately shape results. We recognized an opportunity to create an organization of 'difference makers.'"

- *Fortis*: Leading European banking and insurance provider places a strong emphasis on a "performance driven culture" including a company-wide aligned and calibrated reward model. The company achieved it's 5-year net profit goal in less than 3 years[2] and CEO Jean-Paul Votron was elected as "The Business Leader of the Year" by *BusinessWeek* in January 2007 [3]

- *Hilton Hotels*: Through advanced performance management capabilities and incentive alignment, Hilton continues to win on service. The stock has outperformed the S&P's hotel, restaurant, and leisure index since 2001, as well as that of the competition. Even as the number of facilities directly managed grew from 60 to over 300 in a single year, it successfully aligned and incented all 80,000 people across the organization to "Go for the Green" and pursue performance "perfection."

- *U.S. Department of Veteran's Affairs*: After receiving low quality of care scores and nearly being shut down by Congress, the VA has transformed itself and received modern accolades including two different Harvard awards for their performance management capabilities: "We've completely done a 180-degree change. The VA today is a leader in performance and a model of health care in the United States. It's an exemplary organization, and that's directly attributable to the performance management program."[4]

- *Wells Fargo*: Wells Fargo has a history of strong performance, beating the S&P 500 for a quarter of a century. It is one of only two financial institutions that is AAA rated. The company's cultural mantra, "Run it like you own it," both empowers employees and holds people accountable for results.

- *Whole Foods Market*: Whole Foods stock price has risen nearly 3,000% since its IPO in 1992 and its same-store sales growth is nearly triple the industry average. It is America's most profitable food retailer when measured by profit per square foot. The company applies its "Declaration of Interdependence" mission statement to run high performing teams.[5]

WHY WE WROTE THIS BOOK: A UNIQUE APPROACH

We wrote this book to share a framework that enables organizations to drive business performance—to improve their ability to manage their performance and to deliver better organizational results. This book is more than the result of a research project or a set of case study interviews. Our approach to the book has come from our direct experience and work developing solutions to organizational performance management challenges. We've heard the problems with managing performance directly from Fortune 500 companies and government organizations—and understand the specific challenges faced by their business managers, analysts, and information technology (IT) departments as they try to implement solutions to help them improve their performance. We've discussed the solutions with the usual suspects—the industry analysts who consider how best to approach solutions to performance management problems and the hardware, software, and service providers who are seeking to provide solutions. And every group we've worked with and talked to has its own slant on what's needed to manage performance effectively—each has a piece of the answer.

We captured what we have seen work repeatedly and in this book provide an easily digestible framework which readers can utilize within their own companies. Managing performance is not easy, but we provide specific guidance as to what capabilities organizations need to develop. The model is validated with multiple leading organizations around the world who share their insights on how they have succeeded, and the competitive advantage they are realizing as a result.

Fill the Gap

We also wrote this book to fill a gap in the literature on managing performance. Although many books have been written on performance management, they typically are either too technical to impart business value or too theoretical to provide prescriptive guidance for the reader to take action.

Many business books provide high level statements of value from a few leading organizations, but they lack concrete guidance on how the reader can take action to achieve the same results. These books are compelling to read but not much help in enabling others to try to replicate the success achieved in the case studies. Worse, they can make managing performance seem like a magical or overly complicated endeavor that only a few organizations have miraculously been able to do.

Technical books on performance management have the opposite problem. They are so full of jargon and industry terms that they are inaccessible. Since business leaders rarely read through all the detailed technical descriptions, the ideas are lost before they are adopted.

This book fills the gap.

Get Specific, Make It Actionable

In this book, we seek to ensure that we are specific in describing "how to get it done." First, we describe the business value delivered by performance management capabilities. Then we provide real-world examples of the competitive advantage organizations are experiencing. Next, we break these capabilities down into guiding themes an organization can follow to develop these capabilities. Then, we demystify performance management by removing much of the confusing jargon. Finally, we share some detailed guidance, including the recommended skills and assets needed for organizations to replicate top performers' results. Our goal is to provide a simple, actionable framework that any organization can adopt to more effectively manage performance.

We address questions such as:

- "How do I diagnose my organization's performance management capabilities? How can my organization improve its effectiveness in managing performance?"
- "What does it mean to be able to manage performance—what specifically do I need to be able to do to improve results?"
- "What's possible—how impactful can this be? How can performance management deliver competitive advantage?"
- "What specific skills and assets does an organization need to develop to manage performance more effectively?"
- "How can our organization increase agility, alignment, and accountability?"

We describe detailed best practices for keeping a finger on the pulse of the organization—tips for creating an aware and aligned organization (how to monitor). We also discuss how to deliver analytic capabilities across the organization so everyone is more informed and making better decisions (how to analyze). We discuss how to extend organizational planning, budgeting, and forecasting processes beyond the office of the CFO (how to plan). We explain how strategy execution can become an integrated exercise across the corporate body—so that the organization is coordinated and, as plans change, change is conducted in alignment across the entire organization. It's a collaborative and continuous process with dramatically improved results.

THE SIX STAGES OF PERFORMANCE MANAGEMENT VALUE

We describe six stages of performance management value which organizations that develop performance management capabilities can experience:

1. *Increase Visibility* with data that can be trusted, information that is shared, by execution that is aligned, and by results that are reported. With this visibility,

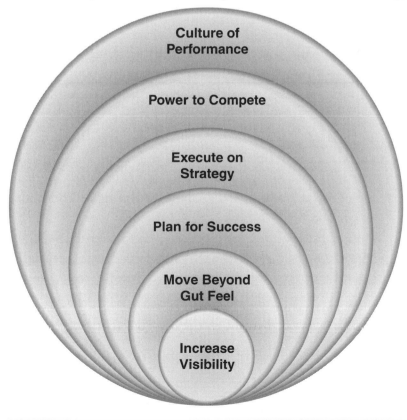

Culture of
Performance

Power to Compete

Execute on
Strategy

Plan for Success

Move Beyond
Gut Feel

Increase
Visibility

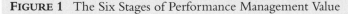

FIGURE 1 The Six Stages of Performance Management Value

organizations understand what is happening across their organization.

2. *Move Beyond Gut Feel* to an organization that operates based on facts and validated information. Companies that are dedicated to making data-driven decisions benefit not only from making better decisions across the organization, but also from having a more disciplined culture.

3. *Plan for Success* with aligned, communicated, and coordinated plans. At this stage, companies can begin to plan, budget, and forecast a desired future state with accuracy and efficiency. Planning becomes a competitive advantage rather than a time-consuming resource drain.

4. *Execute on Strategy* to capture plans and execute in an aligned fashion to reliably deliver the results which were planned. Companies who can execute strategy have the side benefit of developing accountability, alignment, predictability and trust.

5. *Power to Compete*: Understand external factors impacting the business, including changing market conditions or competitive strategies, to manage performance in a way that not only makes the company better, but makes the company better than the competition. Some companies can execute the strategy they planned, but this may still not be enough. Companies that have the power to compete take into account external factors to make sure they are not only performing well, but performing better than the competition.

6. *Culture of Performance*: With highly developed capabilities to monitor, analyze, and plan the business, organizations can create a culture wherein information is a prized asset, aligned execution is the norm, and accountability is inherent in how the company

operates. These organizations operate with transparency and predictability, and are readily adaptive to changing conditions.

These six stages of performance management culminate with the Culture of Performance. So in order to develop a Culture of Performance, organizations first experience the preceding five stages of performance management value.

THE THREE CAPABILITIES: MONITOR, ANALYZE, AND PLAN

But how can you get there? In order to experience any of the six stages, organizations must develop three capabilities: Monitor, Analyze, and Plan. These are three muscles that are flexed in varying degrees of strength to deliver the six stages. Given their essential role, most of this book is focused on how organizations can develop these capabilities.

- *Monitor*: This capability provides the company with the ability to know "*what* is happening" and "*what* has happened."
- *Analyze*: This capability provides the company with the ability to know "*why* what is happening is happening."
- *Plan*: This capability provides the company with the ability to know "*how* to model what should happen."

ABOUT THE READER

Executives

Many readers are executives within their organizations. They have responsibility for groups or teams, profit and loss (P&L), and overall results. They may be accountable to numerous stakeholders—the Board of Directors, shareholders, employees, customers, and partners. The model by which executives affect performance is different from that of other employees. Executives have to work through others to get results. They implement change within an organization through processes, policies, and procedures—frameworks of performance management, which cascade throughout the organization. When asked how the organization is performing, they need to have the facts to explain the team's performance or to direct inquiries to the appropriate owners. Their interest in managing performance may be to:

- *Drive alignment* so that strategies are executed and tactics align to the corporate objectives and commitments executives make.

- *Ensure accountability*: There is a person or group assigned to the success of each objective and when things go awry, they know who is on point for resolving them.

- *Increase agility* to respond to changing market conditions more quickly to beat the competition.

- *Capture and develop best practices* to develop more top performers; understand the specific area of focus for a new market to enter; which segments to target for a product or service; know how to increase results under tight regulations, margins, processes, or markets, which make winning all the more difficult.

Often, executives come across management methodologies like the Balanced Scorecard through business articles or books. Perhaps they see or hear about the cool dashboard that "Sam in Operations" has and can point to and show performance within seconds of when he's asked, or the glossy charts and diagrams (that imply deeper analysis) that other executives are able to show to make their points carry more credibility.

Or perhaps executives are interested in performance management because they read business books like this one, which show the benefits of leading organizations and recognize the advantages this provides them, and wonder: "Is my competitor doing that?" Good question.

Managers

Managers are faced with the difficult task of interpreting organizational strategy to teams to deliver desired results. They are closer to the execution and typically have greater visibility than executives to what is happening with their direct employees, customers, and partners. They are often held accountable for herculean tasks that make more sense in an upper manager's spreadsheet than in the manager's actual environment.

Managers are likely to feel they could do a better job for customers if they just had improved access to better information. Internally, it is managers who feel the direct pain of disconnected systems and processes and invalid information. They still have to generate information for executives in a timely manner, even if the data they need to do their jobs is difficult to find.

Many managers are trying to be the agents of change within their organization by introducing new processes and practices to return better results—techniques for better managing performance often top this list. They often hear about methodologies like the Balanced Scorecard in business classes or from colleagues at work. Managers may be interested in reading this book to diagnose their performance management capabilities against best practices. They may be interested in learning about real-world ways they can get better buy-in for their performance improvement initiatives. They may want to understand how they could better align with and serve those above and below them in the corporate hierarchy if they had improved access to better information.

Individual Contributors

Individual contributors are often the face of the organization to customers and partners. They are the bank tellers, salesmen, and customer service or professional service professionals who work directly with customers. When they don't have an answer or they deliver poor results, the impact is the direct expression of the company brand with the customer. These employees know the actual—rather than implied, philosophical, or hoped for—way in which the company is performing. As we said before, decisions are the act of execution, and individual contributors often make hundreds of tactical decisions throughout the day. Whether they are executing in alignment or against company objectives is often not seen or known until it's too late and the damage done has become a trend.

Individual contributors are likely reading a book such as this to gain insights on how to serve customers better. They want to know how they can improve their personal performance and amplify their individual contribution. Personal performance improvement means better results and greater impact and, possibly, better prospects for the future as a manager or executive.

Analysts

As many of our readers who are analysts will know firsthand, analysts can be either the heroes or the tragically misunderstood and underutilized people in an organization. Which role they end up playing can correlate with the organization's information maturity. If the data is a mess and the company has a "run on gut feel" culture, the analyst is typically used only to manufacture supporting evidence or to "pretty up" reports with a few data points. In an organization where information is highly valued, the analyst can be viewed as a strategic asset utilized to deliver valuable analysis and inform better decisions.

In any case, analysts who are following their calling and have an affinity for objective analysis know the value of inquiry (*you know who you are*). They may be reading this book to find evidence to share with their organization, such as information to help explain the importance of having reliable data, the role of advanced analytic tools, or examples of the strategic role analysts can play within an organization. They may also read a book such as this one to pick up on best practices, which are sprinkled throughout to make sure they are easy to find.

Information Technology Pros

IT professionals have challenging roles in the performance management space. When the executive sees the scorecard and when the analyst sees advanced visualization tools they turn to the IT professional and say, "Can you get me one of those?" What IT professionals recognize is that "one of those" depends on many, many things relating to data quality, budget, resources, and time frame.

Many organizations have already tackled the data warehousing issue of getting the data right. The average enterprise has between 6 and 10 BI systems, and data warehousing has been a key initial step toward delivering better support for decision making. As such, many IT professionals have already been through some BI work as their organization began its BI journey with getting its data integrated. Readers who are in IT may be reading this book to keep up to speed with meeting demands from internal customers as they move from data integration to information management and technologies like scorecards, dashboards, analytics, and planning.

HOW THIS BOOK IS ORGANIZED

The book is structured to present performance management concepts in a logical progression so the reader can understand how the concepts relate to each other and how to implement them within their own organization.

There are three key messages in this book:

1. People drive performance—enabling more people across the enterprise can increase competitive advantage.
2. There are 3 capabilities to effectively manage performance: Monitor, Analyze and Plan.
3. Organization's with these capabilities can experience Six Stages of Performance Management Value.

Chapter 1: The Six Stages of Performance Management

Chapter 1 provides a foundation for the book by orienting the reader to the topic at hand: driving business performance. In this chapter, we discuss why organizations are interested in managing performance. We also note the role of executive commitment to improve performance as well as the importance of intelligent execution over strategy alone. Finally, we introduce the six stages of performance management value.

Chapter 2: Managing Performance

In Chapter 2, we discuss the types of decisions individuals make across an organization to execute their jobs, which collectively comprise the organization's overall performance. We share a philosophy of the three types of trust that need to be developed within an organization to make these decisions most impactful. Finally, we describe the three key capabilities organizations need to develop to drive business performance—monitoring, analyzing, and planning—and how these deliver the six stages of performance management value.

Chapter 3: Monitor

In Chapters 3, 4, and 5, we describe each capability—Monitor, Analyze, and Plan—in more detail. We discuss the guiding principles for each capability and detail the specific skills and assets that organizations need to develop to attain each respective capability. In Chapter 3, we discuss the need for organizations to guarantee consistency of both data and information, and how to drive accountability and ensure alignment. This includes a detailed review of how Key Performance Indicators (KPIs), scorecards, dashboards, and strategy maps are used to monitor performance. Finally, we provide a means for organizations to assess their monitoring capabilities, as well as guidance for how to improve results.

Chapter 4: Analyze

In Chapter 4, we discuss how organizations can analyze and understand information to improve their performance. We discuss the need to make information visual to more readily inform people. We also discuss the importance of the data being presented in an intuitive environment, thus enabling individuals to easily interact with the information. The ability to assess analytic capabilities, as well as suggestions for improving these capabilities, is also provided.

Chapter 5: Plan

Chapter 5 introduces the reader to the concept of modeling performance—to predicting the future and hypothesizing results in order to make more compelling plans and forecasts. The essential roles planning, budgeting, and forecasting play in managing performance are described in detail. Organizations are also invited to diagnose their planning capabilities, and prescriptive guidance is also provided to help improve results.

Chapter 6: Pull It All Together: What's Your Organization's Stage?

The conclusion relates the capabilities back to the six stages of performance management value. Following the three capability chapters—Chapter 3, Monitor; Chapter 4, Analyze; and Chapter 5, Plan—the conclusion provides a framework for assessing where your organization stands today based on the strength of your performance management capabilities (as measured in the Monitor, Analyze, and Plan chapters).

It is our hope that all readers of this book come away with a richer understanding of how they can go about improving performance in their own organizations. The ability to "work smarter" will be a key attribute to future successful companies. We hope this book provides the vision as well as critical guidance in reaching your goals.

NOTES

1. Discussion with Randy Benz, Energizer, September 2007.

2. Jean Paul Votron (Brussels, Investor Day March 2007) http://www
.fortis.com/shareholders/media/pdf/Annual Results 2006
Presentation 0315.pdf

3. Leaders of Europe's BW50 http://images.businessweek.com/ss/05/
06/0526eubw50/6.htm.

4. Discussion with Jack Bates, U.S. Department of Veterans Affairs,
December 2007.

5. Gary Hamel, The Future of Management (Boston, MA: Harvard
Business School Press, 2007).

Acknowledgements

To Bob Kaplan & Dave Norton we extend our deep appreciation for their thoughtful Foreword, as well as their inspirational and groundbreaking work. Your contribution to the discipline of managing performance is unparalleled and we couldn't have wished to work with anyone more qualified or for whom we have so much respect. Thank you!

A special thanks goes to our colleagues and friends Elaine Andersen, Steve Hoberecht, and Tim Kashani. Your deep knowledge and talent was a significant contribution to this book.

We'd like to also thank those who helped ensure that what we were writing made sense. We were fortunate to have a host of reviewers to keep us on track and provide valuable feedback.

We were very fortunate to work with a wonderful editor and friend, Tim Burgard. Thanks for keeping us on track with such patience, kindness and support. We loved working with you and look forward to our continued collaboration.

Our heartfelt thanks go to Bob Fitts, Sr., Bob Fitts, Jr. and John Fitts, for the time, detailed review, and direct and unsaturated critique you provided. We certainly appreciated getting feedback from people who have served in the same roles as many of our readers (CEO, COO, Director/analyst, respectively), who we trust and who we could bother for urgent, lengthy, and untimely reviews. Without your help, we would not have been able to meet our tight timeframe, and even if we had, the resulting book would certainly not have been as high a quality of work. We would also like to thank Karl Ortner and Shelby Goerlitz for their reviews and feedback.

The book would not have been possible without the close collaboration and open dialogue we shared with a number of leaders across different companies, universities and government organizations. You will find their comments throughout the book or interviews on the book websites, and we offer them our sincere gratitude here:

Paul Adams, Bill Baker, Steve Ballmer, Jack Bates, Randy Benz, Thomas Beyer, Scott Brennan, Chris Caren, Michael Contrada, Christophe Couturier, Alan Crowther, Tom Davenport, Howard Dresner, Wayne Eckerson, Allen Emerick, Dave Evans, Scott Farr, Laura Gibbons, Jean-François Gigot, Cary Greene, Ulf Hilton, Jeremy Hope, Andy Hough, Rob Howie Roger Killick, Peter Klein, Chris Liddell, Santosh Mohanty, Walter McFarland, Mazal Tucher, Randy Russell, Eddie Short, Ron Van Zanten, Peter Ward, Stephen Waters, Jens Wittkopf, David White.

~ 1 ~

The Six Stages of Performance Management

> Give employees a large dose of discretion; pro-
> vide them with the information they need to make
> wise decisions; and then hold them accountable for
> results.
>
> —*Gary Hamel,* The Future of Management

WHY MANAGE PERFORMANCE?

Why do companies need to manage performance? For most
organizations, it is crystal clear that they better figure out
how to perform better if they want to better serve their
customers, stay ahead of the competition, and meet shareholder demands.

Drivers for Performance Improvement

What are the catalysts for managing performance? Organizations often embark on a performance improvement initiative within one of the following scenarios:

- *Leadership change.* Often, performance improvement
  initiatives begin with a change in leadership. In case

1

study after case study example in this book, this is a recurring theme—Energizer, Expedia, Fortis, Millipore, the Veteran's Administration—all had new leaders come in with performance management as a priority. When a new leader takes over a division, business unit, or company, they have a green light to be bold in suggesting a performance improvement initiative. The authority and timing is right with a leadership change for performance optimization.

- *Executive request—"top down."* Executives sometimes discover performance benefits achieved by other organizations and want to follow their path with a performance initiative within their own company or group.

  We refer to this scenario as "scorecard envy," when an executive sees the performance management capabilities other executives (inside or outside the company) have and wants these as well.

- *Management best practice—"bottom-up."* This scenario is often the result of a zealous and persistent manager's pioneering performance management results within a team or group, which get discovered and eventually are taken on to be institutionalized across the organization. As we shall see, this "internal guerilla marketing" as Laura Gibbons of Expedia refers to it, is necessary to get buy-in for performance management systems and processes even when executive support is present.

- *Industry/sector awareness.* In some industries, the management practices and systems are very consistent from company to company. When performance management becomes instantiated within a few of these organizations it is not uncommon for others in the industry to follow suit.

  The public sector is a great example of this. Once a few government organizations adopt performance management practices, it soon proliferates across other segments of government.

> There's really a domino effect across the U.S. federal government for performance management adoption. Once the Balanced Scorecard was first adopted in the Army and the Department of Defense, it spread like wild fire.[1]

• *Information technology (IT) driven*: Sometimes the work of IT can help drive the proliferation of tools and applications, which start to effect broad change in how performance is managed. In these scenarios, the organization may view IT as strategic and take guidance on how technologies can improve performance thus having the initiative driven by IT. As IT shares technology capabilities without a business mandate, the "toys" are distributed and then the people discover how to play. This may result in a champion ultimately developing a best practice that bubbles up, and a more formal performance improvement initiative is started. This is not a common scenario, however, as at some point the push must come from the top down. Executive support is necessary for the performance management initiative to become a standard process or practice—to move from an initiative to the way the company does things across the enterprise.

• *Regulations and public reporting*: Regulations can also drive attention to performance management. Many public sector organizations are required to report performance against public metrics, such as the UN's Millennium goals (as we shall discuss in the example of the Development Bank of Southern Africa). Public service organizations are often required to report their impact as well on metrics related to education, health, or safety.

In the private sector, compliance with financial reporting regulations such as Sarbanes Oxley and

Basel II drive a focus on performance management. When the consequences are jail time for executives or fines if the organization is found to be out of compliance, it's no wonder regulations are significant drivers for a more disciplined and transparent management approach.

These scenarios are typical catalysts for performance improvement. In addition to these structural drivers, there are also common business scenarios that compel organizations to better manage performance.

It should also be noted that performance management initiatives do not only occur when times are bad. Clearly, when performance is poor, the interest in performance improvement is increased. However, as professor and author Tom Davenport explains, you shouldn't just manage performance when things are bad.

> Motivation may be lower then (when things are going well), but when things do go bad, you need to know very quickly what the relationships are. So if you see that you are starting to have a problem with employee engagement, for example, you know from previous analysis that this is going to really affect your financial performance if you don't do something about it very quickly. Or maybe you know there is a one year lag, so if we start with a customer royalty problem, it's not going to affect this year's performance but it is going to affect next year's performance. You have to establish that under good times so you can address it quickly during bad.[2]

Good or Bad—You're Making Decisions Today

The question really is not whether an organization will take steps to manage performance; it's just a question of how serious they take performance and how well they'll do it. Even without a formal performance management strategy and systems in place, organizations have some method, process, or habits they've developed to manage performance. Whether this is simply done via informal, status-update conversations, bonus-pay incentives, or a formal management-by-objectives method, these are all approaches to managing performance—it's just the degree to which they are effective that varies.

So, when asked why performance management matters, we often ask in reply, "Why manage anything?"

Let's start with a local business example for familiarity. Suppose you run a retail store and you are interested in making more money to grow your business, pay your people more, or maybe just so you can take a nice family vacation. How will you decide what promotion you are going to run to increase income for your store? This decision could be the difference between success and failure in achieving any of the above objectives.

Viewed differently, which organization would you rather have stock in—the retailer who makes up a promotion in 30 days' time without any data to support the decision and hopes to get lucky? Or the retailer who, also within 30 days' time, (1) segments the local retail market; (2) determines a targeted audience based on local retail market demographics, customer needs, and buying patterns; and (3) offers a promotion on merchandise of top buying interest to this community while also raising prices to increase profit margin on accessories and impulse merchandise? The answer seems obvious.

To believe in the benefits of performance management we assume a belief in the value of data driven decision making, a belief that well informed decisions typically yield better results than uninformed decisions. Thankfully, recent research indicates that "84% of senior executives believe high performing businesses make decisions based on evidence and facts rather than gut feel."[3]

Organizations choose to manage performance for the same reason that organizations choose to have management structures—to provide a disciplined approach and accountability for running the business more effectively. The role of management is to align team efforts with corporate objectives and to be accountable for driving results of the team. Individual contributors are also responsible for individual results and utilize performance management systems to manage and report on this contribution as well. Across the entire enterprise, performance management, as with management itself, exists to help drive strategy execution, accountability, and performance.

Strategy Execution Is a Top Priority

The need and desire to improve performance is as clear as the competition's logo, your own company's ticker symbol or your last lost customer. The key reason why most companies around the world care about performance management is because they want to better execute their strategy.

Indeed, strategy execution is top of mind for global enterprises. In a recent study, the Conference Board asked 658 CEOs from multinational companies to prioritize their most pressing management challenges. "Consistent execution of strategy by top management" ranked first for organizations with revenues greater than $5 billion, and second for smaller organizations (behind "Sustained and steady top line growth").[4] Companies of all sizes seek to realize the benefits of their strategies through better strategy formulation, communication, and, ultimately, execution.

Executing on Strategy Is More Important than the Strategy Itself

It is often believed that it's pure, genius strategy that wins the day. Many assume, "It's the strategy that sets apart the envied market leader. Winning organizations must have great ideas and a novel approach that allows them to blaze a path to glory."

However, we've learned that success hinges more on execution than a prize-winning strategy. Strategies hold potential, but delivering on the potential and contributing to organizational objectives depend on intelligent execution. While at first a controversial view, it is now more accepted to argue for tactical execution over high-level strategy alone. Before we review some of the research, following are some quotes that underscore the "execution" component of "strategy execution":

> You can't build a reputation on what you are going to do.
>
> *Henry Ford*

> However beautiful the strategy, you should occasionally look at the results.
>
> *Winston Churchill*

> I saw that leaders placed too much emphasis on what some call high-level strategy, on intellectualizing and philosophizing, and not enough on implementation. People would agree on a project or initiative, and then nothing would come of it.
>
> *Larry Bossidy and Ram Charan,*
> Execution: The Discipline of Getting
> Things Done

> Flawed decisions well implemented will bring more to the bottom line than the best decision that is not implemented.
>
> *Peter Schutz, former CEO, Porsche*

Perhaps Mae West put it best of all, "An ounce of performance is worth pounds of promises."

You'd Better Execute Better—Research Backs It Up

Fortune estimates that about 70% of companies can't execute on strategy and that only 10% of organizations actually attain their strategic objectives. In the public sector, research by Barron's indicates that out of nearly 800 federal programs studied only 15% achieved their goals.[5]

What's the issue? Why is it so difficult to make strategy reality? A joint study by Renaissance Solutions, Inc., *CFO* magazine, and Business Intelligence helps describe the critical factors that account for failing to execute strategy across the organization:

- *Awareness.* 95% of the typical workforce does not understand the strategy.
- *Financial resources.* 60% of organizations do not link budgets to strategy.
- *Governance.* 44% of board directors cannot identify the key drivers of value in the companies they govern.
- *Executive agenda.* 85% of executive teams spend less than one hour per month discussing strategy.
- *Incentives.* 70% of organizations do not link middle management incentives to strategy.
- *People.* 55% of human resources (HR) organizations either interpret strategy or deal only with operational priorities.[6]

The result of these issues is a confused organization with misaligned tactics, disconnected execution—which can even run counter to organizational objectives—and an inability to reach the goals outlined in the strategy.

When companies execute the wrong things, opportunity is lost. Here are common examples—sound familiar?

- Engineering develops a critical technical capability for a market that is not a priority.
- Marketing develops a global campaign with executive messaging to the CxO-level (CEO, COO, CFO, CIO) audience in companies with greater than

$1 billion in revenue, but the most profitable sales are with line-of-business managers of mid-market organizations between $250 million and $750 million in annual revenues.

- A retailer runs promotions that offer deep discounts on every item in the store and loses out to his savvy competitor who provides an attractive incentive to a targeted audience by simply discounting items that appeal to the local college customer audience and brings them into the store. The profit margin on accessory items is simultaneously increased and thereby maintains profit objectives.

- Two different product planners are working on complementary product enhancements, but the development plans are not integrated, and the strategy for product integration is not yet determined. Without this planning and collaboration, significant enhancements and competitive differentiation in the marketplace for each product goes unrealized.

- A government agency responsible for public health initiatives is unable to prioritize public health requirements and, thus, never seems to have enough resources for those most in need.

HOW PERFORMANCE MANAGEMENT CREATES VALUE

We have identified six stages of performance management value typically attained by organizations (see Figure 1.1):

1. Increase Visibility
2. Move Beyond Gut Feel
3. Plan for Success

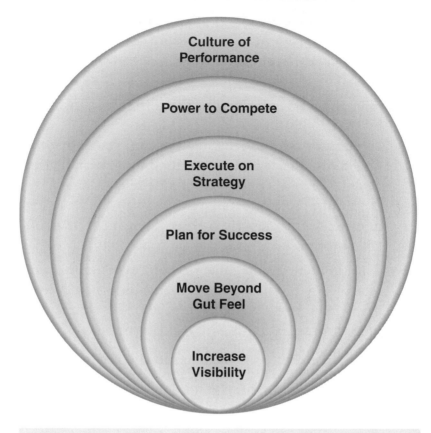

FIGURE 1.1 Six Stages of Performance Management Value

4. Execute on Strategy

5. Power to Compete

6. Culture of Performance

These stages build on each other, leading organizations to establish an environment where managing performance becomes an intrinsic part of how they operate—what we call a "Culture of Performance."

Different organizations (and even different departments within an organization) may recognize the value they receive from managing performance in different ways. Some may benefit from increasing visibility, for example, while others might benefit from planning for success, but none can attain the cumulative benefits derived from a Culture of Performance without developing the other five capabilities.

Increase Visibility

Some organizations simply do not know what they don't know. Since they haven't been closely managing their data and performance information, they lack detailed knowledge of their business to expose issues and opportunities. They focus more on activities than on measured progress toward goals. They may not be aware that they are bleeding, or that there's a pot of gold around the corner because they have not yet developed an analytic capability or implemented the tools to enable rich inquiry.

In cases like these, the organization is not seeking to resolve a performance problem because it doesn't yet know that it has the problem (or opportunity, as the information may reveal). The benefit of managing performance in this case is that it enables the identification of problems and opportunities the company had no knowledge of—and results in the ability to change strategy and operations to produce unexpected improvements.

A leading provider of mobile telecom services, made an interesting discovery as they developed their analytic capabilities.

They identified pockets of customers that were paying less in roaming costs than the company spent to provide the roaming service. Every minute each of these customers used the service in this way cost the provider significant sums—to the tune of around $2 million per month. With this increased visibility, the provider was then able to make the appropriate changes to their rate plans, target the right types of customers, and align their roaming programs with these changes to remove the issues associated with their costliest customer relationships.

Move Beyond Gut Feel

In other cases, organizations seek to investigate a hunch. They know that they're bleeding profits or suspect they may have a potential gold mine—they just don't yet know exactly what's causing the problem or how to reach the gold-mine. They have only guesses without information to draw a meaningful conclusion on the best course of action to take.

The importance of enabling people to move beyond hunches and make fact-based, data-driven decisions is a central theme in this book. Steve Ballmer (CEO, Microsoft) has a favorite story he uses to describe moving from hunches to data driven decisions:

> I was sitting in a plane one day and reading a computer magazine of some sort when the passenger next to me began asking questions about an issue that he thought I could help him with.
>
> "Are you in the computer business?"
>
> I don't know about you, but I am not real fond of talking on airplanes . . . so I answered with a brief "Yep."
>
> "Well, we've got a whole lot of computers in my company." I was beginning to get a little afraid there was a tech support question coming . . . .
>
> "I've got a question for you. . . . " I'm thinking at this point, here it comes . . . but he continued,
>
> "My job is setting the price of auto insurance in the State of Colorado. Every state is regulated individually, and I have Colorado. Here's my problem. I believe people who buy auto insurance policies between Christmas and New Year's should be charged a higher rate than anyone else we sell to."
>
> "Why's that?" I asked.
>
> "I honestly believe that if you're buying auto insurance that week, you're probably planning on drinking for New Year's Eve, and I think we should charge a risk premium for that."
>
> The guy was dead serious, and, actually, it's sort of logical to me. "So what's the issue?"

"I know someplace, in our computers, we know what our actual experience has been with people who we've written policies for that week. I know if I could just get at it, I could either prove my theory and I could go to the regulators and recommend we charge more, or I would abandon my theory and move on."[7]

The insurance analyst in this story is seeking to make a decision based on facts, rather than his intuition—he wants to move beyond gut feel. But even if he had access to this data, could he trust it? Could he get this information in time—before New Year's, when he can still do something about it? Could he validate his hunch based on historical patterns and trends? Could he take into account other potential factors such as weather conditions, age, sex, marital status of the policy holders, or differences across geographies? Better still, could he forecast and plan better based on correlations found between those factors? Could he model the different types of actions he may take to see what changes in the policies may yield?

Organizations realize the benefit of moving beyond gut feel when they are able to make informed decisions and move past speculation to validation. They don't guess, they know.

Plan for Success

As Steve Ballmer describes above, with a common trust of data and respect for facts, organizations can begin to develop reliable plans and strategies to capture "how we win." They plan for success—they say what they are going to do. In this stage, organizations are planning for success by anticipating future results and accurately forecasting their desired future state.

Companies seem to consistently struggle with the fact that the processes they're involved in rarely enable the execution of strategy—often because they are executed in silos and don't relate to each other. Most every organization does planning, budgeting, and forecasting of some sort—the depth, discipline, and effectiveness varies, but these practices are established as a part of doing business. It is both ironic and tragic that these foundational, rudimentary business activities that are core to doing business are also so poorly executed. As Eddie Short, Global Head and VP of Business and Information Management at Capgemini, puts it:

> Today for many organizations, there is a disconnect in the core management planning and control processes, for example, between setting targets, formulating strategy, planning, forecasting, risk management, investment planning, performance feedback, and financial consolidation. The annual budget, driven by Finance, frequently dominates the process, and the value it adds in its current form is increasingly being questioned. These processes need to be linked together in a better way, making use of three loops of feedback and control at three levels: Strategic, Operational, and Activities levels. What is required is step-by-step progress through the enterprise's processes, methodologies, metrics and technologies. Merely implementing a business intelligence tool is not the answer.[8]

The typical organization's planning, budgeting, and forecasting processes today are fragmented, slow, labor intensive, costly, and ineffective. Organizations that move from annual disconnected processes to collaborative, continuous execution achieve significant competitive advantage. They have increased agility as they streamline these processes and improve results through faster, more accurate, and better-communicated plans, budgets, and forecasts.

Execute on Strategy

We've discussed the fact that a primary reason companies seek to develop their performance management capabilities is to improve strategy execution. Executives often launch performance management initiatives when they see their strategies continuing to fail to be implemented. Removing obstacles to effectively execute on strategy is critical,

Author Michael Treacy refers to this as "performance discipline." As he defines it, "A company achieves a performance discipline when the risks of high performance have largely been eliminated and all that remains is hard work."[9] With this discipline, organizations can set an objective and know they will achieve it because they have the confidence that they will perform to plan. As Bob Baker, Vice President, Mobil, puts it, "I firmly believe that if I change one measure on my scorecard, change will happen."

Premier Bankcard, a leading credit card provider, provides a good example of the ability to execute on strategy. The company enables its employees to reach their goals with maximum predictability and confidence.

> We have a process we implement as the month is coming to a close called 'the Goal.' Managers had already decided their goal for the month, how many and which type of applicants they want approved. Now as the month progresses, they have real time stats showing them where they are against the goal. That was something they didn't have previously during the month or during the day—to know that 20,000 or 200,000 was the right number based on various dynamic contributing factors throughout the month . . . to know that this is the most profitable number—right here, right now. To know that we start getting a diminishing return if it goes higher than this and being able to come in at the right number with predictability provides us with a competitive advantage.[10]

When companies commit to a strategy and communicate "This is how we win," and can align execution with corporate objectives, they begin to create a Culture of Performance. Beyond communicating their strategy, best-practice companies are able to instill in the minds of their employees the discipline of execution, enabling their people to become the "agents of change" across the organization. This moves the organization from disconnected pockets of decisions made in silos to informed decision making tied to common and aligned objectives.

Performance improvement should be an empowering and strategic focus for the entire company. Strategy execution takes a coordinated and aligned organization, from top to bottom, side to side. As Allen Emerick, Director of IT at Skanska, a top five global leader in construction services with annual revenues of $17 billion, says, "We believe that performance management is for every individual in the organization because every individual needs to be able to make better, more informed decisions." At Skanska, they execute on strategy—they do what they say they are going to do.

Power to Compete

Up to now, we've talked about how companies can manage themselves better internally. But how do you know if your best is good enough? Even if you are predictably achieving 100% of your goals, that still may be 50% of your competition's performance. Companies need to have context for their metrics outside of the organization to ensure they are not only performing well, but performing better than the competition, and giving customers a reason to buy their products and services, and shareholders a reason to buy their stock.

To do this, companies need to benchmark results against the rest of the industry and make the fact that they execute better on these metrics a competitive advantage. For example, say you're a services company and your goal is a 20% operational margin, which means the difference between the cost of providing services versus the income associated with delivering services is 20%. But your number one competitor has an operational margin of 30%. In order to grow you have to operate better than your competitor. Beating your competitor on profitability means your goal is not 20%; it is now anything above 30%, all other factors being equal. By focusing on beating this new margin objective internally, you're creating a proof point that you're beating the competition. You're operating better than they are, and the fact that your margin is higher is proof of that. What are the associated customer benefits? Customers have higher confidence in your operational effectiveness—that you will deliver quality services on time and within budget. This helps you secure your base and win customers because you can say with confidence that you're operationally better than the customer's alternatives.

"Making better decisions faster potentially means millions of dollars to us over the course of a year" says Skanska's Emerick.[11] But Skanska goes a step further to compete more effectively. Not only do they have the information to tell them what their profit margin is, but they also have industry benchmarks to show the context of this performance versus their competition. Finally, they have the ability to forecast their performance versus the competition to define success for their shareholders. Internally, they are able to communicate plans with what they call "outperform" objectives—which, when met, enable them to exceed stakeholder expectations and win. Hospitality leader Hilton Hotels has a similar metric approach that they refer to as "perfection."

The power to compete doesn't just exist in the private sector. Public-sector organizations like the Development Bank of Southern Africa (DBSA) compete for public support, government aid, and private-sector sponsorship. The DBSA is a good example of how to align to public objectives that stakeholders have defined as success.

Dave Evans, Executive Coordinator, Group Risk Assurance Division for DBSA, explains:

> Our government has a 10 year plan called "The People's Contract" which was put together in 2004. There are measures that

have to do with reducing poverty levels, and the number of households without access to clean water and electricity. We also have the UN Millennium Development Goals which relate to things like reducing mother mortality from childbirth, improving education—percentage of females in school—hygiene, health (with diseases like malaria and AIDS), sanitation, etc. The Balanced Scorecard gives us a framework to see how we're impacting against those goals. The report of how we're doing on our Balanced Scorecard is a separate section in our annual report and is vetted by our external auditors.[12]

External benchmarks are important indicators of the bank's effectiveness relative to the other options that their stakeholders may have for development activity. Dave continues:

Our scorecard contains benchmarks that relate to maintaining targets with international rating agencies (like Moody's), which provide ratings of creditworthiness of organizations like ours who sometimes seek to raise money on the global markets. Benchmarking also shows up with global risk standards, like Basel II. Those who are processing loans look at things like turnaround times for appraisals relative to the competition. Sometimes this is from benchmarks, sometimes from surveys to understand how we compare to the competition.[13]

Culture of Performance

As industries continue to move more and more to information-based work, empowering the information worker becomes a greater responsibility. A Culture of Performance needs to be created that enables the individual to make good decisions to better serve customers, the company, and other stakeholders. You can have the right people, the right processes, the most enabling technology, but each of these alone no longer delivers strong competitive advantage. As the Balanced Scorecard Collaborative warns, you can have great people effectively executing the wrong things. The key is to make sure you can effectively execute the right things. "The main thing is to keep the main thing the main thing."[14]

Organizations achieve a competitive advantage when they develop a culture that fosters improved performance—one that holds facts in high regard; one that is customer-centric; one that competes from a common playbook, makes data-driven decisions, and promotes cross-group collaboration, alignment, and execution.

Capgemini's Short often discusses the processes, methodologies, metrics, and technologies that enable the "Intelligent Enterprise." He uses a line that we love—*"It's time to put the 'I' back into IT"* (Information back into Information Technology)—to underscore how "masters of performance management" view information as a critical corporate asset.[15]

The people who decide to develop an organization's performance management capability cite an interesting motivator: organizational credibility. They know what they don't know—and they know what capabilities they lack that they feel they should have. Rather than accepting that their organization is simply not going to be able to model multiple business scenarios to anticipate results and easily support strategic decision making, they take action to deliver these capabilities. They are driven to answer their own burning questions, and after they have experienced the benefits, they want to empower others across the organization with this ability as well.

"I want the credibility both internally and with our customers—the retailers who distribute our products—that our capabilities are world class and we're the most capable business partner they can possibly have. When they propose hypothetical scenarios and new ideas on how to package products for retail distribution, I want our people to be knowledgeable and flexible enough to brainstorm with them with absolute confidence that we're not only meeting their needs, but our own as well," says Randy Benz,

CIO of Energizer Holdings, Inc., a leading global manufacturer and provider of batteries and flashlights (under the Energizer and Eveready brands) and the second largest manufacturer of wet-shaving products (under the Schick and Wilkinson Sword brands). While other organizations may accept their limitations, Energizer is ensuring they can exceed expectations and compete more effectively.

When it comes to organizational competition, the company that removes employees' information limitations and provides them with the information capabilities they need to excel at their jobs gives itself the best chance of winning.

The right people, tools, and processes will not deliver results if they are executed in an environment that does not support them. They become as ineffective as an organ rejected by the host body. Effective performance management delivers competitive advantage by enabling a Culture of Performance—managing performance must become a part of the organization's DNA. As companies develop a Culture of Performance, their performance improvement initiatives move from initiatives to simply, "how we do things around here."

Leading companies like Expedia are developing a culture of performance by building performance management capabilities into the new hire training every employee attends—it becomes a part of how Expedia operates and communicates.

> Every new employee goes through training on 'what is performance management?' and how to do it at Expedia. They are asked what groups they are joining and they are shown how to manage and even build their own scorecards for their respective jobs. They understand how performance is managed and communicated for their respective team and how this impacts organizational objectives.[16]

And they are recognizing the results.

> We're extremely fast at making decisions now. Before, we were really flying blind. The competitive advantage is like night and

day. If you could see where we were with our lack of reporting capabilities, and now the way the business talks in terms of "reds, yellows, and greens." It's truly an impressive feat for Expedia . . . we're developing a Culture of Performance and it's a real differentiator."[17]

CONCLUSION

In this chapter we have discussed why organizations are interested in managing performance. We have noted the role of executive commitment to improve performance as well as the importance of intelligent execution over strategy alone. Finally, we have introduced the six stages of performance management value. We will come back to these stages and enable you to determine your organization's stage later in this book. However, before organizations can diagnose their stage, they need to first understand and assess performance management capabilities.

This is why we now turn our attention to the capabilities that deliver this success. The six stages are the goals of managing performance—and they are the typical evolution that companies will go through on their path to the Culture of Performance. The capabilities are what enable organizations to go through these stages.

~ 1 ~

Appendix

In addition to the intended benefits of improving organizational performance, performance management also offers unintended benefits. These ancillary benefits can be as beneficial to the organization as the targeted performance improvement and are great examples of the impact of creating a Culture of Performance, not just implementing separate people, process, or technology changes alone.

Great thinkers, past and present, have offered thoughtful pearls of wisdom that, shown through a performance management prism, can illuminate further the power and potential that comes with a Culture of Performance:

> After all is said and done, more is said than done.
>
> *Aesop*

Strategy execution and results are the primary benefit of managing performance. The side benefit is creating a culture which respects results and fosters accountability.

> We can have facts without thinking but we cannot have thinking without facts.
>
> *John Dewey (1859–1952)*

Creating an organizational culture that values facts can be challenging when "gut feel" has been the decision support tool of record. However, it's difficult to argue against a verifiable fact. Creating a fact-based culture provides the added benefit of making better, data-driven decisions.

> The great thing about fact-based decisions is that
> they overrule the hierarchy.
>
> *Jeff Bezos, Founder, Amazon.com*

Many companies find that moving from decisions based on emotion and politics to decisions made on facts and reliable data neutralizes the political charge within an organization. The culture of respect for facts must get interwoven into the thread of the organization. With verifiable facts, which groups adhere to, organizations can remove the degrading effects of multiple theories and strategies that result from an environment "where facts are few, experts are many."[18]

> We each have only enough strength to complete
> those assignments that we are fully convinced are
> important.
>
> *Johann Wolfgang von Goethe*

The increased focus that is enabled by the introduction of performance management within an organization is immensely valuable. When we know what the organization is trying to accomplish and how our work contributes to it, it is much easier to identify what contributions are the most prioritized and what work is less impactful.

> Technology is dominated by two types of people:
> those who understand what they do not manage,
> and those who manage what they do not understand.
>
> *Archibald Putt*

Performance management allows the accurate reporting of both group and personal impact to organizational objectives such that both the boss and the employee understand not only how the company is performing, but also how the group and individual are contributing.

> Things do not just happen; things are made to
> happen.
>
> *John F. Kennedy*

Miracles are better explained when we are actively managing performance as we are able to see contribution and account for our success . . . and replicate miraculous results!

Good marketers measure.

Seth Godin

Performance management also introduces accountability to departments within an organization for whom measured impact may not be well known. This allows for better allocation of resources and investments toward these departments as return on investment and impact are better understood.

There is nothing so useless as doing efficiently that which should not be done at all.

Peter Drucker

Focusing and executing on the wrong things is a common, damaging problem for many organizations. Performance management does not just introduce good new habits—it can also get rid of old habits that were detrimental to performance.

If the only tool you have is a hammer, you tend to see every problem as a nail.

Abraham Maslow

To an organization without data and facts, every issue may be solved with the same blind inaccuracy, and solutions to singular problems can be overextended to apply to various complex problems.

It is a very sad thing that nowadays there is so little useless information.

Oscar Wilde

This may be the lament of a few who formerly got by through obfuscating the facts with misinformation or hiding from accountability in misprioritized initiatives.

> Deprived of meaningful work, men and women
> lose their reason for existence; they go stark, raving
> mad.
>
> *Fyodor Dostoevsky*

While employees often get concerned when first introduced to performance metrics, it's always rewarding to see the recognition of the benefits it provides them: They can defend themselves with data, they can make more informed decisions, and they can ensure their good work is accounted for—all of which help to arm the employee in performance reviews as well as increase the feeling of contribution and value to the organization. In this way, performance management can provide a morale boost and "power to the people."

NOTES

1. Discussion with Thomas Beyer, Global Government Administration Competency Leader, Bearing Point.
2. Conversation with Tom Davenport, November 2007.
3. Capgemini Intelligent Enterprise CXO Survey, December 2007.
4. Linda Barrington, Henry Silvert, and Rachel Ginsberg, *CEO Challenge 2006: Top 10 Challenges* (The Conference Board, November 2005).
5. See http://online.barrons.com/public/main.
6. *Translating Strategy into Action*, joint study by Renaissance, *CFO* magazine, and Business Intelligence, 1996.
7. From Steve Ballmer's keynote at the inaugural Microsoft BI Conference, May 2007.
8. Capgemini white paper "How the Intelligent Enterprise Delivers Performance Management, 2007
9. See http://www.marketingpower.com/content/Treacy-Reinventing%20Innovation%20in%20Consumer%20Products.pdf.
10. Discussion with Ron Van Zanten, Premier Bankcard, November 2007.
11. See www.microsoft.com/presspass/features/2007/may07/05-09 BusinessIntelligence.mspx.
12. Discussion with Dave Evans, Development Bank of Southern Africa, November 2007.

13. *Ibid.*

14. Stephen R. Covey, A. Roger Merrill, and Rebecca R. Merrill, *First Things First* (New York: Fireside, 1994).

15. Eddie Short, "The Intelligent Enterprise" (Capgemini white paper, March 2007).

16. Discussion with Laura Gibbons, manager, BI and Performance Management, Expedia.

17. *Ibid.*

18. Attributed to Donald R. Gannon.

— 2 —

Managing Performance

The most valuable assets of a 21st century institution, whether business or non-business, will be its knowledge workers and their productivity.

Peter F. Drucker,
Management Challenges for the 21st Century

IN THIS CHAPTER

We've introduced the six stages of performance management and explained how the goal is to involve more people and create a Culture of Performance. However, we can't just give guidance that "it's good to have a Culture of Performance." Instead, we need to get specific in explaining what you need and how to get there.

The primary focus of this chapter is to introduce the three capabilities organizations need to develop to effectively manage performance: Monitor, Analyze, and Plan.

Let's begin by understanding the types of decisions that are made across organizations, since, as we mentioned earlier, decisions *are* the act of execution.

STRATEGIC, OPERATIONAL, AND
TACTICAL DECISIONS

At any company, any day of the week, hundreds or even thousands of decisions are made. Each of these decisions has a particular impact on the business, positive or negative, large or small scale. These decisions are the way the company operates; this is how execution happens. So how can organizations impact the quality of these decisions to improve their performance? They need to first understand what these decisions are and how these decisions are made. There are three types of decisions that drive business performance: strategic, tactical, and operational (Figure 2.1).

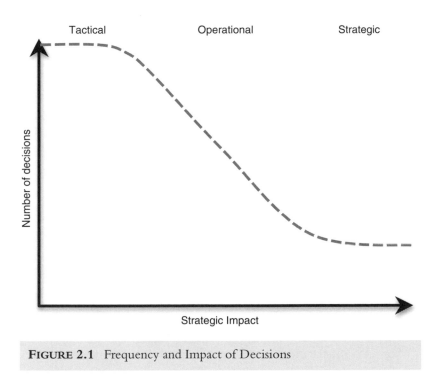

FIGURE 2.1 Frequency and Impact of Decisions

Strategic Decisions

Strategic decisions are typically made by executives. These decisions might influence the direction of a corporation, the type of business it wants to be in, or the mission it will try to accomplish. While there tend to be few of these decisions made throughout the year, they require a large amount of information, and their implications are significant. Repercussions can be dramatic, and careful thinking and time are required to make these decisions. They also have a particularly significant impact on the entire organization. Due to the scope of these decisions, everyone within the organization needs to align to them and "sign up" for their contribution. These decisions can have a serious effect on the future of the corporation, and they are discussed and often debated before they are committed. At least for the major decisions, organizations often go through due diligence exercises and review of the impact of the various possible avenues. Examples of strategic decisions include:

- *Target-setting.* A company might decide to grow its business by 10% over the next two years. Internal stakeholders will need to align and provide bottom-up goal setting and tactical plans to align with the organizations 10% growth goals.
- *Acquisition.* Merger and acquisition (M&A) activity requires significant capital and risk. Due to the investment, organizational impact (head count, alignment, retention plans, etc.) and time to complete the task, these are weighty decisions with significant analysis.

As is typical with many strategic decisions, both of the preceding examples require the ability to model multiple business scenarios and compare them in order to determine the best possible outcome before making the strategic decision.

Operational Decisions

Operational decisions are decisions made by line-of-business managers about the operations of their business. They might relate to allocation of people, time, or money to accomplish a planned objective. These decisions require contextual information of the operational environment—"Do I know that this decision will give me the expected outcome in the expected time frame?" As opposed to strategic decisions, operational decisions are ones whose consequences can be observed more immediately and may also have the benefit of being modified more readily. These decisions may be partially data driven and based on verifiable facts, but most often they are based on managers' judgment. Examples of operational decisions include:

- *Manufacturing.* A line-of-business manager has less than a week to reforecast production of a particular item to meet increased demand (and will need to model sales and supply-chain information to understand the consequences of the proposed decision).
- *Retail.* A floor manager needs to reallocate this month's supply to maximize shelf space and profitability. In order to place the right products in the right places to maximize supply and profitability, the floor manager needs to understand customer buying patterns as they relate to product placement.

As is typical with many operational decisions, both of the preceding examples require the ability to have relevant information available in the hands of the managers who are making these decisions, as well as the analytic and forecasting capabilities to make the right decisions quickly.

Tactical Decisions

Tactical decisions occur much more frequently than strategic and operational decisions. They are made by all types of employees across the organization and have various levels of impact to the company's bottom line. They often offer little opportunity for investigation—their impact is thought to be so low that extensive research would be more labor intensive than the impact of the decision itself. They are often made on gut feel and habits more than facts. Examples of tactical decisions include:

- *Retail Banking.* A bank teller needs to know what to offer a customer she is serving (right now). She needs to know whether the customer is a good candidate for additional services, such as a mortgage or a home loan. If the teller can see that the customer already has checking, savings, loan, and credit assets that, when combined with the mortgage or home loan, would bring more value to both the customer and the bank, she can recommend consolidating these accounts.
- *Telecom.* A customer service representative needs to know which services a customer would be a good candidate for, which offers to make to keep the customer from canceling their service, or which rate plan best fits the customer's needs based on the customer's travel schedule (for roaming) and calling patterns.

As is typical with many tactical decisions, both of the preceding examples require the ability to have real-time information available to these employees to better serve, retain, or up-sell customers. Tactical decisions need to be made rapidly, on the spot, and often directly with the customer. As these decisions are made repeatedly throughout the day, the combined impact to the organization grows more significant. These decisions represent the face of the organization to customers. Cumulatively, these decisions can define customer opinion and determine whether the overall voice of the customer is satisfied or dissatisfied.

THE FOUNDATION FOR DECISIONS

The foundation for informed decision making is not only information, but also trust. Performance management is based on the ability for organizations to trust their data, trust their insights, and ultimately trust their decisions.

Trust Your Data

Before any employee capabilities can be enabled—before any employee can trust that they're gleaning the right trends or patterns of business activity and performance, before any decision can truly be called informed—the data must be trusted. Is it current? Accurate? Consistent? Can employees rely on the quality of their corporate data? If a company believes that both people and information are key assets to their success, they have to think about how to bring the two together in a more integrated fashion.

Consider the following scenarios:

- *Data accuracy*. A business analyst spends hours cobbling multiple data points into a spreadsheet in order to analyze the impact of a given marketing campaign. New decisions such as budget cuts and investments are made based on this information—only to discover later on that the data were inaccurate and didn't reflect some of the latest data refreshes.

- *Data consistency*. Finance and Marketing officers discuss at length their initiatives around "margin growth." They compare and contrast the result of initiatives across countries, rank these countries, and start building a plan, only to realize that the definition of "margin growth" was not shared across the groups or the countries, making it impossible to drive consistency of execution or even compare results. This syndrome has been brilliantly coined by Peter Klein, Corporate VP and CFO of Microsoft Business Division, as the "Tower of Babel" effect:

When employees can't rely on the validity of the data, share the same understanding of performance, their discussions become fruitless. If they understand the same piece of data to mean different things, they effectively talk a different language of performance, they can't reconcile their thoughts and processes—they live on the Tower of Babel of data.[1]

Both of the examples above will result in the same consequence: lack of trust and credibility. If employees can't trust their data, if they cannot store it in a place that is secure, reliable, and open enough to make the consumption of this information ubiquitous, then insights and decisions are worthless. In fact, doesn't most every fact-based business decision start with the following questions?

- Where does this data come from?
- How old is it?
- What does it include?
- What does it not include?
- When is it refreshed?

Data skepticism is a good thing when it helps corporations get better at managing data. It is a bad thing, though, when it discourages companies from getting better at managing their data and building a sound and reliable foundation for information. As the adage says: "garbage in, garbage out." Even if employees have the best personal tools to slice and dice information, with poor data quality practices,

their insights and decisions will remain unfounded and misguided. To underscore this critical point, *the ability to trust
data is a prerequisite to managing performance.*

Trust Your Insights

Once employees can trust that the data has integrity, they
can begin to derive insights they can trust—they can turn
data into insights. Insights are defined as the ability for an
individual to develop "clear or deep perception of a situation." This perception is enabled by trustworthy data.
When data can be trusted, individuals, groups, and, ultimately, the whole of the organization can recognize trends
with confidence that the data actually support what they
are seeing. They can recognize patterns in the data that inform them of where the business is heading, which factors
are reliably contributing, and trust that their insights have
integrity based on sound data.

Consider the following scenarios:

- *Insights at the right time, right place.* A line-of-business
  manager looks at information from his Customer Relationship Management (CRM) system, from his pro-
  curement system, his ordering system, and revenue
  report systems. The amount of information, although
  accurate, is dispersed through so many systems, across
  so many different dimensions ("time," "geography")
  and attributes ("presales," "after margins") that it becomes overwhelming. When the manager can't reconcile any of the common threads of data, he gives up
  and goes back to doing "what feels right."

- *Sharing insights broadly.* A business analyst spends hours
  combing through a large amount of information in
  order to find a trend, an indication of where the organization is heading. Once a trend has been found,

the analyst has to develop a complex and convoluted set of explanations to communicate findings to the executive team. The information is discarded because it's deemed too complex. The analysts might think that the executives are ignoring an important detail—that they are managing by simple and easy to understand "sound bites" alone. The executives . . . well . . . they figure that if the analyst wants to be understood, he needs to put his insights into a digestible and actionable format. Later down the line, the organization experiences challenges that were originally identified in the analyst's insights. They could have been avoided if only the analyst had a better way to communicate his insights—if he could have made the complex information more readily understood by others in the organization.

Both of the preceding examples result in the same consequence: insights made nonactionable. We talked earlier of the importance for a company to capitalize on the incredible asset that trustable data represent. Insights come from employees—the most important organizational asset. The more employees can easily understand what works and what doesn't and can broadly share these insights, the more impact these insights can have on the performance of an organization. By enabling employees to understand complex information more quickly, and to communicate these insights simply and effectively to management, organizations use information assets to positively affect business decision quality and agility.

Trust Your Decisions

Ultimately, better business performance is determined by an organization's ability to provide employees with better capabilities to make better decisions faster. Providing broader access to reliable data and delivering the right mechanisms to share better insights are key components to enabling better decisions. And better decisions are the ultimate goal. Knowing is powerful, but acting based on knowledge is what creates true value to the bottom line.

Decisional Context   We discussed how a poorly communicated insight can result in no action, negating the value of the insight in the first place. Knowing how to share insights and linking these to beneficial action is a concept we call "decisional context." Decisional context occurs when the decision of an individual or a group is not solely based on the individual's or group's interests alone, but also factors in the business imperatives of other groups or the organization as a whole.

Imagine that an operations manager has just found out that, in order to meet demand, she will have to outsource some of the production to an external company. The outsourcer pricing is highly competitive, and insights drawn from historic supplier data allows her to predict that the outsourcer has faster turn times than their competitors when certain market conditions are met. They can likely fulfill the order on time and at an attractive price point.

However, when the operations manager's company outsources from outside companies, marketing incurs costs related to the positioning of the new offering. They may have to rebrand some products for distribution relationships this company has with large distributors and retailers. These distributors also have strict quality control standards and punishing return policies, which are of great concern to the Sales, Support, and Finance departments. If the quality of these products is below standard, it will damage the company's sales, distribution relationships, customer loyalty, and brand equity.

While outsourcing production may make sense strictly for the operations manager who's trying to meet demand, it might not make sense for the organization as a whole. It's critical to have context for what the organization is trying to accomplish. If the company competes on quality, if they position their products as "best of breed" or "top of the line," the risks may outweigh the benefits.

Making a decision in a vacuum based solely on operations objectives might be easy, but the right decision is to incorporate the organizational context.

Decisions Accountability   What's the difference between insights and decisions? Insights can be the basis for decisions, while decisions imply action and, ultimately, accountability. *Compliance* and *auditing* have been common terms in the accountability register. Decision accountability is the ability to move beyond insights to drive decisions and also understand decisional impact. The value chain of information progresses from data to impact in this way:

- Data
- Information
- Insight
- Decision
- Impact, Results

Implementing accountability is a major component of driving business performance. Knowing that someone is supposed to take action is critical, and responsibility for the impact or results determines the value of that decision-making ability. For best-practice companies, the relationship between the person making the decision and the decision itself doesn't stop at impact or results. They account for what works and what doesn't. They leverage the individual's impact to help the organization determine how to do more of the things they did well and fewer of the things they did poorly.

THE THREE CORE CAPABILITIES TO MANAGE PERFORMANCE: MONITOR, ANALYZE, AND PLAN

Once organizations understand the importance of data and information management and how this enables trustworthy decision making, they must develop their performance management skills (see Figure 2.2). In order to effectively manage performance, organizations must develop Monitor, Analyze, and Plan (MAP) capabilities:

- *Monitor*: This capability provides the company with the ability to know "*what* is happening" and "*what* has happened." Organizations implement cockpits, dashboards, scorecards, or simply reports to monitor their performance. These visual applications allow executives, managers, analysts, and other information workers to keep an eye on important indicators of their group's or company's health.

- *Analyze*: This capability provides the company with the ability to know "*why* what is happening is happening." To analyze performance, organizations

In order to manage performance, organizations must be able answer three fundamental questions:
  1. Monitoring: What has happened? What is happening?
  2. Analytics: Why is this happening?
  3. Planning: What do we want to see happen?

FIGURE 2.2 **Three Capabilities to Manage Performance**

implement solutions that are often very interactive in nature and allow managers and analysts to investigate the root cause of issues they see in their cockpits, dashboards, scorecards, or reports.

- *Plan*: This capability provides the company with the ability to know "*how* to model what should happen." Organizations develop processes and tools to conduct the essential planning, budgeting, and forecasting exercises. These processes, often driven by the financial community, first allow executives and managers to align groups and individuals around the metrics that drive the business—for instance, "What is our margin target?," "What percentage is our control spend to revenue?"

It should be noted that any capability can be developed first, but we commonly see organizations begin with monitoring or analyzing capabilities before moving into developing their planning capabilities. This may seem backward, as it may seem logical that the first capability to be developed would be planning, since a plan is crafted before it is monitored and analyzed.

However, the Monitor capability is listed first because most organizations are already in motion when they begin their performance management initiatives. They often first seek to have the ability to know "what is happening."

Despite the order in which they are developed, without all three of these capabilities, organizations cannot attain the six stages of performance management value. It is critical to understand that these capabilities are integrated, and the combination and interplay of all three is required to successfully manage performance. In fact, you will see this point underscored as the same leading companies are highlighted across multiple capabilities—we highlight their advanced skills in each of the Monitor, Analyze, and Plan chapters. Let's take a closer look at each.

Monitor

Organizations need to first know how their business is running before they can improve their performance. Understanding how the business is performing is critical to managing performance. Surprisingly, many Fortune 500 organizations do not know who is buying their products, where they are being used, where or how they were purchased, how and if they were paid—things that were much simpler to know when we were children selling lemonade at a corner stand. However, these operations are significantly more complex than the corner lemonade stand. Issues arise as the number of customers and transactions increase; it gets more difficult to track. There are data management complexities of running multiple systems, complex distribution models to account for, privacy concerns over sharing customer data, and global business models, multiple currencies, returns, rebates—the list goes on. Keeping a finger on the pulse of the business can be very difficult.

Challenges   When organizations lack the ability to monitor their performance, they limit their impact. Being deficient in the monitoring capability can result in:

- *Shortsightedness.* When organizations lack visibility in into their performance, they are often shortsighted in their recognition of problems and proposed solutions. They lack insight to the root causes of problems.

- *Managing by conjecture and sound bites.* Lacking facts and data to drive their decisions, these organizations often make decisions based on hunches and hearsay. However, as has been said, "The plural of anecdote is not data."[2]

- *Aimlessness and speculation.* Without focus, direction, and accountability, people are simply doing things— the activities that they are driving may not align to the results that the organization is seeking. This environment also suffers from countless theories and personal takes on the direction the company is trying to go. Each employee has a different definition of the mission statement or group charter. Put best, "Where facts are few, experts are many."[3]

- *Misalignment.* As different groups march to the beat of their own drum, the band breaks apart and the organization is uncoordinated and out of step. It trips over itself. Redundant and even conflicting agendas are typical in these environments.

- *Inability to execute strategy.* It is nearly impossible in this environment for the plans of a few disconnected executives to get transposed into group and individual tactics.

In the next chapter, we discuss the specific skills and assets needed to monitor performance. We begin the chapter with the story of how Expedia developed its performance management capabilities. To further demonstrate the concepts and recommendations, we highlight how leading companies like Expedia, Hilton Hotels, Millipore, Siemens, and Skanska have developed these skills and the benefit it provides them. We then provide a self-exam that allows the organization to assess its ability to monitor and provides guidance for improving these capabilities.

Analyze

Once organizations understand what is occurring in their business, they need to understand why. Many organizations continue to see problems within their business but are unable to identify the cause and take action to rectify the issues. With all the possible reasons that could account for a given business issue and with no ability to identify the real issue, the organization is left to draw insights from conjecture.

Larger organizations employ specialized professionals, analysts, to do this very work—dig into the data to derive insights about which markets to penetrate, understand the voice of the customer, or determine cost-saving moves the company can make. While this supports the needs of strategic decisions, this doesn't work for tactical and operational decisions. Having specialists who do deliver insights for tactical decisions is akin to the couriers of yesteryear. The technologies are available today to expand this capability to the people who need it, when and where they need it. Businesses no longer need to wait for their insights to be delivered to them from a specialized service bureau.

Challenges   Organizations are often frustrated by their inability to know the details of their business. Without an analytic capability, they are unable to query their data to understand why their business is experiencing problems. When organizations lack the ability to analyze their performance, they limit their impact. These companies suffer from:

- *Blindness and learning disability*. Without an analytic capability, organizations often repeat the same mistakes without knowing it. Since they are unaware of the linkage between their action and the problems they are experiencing, they continue to feel the pain.

- *Missed opportunities*. Since organizations are unable to analyze their information, they miss the insights that could yield great returns. Even when they suspect an opportunity may exist or have a hunch on how to solve a problem, they are unable to conduct meaningful analysis to discover their opportunity. Missed opportunities can also arise from restricted analytic capabilities within the organization—the intelligence is too hard to get to for the opportunity to be seized (the customer service rep may not recognize the up-sell/retention opportunity).

- *Multiple theories.* Without insights based on data, the organization becomes a breeding ground for theorists—people across the organization with their own guesses at what is really impacting the business. This undermines executive leadership and creates potentially divisive debate. Without data to have constructive queries, this environment is left to political clout alone to decide direction.

- *Uninformed planning.* Without the ability to recognize patterns and trends in their performance, and unable to see correlations between their actions, organizations without the ability to analyze are unable to develop solid plans.

In Chapter 4 we focus specifically on the Analyze capability. We begin the chapter by telling the heroic story of the U.S. Department of Veterans Affairs and the success they've had managing performance. We also highlight the skills of the world's second largest health maintenance organization (Clalit), Hilton Hotels, and Premier Bankcard to provide examples of how the skills and assets we cover are applied in the real world. At the conclusion of the chapter, readers can assess their organization's Analyze capabilities.

Plan

Whether at the beginning (Plan, Monitor, Analyze) or the end (Monitor, Analyze, Plan) of the performance management cycle, planning is a critical process for driving business performance. When organizations are first determining their strategy, they need to accurately capture and develop the plan, budget resources, and forecast future results.

Planning is equally important for organizations already in motion. Once an issue has been identified using monitoring capabilities, and the reason for the issue is understood through analytics, the logical next step is to do something about it—develop a plan of corrective action.

While planning, budgeting, and forecasting (collectively, the Plan capability) are essential business practices, it is unnerving how few of us are able to do it effectively. The typical enterprise utilizes "10 general ledger systems, 12 different budgeting systems, 13 different reporting systems," and takes "6 months for planning, 5 months for budgeting, 2 weeks to develop a forecast."[4] Such disparate information and slow execution make the basic practices of performance management a real challenge for most companies.

Challenges   Organizations are often frustrated at the time, effort, and errors they encounter in the planning, budgeting, and forecasting processes. It is often an annual pain across the company. As they struggle to accurately capture their plans, develop their budgets, and close their forecasts, these companies suffer from:

- *Being out of step with the market.* Without the ability to work plans, budgets, and forecasts continuously, organizations move slowly at scheduled rhythms. They are too slow to meet the needs of the customer, the pace of competition, and the movement of the markets, which move faster and in different cycles. While they may plan annually, their business environment is changing monthly. These organizations lack agility to keep pace with their continuously changing markets.

- *Planning in a vacuum.* The process of predicting the direction of the business is the responsibility of everyone in the company. Companies who run budgets, forecasts, and plans in the confined walls of the Office of the CFO have rendered the broad collaboration of the remainder of the business impossible, either because they don't want to enable it or because the other business units perceived the effort fruitless.

- *Disconnected solutions.* Many companies have a large number of systems to run budgets, forecasts, and plans. Companies have to weigh the benefits of having a large selection of best-of-breed point solutions that don't talk to each other versus having fewer applications that can further integrate and enable more constituents to participate in the performance management process.

- *Continuous realignment.* Since the needs of all employees in respective departments are not accounted for, the company is constantly repositioning as it struggles to keep a handle on its needs and changing plans.

Chapter 5 begins with the story of Energizer and its transformation to a company full of "difference makers." We then detail the specific planning, budgeting, and forecasting skills being utilized by Energizer and other leading organizations, such as Hilton Hotels, Millipore, Oticon, and Premier Bankcard. Finally, we conclude with an assessment to allow the reader to determine the quality of their Plan capabilities and guidance on how they can improve their results.

CONCLUSION

Having discussed the types of decisions organizations make—strategic, operational and tactical—we now know what decisions we're trying to impact. We also have an understanding for the types of trust organizations need to provide: trust of (1) data, so people can trust their (2) insights and, ultimately, trust their (3) decisions.

We have also introduced a key concept of this book—that there are three capabilities organizations need to drive performance: Monitor, Analyze, and Plan. These capabilities are integrated and together allow organizations to begin to realize the value they seek from managing performance.

In the following three chapters, we begin to get a much deeper understanding of these three capabilities and the specific skills and assets needed to attain them. We start with the ability to monitor in Chapter 3.

NOTES

1. Peter Klein, keynote presentation, New York, September 2007.
2. Attributed to Frank Kotsonis.
3. Attributed to Donald R. Gannon.
4. David A. J. Axson, *Best Practices in Planning and Management Reporting* (Hoboken, NJ: John Wiley & Sons, 2003).

3

Monitor

Strategy without execution is a daydream, execution without strategy is a nightmare.

Japanese proverb

We begin this chapter with the Expedia performance management story. This introductory story is a firsthand account of the typical challenges faced by organizations as they embark on their performance management journey. It sets the stage for the rest of the chapter and the remainder of the book.

Expedia has developed skills and assets across all three capabilities: Monitor, Analyze, and Plan. Here, we highlight their advanced monitoring capabilities in particular, and also identify their progression through the various stages of managing performance.

THE EXPEDIA STORY

Once an Internet start-up, Expedia, Inc. is now one of the largest travel and hospitality companies in the world, with operations in North America, South America, Latin America, Europe, the Middle East, Africa, and Asia Pacific. Its portfolio of brands includes Expedia.com, Hotels.com,

Hotwire, Expedia Corporate Travel, TripAdvisor, Expedia Local Expert, Classic Vacations, and eLong. Expedia, Inc. is also a member of the Nasdaq 100 and was recently added to the S&P 500 index. So not only are the world's travelers watching their performance, but so are the stock markets.

New Leadership

In 2006, following two spin-offs of the company and a change in stock price from a high of $86 in 2001 to a low of $14 in 2006, Expedia appointed Paul Brown as President. He was chartered with the mission to drive growth, reinvigorate the company, and show the value still attainable in the model. Brown introduced an initiative to drive performance and established rigor in the organization with aligned execution toward common goals.

Getting Started

When Brown arrived at Expedia, he asked Laura Gibbons, Manager of BI and Performance Management, to spearhead the performance management initiative. As Gibbons explains, "We discussed a way to use the Balanced Scorecard to improve performance and drive change throughout the organization, and asked, 'Can we do this?'"[1]

Your Numbers Must Be Wrong   Gibbons continues:

> We have six lines of business—flights, hotels, cars, cruises, packages, and destination services—and so we went to the leaders of each of these groups and asked, "What are your metrics? How do you measure success?" Distilling everything that was measureable down to 30 metrics was the result of meetings with the Senior VPs across the company . . . lots of voting and negotiating.[2]

The common difficulty with trusting the numbers, typical at the start of a performance management initiative, made it a difficult road in the beginning. Gibbons adds,

It was very painful at the beginning, because after all the work done to collect and integrate data, analysts would still get berated in meetings with "Your number's wrong. I'm sure your number is wrong. That can't be right." We spent a lot of time debating whether our data had any integrity versus actually focusing on the reds, yellows, and greens themselves.[3]

(*Note*: For those who do not already know what "reds, yellows, and greens" mean, never fear—you will know shortly).

The process was very lengthy: three months to determine the right KPIs [key performance indicators] and another two months to make sure they were accurate. Then, we developed these 10MB spreadsheet workbooks with the KPIs and charts to use as rudimentary scorecards to help us monitor progress. They were bulky, outdated books that were too cumbersome to actually get through in a meeting. It really was a matter of bandwidth as to what we managed and what we couldn't get to in the spreadsheet didn't get covered.[4]

Baby Steps Beyond the numbers, Expedia wanted additional context about the information and the ability to see more detailed explanations. The information was not in a state where it could allow questioning to explain the numbers and so employees could quickly understand what was actually happening across the organization. Gibbons explains,

The rudimentary scorecard told us the "what"; we needed to add supplemental information to tell us the "how." The "why" came in when we started to overlay different dashboards by line of business—things like revenue per customer and normalization factors such as calls per transaction. So rather than only showing absolute numbers, we started to create more of a dashboard approach off of these six top line scorecards.[5]

Expedia needed to build cascading and aligned scorecards, starting from the top. "Every day there was a request to compile a handful of metrics for the CEO and President—things like revenues, customer satisfaction, visitors, etc. We had all the data points, so we started publishing an executive scorecard, which is now called 'the Heartbeat.'"

Here Comes the Flood

What happened next is typical as companies increase visibility and move beyond gut feel—they get flooded with additional requests: "We suddenly got an immense amount of requests. Everyone wanted a dashboard, saying, 'My boss wants to know why this measure is turning red.'" These requests required Expedia's analysts to spend more than half their time scurrying around trying to find the data.

While the manual collection of data was an unfortunate consequence of an immature performance management system, the fact that management was starting to look for information was a positive sign of adoption. The measures now meant something for Expedia—the expectation was that employees would now have data to back up their claims and to show progress toward goals. "And adoption is one area that most people gloss over. But adoption will make it or break it with performance management. If people don't buy into it, you're never going to get them to manage their performance," Gibbons adds.

Top Down, Over, and Across

Today, "the Heartbeat" is felt across the organization. "We now have scorecards cascading across lines of business (air, car, flights, hotels), across channels (search engines), and cascading all the way down to the call center and agent level – top to bottom. We did it by Balanced Scorecard perspective – once a perspective was done, we moved on to the next."[6]

Developing a Culture of Performance

The company has turned the initiative into standard operating practices to make performance management part of the Expedia culture.

"We had the mandate, but we still needed to be able to drive adoption and buy-in to start to create a Culture of Performance. It was internal guerilla marketing," explains Gibbons. Gibbons's team developed training programs to drive performance management capabilities across the organization. They hosted "lunch and learns" and discussed performance management during new hire trainings:

"Every new employee goes through training on 'what is performance management?' and how to do it at Expedia. They are asked which groups they are joining and they are shown how to manage and even build their own scorecards for their respective jobs. They understand how performance is managed and communicated for their respective teams and how this impacts organizational objectives."

Expedia even created a brand to certify their agreed-upon understanding of "truth." "We created an icon with an Expedia logo on it (a 'Data Quality & Accuracy Seal') to certify the information and created a tag line, 'How satisfied are your customers?' We also had an internal communication campaign and did not ever wait more than 30 days without giving a piece of information about our performance management culture, which was really effective."

Employees were made well aware of the culture shift, and they were provided the tools to better embrace it. The Data Quality & Accuracy Seal that they saw on reports and scorecards increased their trust in the numbers and the emphasis on performance management altogether.

Further, teams across the organization conducted contests to engage employees and help them understand they were participants in performance improvement. For instance, airline tickets would be given to whoever could get the closest to forecast without going over, within a 5% variance. So teams were competing to see how closely they could stay to forecast. "It's really about finding out what motivates your employees and then finding ways to incent them to actually use the system and drive the desired results," concludes Gibbons.

Now that the organization was better engaged, it was time to tie corporate performance to individual compensation. Expedia accomplished this by integrating their performance management systems with their human resource (HR) systems. This helped employees see the connection between their actions, the bottom line, and their compensation. This required a cultural and mental shift. "After all, performance is personal. Better overall performance starts with better individual accountability," explains Gibbons.

After five years of developing world-class capabilities, Expedia is a prime example of how to approach performance management. "The results have been extraordinary. We're extremely fast at making decisions now. Before, we were really flying blind. . . . Now, our business is almost running truly like a heartbeat, where it's monitoring and alerting itself. We used to lack basic reporting capabilities, and now our people talk in terms of reds, yellows, and greens. It's truly an impressive feat for Expedia—and a real differentiator and competitive advantage."

Realizing the Six Stages of Performance Management Value

So how have Expedia's capabilities helped them? Let's review how Expedia is realizing the six stages of performance management value:

1. *Increase Visibility.* This is achieved with an understanding of what is happening across the organization

through cascaded and aligned scorecards. Trusting information is key here, and Expedia's "Data Quality & Accuracy Seal" ensured that their visibility was not only increased, but also improved, since they now had better views of numbers that could be trusted and acted upon.

2. *Move Beyond Gut Feel*. Expedia transitioned to a fact-based and data-driven culture by developing consistent and reliable data and information and creating a culture where facts are held in high regard and supersede politics. For example, Expedia ties together the performance management and HR review systems so they can communicate with and evaluate employees based on facts. Gibbons provides an example of how Expedia has moved to fact-based decisions:

> There are three key metrics that relate to how we're doing with customer interactions and the call centers have access to these metrics. Our call center personnel have the authority to waive fees and, while that can have a negative impact on revenue, it can also have a positive impact on customer retention. In some cases, we had found that 60% of the agents were waiving these fees every month. So we wondered, if we're losing customers and we're waiving fees more than half the time every month anyway, why are we even charging it? As a consequence, our Hotels.com brand eliminated fees and they did that because we published the metric that showed the large percentage we were waiving. Along with that, they were able to drill in and find out that retention was suffering and we weren't making as much money as we thought anyway since we were waiving the fees so often. So it was a great way to see how one little metric on our scorecard has now translated globally across our different brands to serve customers better.[7]

3. *Plan for Success*: We cover Expedia's planning capabilities in more detail in Chapter 5. However, it is worth noting how they've developed these capabilities, and

how, along with the monitoring capability, they utilize them to better plan.

> With Finance came our first foray into taking planning one step further. We automated a forecasting portal, so that while they were going through the planning process, they could adjust their plan or forecast based on what they saw on the portal. The portal incorporates six years worth of "day of the week" factors—for every day of every year, we logged in every event that occurred that could affect travel—like weather events (storms, hurricanes), political events (terrorist activities), and holidays and sporting events, for instance. We had the ability on our charts and graphs to annotate why there were fluctuations. We finally got this in an integrated environment, where financial analysts can integrate their planning activities.[8]

4. *Execute on Strategy.* When plans are developed, there is greater confidence that the anticipated results will be achieved. Expedia uses strategy maps to capture and communicate the strategy broadly. The company has aligned goals, active monitoring of business performance, visibility into operations, and a clear line of sight from the call center to the Board of Directors.

5. *Power to Compete.* By delivering daily snapshots of "Heartbeat" metrics, with thresholds and tolerances set in line with company goals, employees have been able to hear the voice of their customers and their suppliers, helping the company to exceed investors' expectations. Indentifying what metrics should be classified as "Heartbeat-worthy"— meaning metrics that executives cannot do their jobs without knowing—is an important and fundamental step in creating Expedia's Balanced Scorecard program. With that knowledge, Expedia made all of their objectives available to all employees providing an unprecedented level of focus across the company.

Furthermore, employees and executives constantly challenged existing metrics and brainstormed to prioritize potential Heartbeat metrics. The company developed the ability to collaborate in ways they hadn't before, ultimately, spotting trends much earlier than in the past.

One of those very trends related to "guaranteed price programs" that some of Expedia's competitors were developing. "Guaranteed price programs" referred to the guarantee by which customers were assured that travel providers would match any deal customers found to be lower than the price booked with that provider. Expedia was able to quickly build its program, "Best Price Guarantee," to counteract anticipated external pressure. However, before their performance management system was in place, executives had little insight other than gut feel as to how customers really perceived Expedia's prices and value.

Once the scorecards were used throughout the organization, special alerting capability was added. This meant anybody in the organization could sign up to be notified when a particular metric of interest either increased or decreased beyond an expected value. It was this very concept that drove a series of alerts related to competitive guaranteed price programs. Because Expedia realized the impact to their financials so quickly, they were able to dial up the heat in implementing what it dubbed the "industry's first comprehensive price guarantee offer."[9]

6. *Culture of Performance.* With employees understanding the corporate strategy, their responsibilities, and how they can actively manage their performance, the focus on intelligent execution became part of the culture. The "Heartbeat" was a key part of Expedia's efforts in developing such a culture. The term *Heartbeat* extends way beyond the management suite: "Everyone

inside of the company understands what the 'Heartbeat' is, how they align to it, and, more importantly, how they can impact it," Gibbons explains. "Incorporating performance management into new hire training and tying individual performance assessments to the corporate scorecards are tactics that further develop the right types of behaviors." Transparency of measurements and internal marketing initiatives such as trustworthy information branding made it easier for each employee to embrace the change in culture.

In order to develop a culture of performance, Expedia was guided by the principles of consistency, accountability, and alignment. In this chapter, we detail how you can also follow these guiding principles and develop a performance-focused culture at your company, too.

IN THIS CHAPTER

So how can you get started? Our goal is to help you start your journey toward better performance.

This chapter focuses on the Monitor capability. We describe the three guiding principles that best-practice companies follow in order to effectively monitor their performance as well as the specific skills and assets needed to implement the capability (see Figure 3.1).

The three guiding principles companies focus on to help them develop the Monitor capability are:

1. *Consistency*: both in terms of data and information and including the effective use of KPIs to drive consistency across the organization.
2. *Accountability*: making objectives and measures personal and driving ownership of execution.

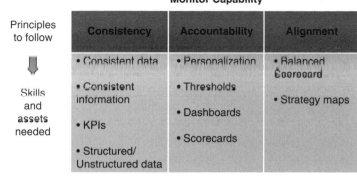

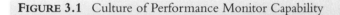

FIGURE 3.1 Culture of Performance Monitor Capability

3. *Alignment*: in both objectives and execution with tools like strategy maps and the Balanced Scorecard.

Let's take a closer look at how companies can think about consistency to guide them to effectively monitor their performance.

CONSISTENCY

A key challenge with driving performance across an organization is the ability to deliver consistent information. People often aspire to attain "one version of the truth," making sure, for example, that when everyone sees revenues across different product groups, they're all, in fact, looking at the same, consistent numbers.

One Version of the Truth?

Companies spend significant amounts of time and money storing all their enterprise data in a data warehouse to have "one version of the truth," but they often still can't get their management to agree on how to communicate about metrics of performance in a consistent manner. As Jeanne Harris of Accenture's Research Labs discovered, "We found that the average large company has 17 different definitions of the term *customer*—and some even have up to 400."[10]

This is reminiscent of the Tower of Babel comparison we previously discussed:

> When employees can't rely on the validity of the data—share the same understanding of performance, their discussions become fruitless. If they understand the same piece of data to mean different things, they effectively speak a different language of performance—they can't reconcile their thoughts and processes—they live on the Tower of Babel. They have been punished to speak different languages of performance.[11]

How can you ensure that people are speaking the same language? First, people must use the same words, which in an organizational sense means using common and consistent data. They also need to use consistent grammar, which, in terms of performance management, means having consistent business logic. The combination of both data consistency and consistent business logic creates "information consistency" and is the basis of a language of performance as shown in Figure 3.2.

Trusting the Numbers

When an organization has consistent data, the numbers are reliably valid. The $6 million sales goal is the real, accurate,

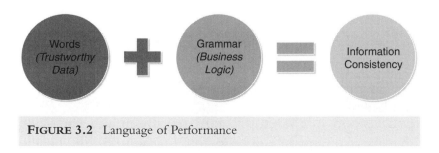

FIGURE 3.2 Language of Performance

and valid number to which the entire organization can refer. If the organization wants to change this number to $8 million, that change will be reflected to all systems that report from that "one version of the truth": the data warehouse.

Being able to trust *data* is the foundation for trusting *information*. If the data is consistent, you can trust the systems and people who are reporting it. Imagine that you received two reports telling you that your sales last year were "10" in one report and "20" in the other. What feeling would that data give you? Would you trust your analysts or the systems from which that piece of data is coming? Probably not. Many companies find themselves in this situation today and question whether the different numbers they hear across the organization can be trusted.

But providing trustworthy data alone doesn't solve the problem. Having consistent and reliable data does not necessarily mean that the information people are working with is consistent and reliable—data consistency is different than information consistency. To understand this better, we need to first discuss what information really is.

Using the Numbers

In technical terms, information could be called "business logic." Business logic is what defines data, what people do with the data, and how they use it to measure performance in their own business terms.

Bill Baker, Distinguished Engineer and GM, Business Intelligence for Microsoft, provides a great example of business logic:

> Think of a regional manager with a couple of hundred stores. He may have a hunch that the high-growth stores have different needs, that if satisfied, yield some special opportunity to the company. To drive this hunch to a real insight, he gathers some data for all his stores and sorts the stores by high or low growth.

But it's not just a matter of the absolute growth rate. He may want to exclude very new stores since their growth rate may be distorted by their relative size. And very small stores that may not be as relevant for what the manager is trying to determine. And maybe he knows the company is selling the two stores over there, so he wants to account for that. And he also knows that these two stores over here, while not in the same growth range as some others, fit the profile of what he wants to do. What he's done is create a small nugget of business logic. It's his working definition of "high-growth stores." And if that definition remains private to him, that's ok, he got what he needed. He either figures out these stores are special or not and either decides to do something different for or with them, or not. But at the moment he puts a program in place for these stores, it becomes important to share the definition of high-growth stores with the rest of the organization, at least at the regional level. And if his program works, we should want his creativity to apply across the whole organization. In other words his definition of high-growth stores (and his program for them) gets shared across the company.[12]

In other words, trusted data alone is necessary but insufficient in driving better performance. Institutionalizing business logic is an important complementary asset to develop because it describes how data is interpreted to drive performance. As we can see in the preceding example, business logic is often required to allow more flexibility and personal management of the data. Business logic provides the flexibility businesspeople need to address changing business challenges. One year, the definition of "high-growth stores" might include some stores, and the next year it might exclude them based on new requirements.

Information Consistency

Information consistency is reached when data can be trusted, when business logic reflects the definitions and approach of the organization, and when both of these assets are shared across the organization. As we discussed earlier, there is a formula for a language of performance—everyone understands the same words (consistent data) and uses common grammar (consistent information). Each of these components is an enabler to better execution and better performance, and when they are combined, they can deliver competitive advantage.

Organizations that have developed just one of these assets—they have consistent data *or* business logic but not both—might be left wondering why their marketing team argues with their finance organization about the definition of "high-growth stores." Often, they argue about the data not being right or that the data should be interpreted differently (depending on which departmental agenda is favored). This situation is far too common and is counterproductive to overall business performance. With consistent information, organizations are able to focus their employees to work toward the same goals and objectives, reliably, across the organization.

Once consistent information has been gained, it needs to be communicated widely throughout the organization. Leading organizations such as Siemens and Expedia have actually created a logo for their "One Version of the Truth." Siemens Data Drives division in Congleton, United Kingdom, created a logo to certify information as accurate and trustworthy as a part of their performance improvement initiative called Congleton Business Reporting and Analysis, or COBRA (see Figure 3.3).

In order to determine if information is valid—not just the data—employees simply check to see if their information is "Powered by COBRA," whether on reports, in their scorecards or dashboards, or on their portal (see Figure 3.4).

This is similar to the approach Expedia took in branding their trustworthy information. (See Figure 3.5 and 3.6.)

FIGURE 3.3 COBRA Poster

Consistent Definitions Lead to Consistent Execution

Now that we understand the importance of consistent information, how do we utilize this to better manage our business? Execution is key to business performance. Leading

FIGURE 3.4 Powered by COBRA

FIGURE 3.5 Expedia Data Quality Seal

FIGURE 3.6 Expedia "How Satisfied Are Your Customers?"

companies don't just win because they can monitor better, they win because they can monitor *and* execute better.

We often hear about *information overload*, a term that describes how as more and more data is being tracked, reported, and communicated, it becomes increasingly difficult for people to get to the specific information they need. In a work environment, this often comes in the form of a deluge of e-mails, voice mails, project updates, and requests, which may or may not align with the employee's performance objectives and focus. According to research by Accenture, "the average middle manager is swamped by useless information and spends about a quarter of work time—or two hours a day— looking for the data they need. . . . And despite the time spent hunting for the information, once they obtain it, half of the information has no value to their jobs."[13]

Given this dynamic, it is important to communicate information in a format that is quickly and easily understandable to make it more easily consumable. Newspapers have followed this model well, as summary pie charts and graphs quickly and simply convey the message.

Take a look at the difference in the way information can be presented in Figure 3.7. On the right you see a dashboard. On the left you see a report in print format that tracks the same information.

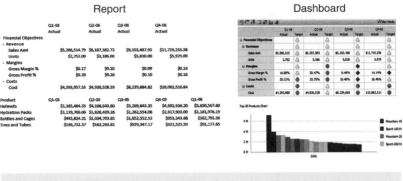

FIGURE 3.7 Report versus Dashboard

Which of these two provides a better snapshot of this organization's performance? Clearly, the dashboard on the right provides greater visual indicators to quickly communicate the information of what is happening in the business and the context for how this relates to other factors impacting performance.

Visualization is all the more impactful when it enables better communication of consistent information—data that can be trusted and logic that can be shared, accepted, and acted upon. Organizations that effectively monitor their performance provide quick and easy explanations of information that can be trusted and in terms that have been agreed upon and are understood. As the ability to create and consume information in this way spreads across the organization, the organization is better able to monitor its performance.

It's not surprising that the terms *scorecards, cockpits,* and *dashboards* have become buzzwords within the business community. These technologies are in high demand. Performance management is the top spend priority for CIOs; as Hoover's and Forrester estimate, these strategy and measurement solutions are the fastest-growing segment within the hot performance management space.[14]

But before rushing into these technologies, it's important to understand the differences between these highly visual applications. With this knowledge, organizations can understand how best they can be used to monitor business performance.

Key Performance Indicators

Key Performance Indicators, also known as KPIs, are predefined measures that are used to track performance of goals, objectives, plans, initiatives or processes.

KPIs are great visual decision-making tools that are meant to prompt action when things have gone poorly (red), alert when performance is deteriorating (yellow), and motivate when everything is well (green). Organizations often refer to the status of projects or performance in these KPI terms. They use expressions like "we should have a 'red, yellow, green' on this project to monitor how it's progressing"—very much like the Expedia example discussed earlier.

A KPI's utility rests on employees' ability to trust the underlying data and trust the business logic that makes it red, yellow, or green. KPIs are the way to deliver consistent information. KPIs are the way organizations can:

- *Express strategy and objectives.* A KPI can describe a particular metric (such as "revenue" or "margin") or describe an initiative (such as "create great customer experience").
- *Define success.* KPIs are matched with a target or goal measure symbolizing what failure (red), average results (yellow), and success (green) look like.
- *Hold individuals and teams accountable.* KPIs are created for a reason—to drive results. KPIs don't drive results by themselves—people do! Therefore, KPIs need to be associated with an owner, an individual who is responsible for the performance of that metric.

KPIs, Like People, Need Goals   As organizations incorporate KPIs in their systems for managing performance, it is important to remember that a KPI is evaluated against a target. The following example illustrates why this point is key.

Excel is the most popular environment within which organizations model their business. This is the tool individuals and companies turn to for developing plans, budgets, and forecasts. This application is particularly powerful and offers tools to allow people to model and graph information with even greater ease. Since this application is on employees' desktops, people can use it across the organization.

A popular feature within Excel is called "conditional formatting." Conditional formatting allows people to select a "traffic light" indicator from among a set of different icons and then apply this indicator to a range of numbers.

In the following example, conditional formatting has been applied to a range of numbers. Selecting the stoplight makes it easy to quickly understand trends and context for how the range of numbers relate to each other.

While this feature is extremely useful for comparing a range of numbers, it is important to note that this type of indicator is *not* a KPI. This distinction is more than just semantics. When performance indicators lack context of actual versus target, they lack critical information to enable better decision making (see Figure 3.8).

So what makes an effective KPI? A KPI is differentiated by the presence of two critical values that together enable meaningful interpretation of performance data. These values are:

1. *Actual value.* The "actual" value is the number an employee wants to look at to understand current status. For example, the manager of a consulting firm may want to see a KPI that indicates the percentage of customers surveyed who rate her company as their top source of advice. Or the regional manager of a

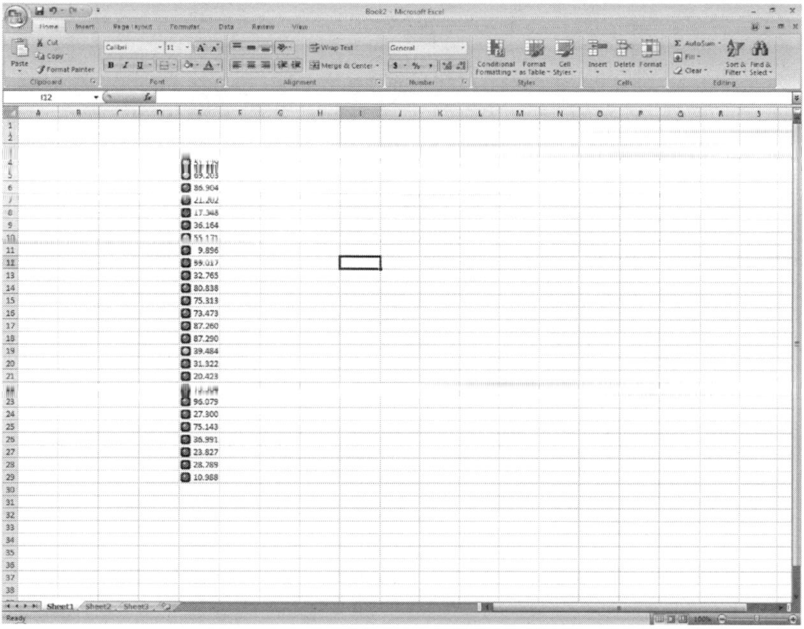

FIGURE 3.8 Spreadsheet Metrics

real estate company may want to see how many properties were sold in the last quarter. The data collected to support this indicator is the actual value.

2. *Target value.* The "target" value is different but related to the actual value. The target value is determined by answering the following question: "What do you want to achieve?" For example, how many customers do you want to acquire who view your consulting firm as their primary source of advice? How many properties do you want your regional office to sell this quarter?

Together, the actual and the target values facilitate business decisions that are informed by facts and common goals. The target value determines whether an outcome or result is good or bad. A sales executive may say, "I sold $3 million

FIGURE 3.9 Objectives, KPIs, and Targets

worth of goods this quarter." Is this a good or bad result? It depends on the target value. If the target value of sales for the quarter is set at $10 million, this is obviously not a good result. If the target value is set at $1.5 million, on the other end, this executive deserves a bonus. (See Figure 3.9.)

Energizer is a good example of a company that utilizes actuals and targets effectively.

> Having a strong performance management system in place also positions Energizer toward a Culture of Performance in which employees throughout the company have constant access to the accurate, up-to-date information they need to make smart business decisions. With the ability to monitor KPIs and compare actual results to pre-defined targets, both the company's 'difference makers' and high-level decision makers can take immediate actions to correct problems or to replicate one region's or country's success.[15]

KPIs Fit in a Broader Context However, KPIs are about more than just actual and target values. When done well, KPIs deliver organizational consistency: They can be relied upon and they can be shared across groups. They align to the organization's objectives, and their targets have been set appropriately to hit the organization's goals. As Allen Emerick, Director of IT at Skanska says:

Often, people think KPIs, scorecards, and dashboards to be the solution to their performance management problems. However, these technologies are merely the outputs of the efforts a company puts in determining what is core to its business, its objectives and how it defines performance.[16]

Determining What Matters   One of the first challenges an organization faces in determining KPIs is to know "the measures that matter." It may seem easy to know what an organization cares about, but the identification of KPIs can be one of the most time-consuming and arduous tasks in the performance management process. What makes it so difficult?

- *Focus is difficult.* Prioritizing objectives, determining which to focus on and which to remove, is very difficult. Executive leadership is required to clarify focus, provide direction, and determine which results are most critical.
- *What matters depends on whom you ask.* Different groups have different definitions of success. Even if the corporate objectives seem clear, the way teams or groups interpret how they can contribute to this success often varies.
- *Prioritizing metrics is difficult.* Determining which weights to assign to which objectives is a revealing endeavor: Is high customer satisfaction more important than maintaining budget or reduced expenses? All of these are likely important metrics, and it is necessary to capture them in some sort of grouping, perhaps relating to a particular methodology (such as the Balanced Scorecard, LEAN, Six Sigma, Total Quality Management, Economic Value Add, etc).
- *Metric relationships are difficult to map.* Understanding how metrics from different groups align and support each other is challenging. How does customer satisfaction relate to increasing shareholder value?

Leading organizations like Harrah's have derived competitive advantage by knowing this linkage: They "can measure the revenue they will gain by moving a customer to a higher satisfaction level."[17] Hilton Hotels has even identified a link between customer loyalty and revenue—a 5% increase in the former associates with a 1.1% increase in the latter.[18] Unfortunately, for many organizations, not only is the linkage not known, but they actually have redundant or misaligned, if not contradictory, metrics.

- *Valuing intangible assets.* As authors Jon Low and Pam Kalafut estimate, "Fully one-third of an organization's value is derived from elements that can't be seen, such as brand equity, strategy execution, reputation, and innovative culture."[19] Determining how to capture and manage intangible assets can pose significant challenges. "Intangibles such as R&D, proprietary know-how, intellectual property and workforce skills, world-class supply networks and brands are now the key drivers of wealth production while physical and financial assets are increasingly regarded as commodities."[20]

In summary, KPIs represent the measures that an organization relies on to monitor and drive business performance. Companies such as Hilton innovate in their use of KPIs and, specifically, targets. As they show, targets neither need be static nor have a one-to-one relationship to each KPI.

Hilton Hotels has a very creative way of motivating their employees to achieve "perfection" by setting up multiple targets to the same KPI:

For nonfinancial measures, we would set up a number that we called "perfection." This number was statistically calculated. It looked at the performance of all the hotels across the firm and determined what a perfect score would be. Then, we would establish for each property a plan to decrease the gap between their actual performance and "perfection." For some hotels, we would set a plan to decrease the gap by 10% each year. Of course, as everyone's performance would increase, the statistical number for "perfection" would increase as well, so this system would constantly pull our properties' performance up. In addition, we had something we called the "red zone." The red zone was the opposite of "perfection." It was the area that no hotel should be in. So, by creating a zone between which identifies the minimum level of performance, an unacceptable area (the "red zone") and an aspiration ("perfection") for each hotel, we could motivate people to move up the performance ladder.[21]

Doing so required the ability to establish multiple targets for the same KPI and reevaluating targets ongoing. Establishing these barriers with multiple targets for the same KPI is becoming a more common approach for many companies as their performance management capabilities mature.

Not All that Is Measured Is Managed As more and more teams "measure what they manage," KPIs proliferate. There's a temptation to measure everything. Many companies watch tens, hundreds, and some even thousands of metrics.

However, in the words of Einstein, "Everything that can be counted does not necessarily count and everything that counts cannot necessarily be counted." Not all that is measured should be managed. Organizations and managers simply don't have the bandwidth—there's only so much information to which people can attune.

> One of the big differentiators for Expedia is that we measure things we can actually do something about. We're a big actionability company. We care about what's actionable—information that we can actually do something about—because this provides great focus and alignment across the company.[22]

Leading organizations focus on only a few summary metrics that accurately represent their strategy, the performance against which determines their success. These are often financial metrics such as "revenue," "profit," or "market share," but as noted above, these should also include nonfinancial and intangible assets which often also have a significant impact on performance.

Given the importance of these "bottom-line" metrics, it's important that the KPIs line up to these objectives. Progress on tactical metrics at the individual contributor, team, and group levels actually affect performance against these top objectives.

It is understandably common, then, that related KPIs are often combined and measured at different levels of the organization. For instance, the combination of the German, French, and U.K. revenue KPIs make up the "Europe revenue" KPI results. Sometimes the same principle might apply across KPIs: Revenue KPIs and cost KPIs both impact margin KPIs.

The sales scorecard in Figure 3.10 is an example of how this may look. There are KPIs for Revenue items such as Sales Amount and Units. For Margins, the KPIs measure Gross Margin percentage and Gross Profit revenue while

	Q1-06		Q2-06		Q3-06	
	Actual	Target	Actual	Target	Actual	Target
⊟ Sales Objectives		●		●		△
⊟ Revenue		△		△		△
Sales Amt	$25,663,364	△	$34,366,793	△	$48,122,573	△
Units	14,005	△	18,752	△	24,057	△
⊟ Margins		●		●		△
Gross Margin %	19.89%	●	19.84%	●	16.52%	△
Gross Profit %	24.83%	●	24.76%	●	19.78%	△
⊟ Costs		●		●		●
Cost	$20,558,319	●	$27,546,799	●	$40,174,195	●

FIGURE 3.10 Sales Scorecard

Costs has one KPI to measure: Cost. These KPIs are organized hierarchically, with the lower-level KPIs rolling up to the higher-level categories—Revenue, Margins, and Costs—which also have KPIs assigned. Notice also that these higher-level categories in turn roll up to an overall "Financial Objectives" level with its own KPI.

The Sales Amount KPI above serves as a good example of how comparison and evaluation occur. This KPI has an actual value and a target value. The scorecard displays a number for the actual value, while the target appears as an indicator that ranks the performance of the organization in this area. In this case, a sales manager can look at the KPIs and quickly determine that for Q4 the Sales Amount is below the projected target but the overall Financial Objectives are on target.

Suffice it to say that defining the right KPIs is a difficult task: They not only have to rest on data the company can rely on (trusted data), and reflect the way a company measures performance (business logic), but they also have to be linked across all levels of the organization to drive consistent execution. Rushing to build dashboards or scorecards without considering the above requirements on information consistency often results in resources and money spent chasing the wrong objectives.

Determining the right *number* of KPIs to measure your business is also a challenging exercise. Sometimes, a few KPIs are enough to drive focus, while in other situations a larger number is required. For an executive scorecard, a summary set of 5 to 10 KPIs might be the right number at first. When deploying operational scorecards, however, organizations might need to produce 10, 20, and sometimes even 30 KPIs to meet the needs of a more operational audience. A dashboard with more than 30 KPIs, however, can become too much information to digest at once and therefore be nonactionable.

We advise that you look at the type of employees that the scorecard serves (e.g., executive, middle manager, operational manager, or business analyst) and then determine the appropriate level of detail and number of KPIs they need.

We also suggest that you think of KPIs as "recyclable" items. For instance, you might want to revisit your KPI portfolio each quarter, allowing your employees to focus on a smaller number of KPIs at a time. Once you've executed on this smaller number of KPIs and attained these goals, you may want to create new ones.

Millipore, a leading life sciences company included in the S&P 500 with operations in more than 47 countries, uses specifically this best practice of recycling KPIs. Christophe Couturier, VP Corporate Planning and Strategy Management, explains:

> Today, our operational dashboard has about 30 metrics. These are the key metrics that we want to work on today—they are the things that we want to focus on, they are the top 30 things that are important for our performance. Once we solve those, we will find more and keep the ones we now can execute on with confidence, in the background—we will check those maybe once a year. A great example is to think about how we work with KPIs. First, we define what we want to measure. Then, we measure and analyze. Finally, we investigate the source (or driver) of a KPI's performance (good or bad) and sometimes determine that one of its drivers is a better KPI to monitor. So we switch our KPI to that driver. This provides focus and this is really important for us. Some companies might monitor 200 KPIs at a time. Great for them, but doing so doesn't allow your organization to prioritize execution, which is what KPIs are all about.
>
> In fact, if you think about your KPIs, they truly represent an execution roadmap for your company. You need to think long-term but you also need to have flexibility. What matters is not how many metrics you have—but it is the flexibility that you can have to decide to work on one versus the other.[23]

Your World Is Not Defined in Rows and Columns   Thus far, we've discussed how organizations can more effectively monitor their business by implementing consistency in their data and information and in their use of KPIs. The common theme for each of these is not only that they drive consistency, but also that each is based on data that is structured in nature—it comes from systems across the organization.

The information that people need to make decisions, however, takes various forms. Some information can be stored in a database (called "structured data"), while other information is just too fluid and variable to be constrained to the rows and columns of database applications ("unstructured data").

In order to drive consistent execution, organizations need to understand how to empower their employees with additional information that is not system generated yet is very useful in enabling them to execute better decisions more rapidly. In fact, recent research indicates "81% of senior business executives believe they are increasingly having to join up information from different sources about people, objects, locations and events to be successful."[24]

Decisions Are Based on Structured and Unstructured Data   The best way to define the terms *structured data* and *unstructured data* is by example.

Structured data is data that can be structured in rows and columns in spreadsheets or databases. The scorecard on the top left of the image shown in Figure 3.11 is an example of structured data. The data is constructed and presented so that it tells a specific story about the organization. KPIs have been defined to measure and track Revenue, Costs, and Net Profit with Actual, Plan, and Trend information available by Quarter for each category. The scorecard measures business objectives and results and provides an overall view of business goals. A quick glance tells you that Product Revenue trends are good but Gross Profit Margin % trends are not.

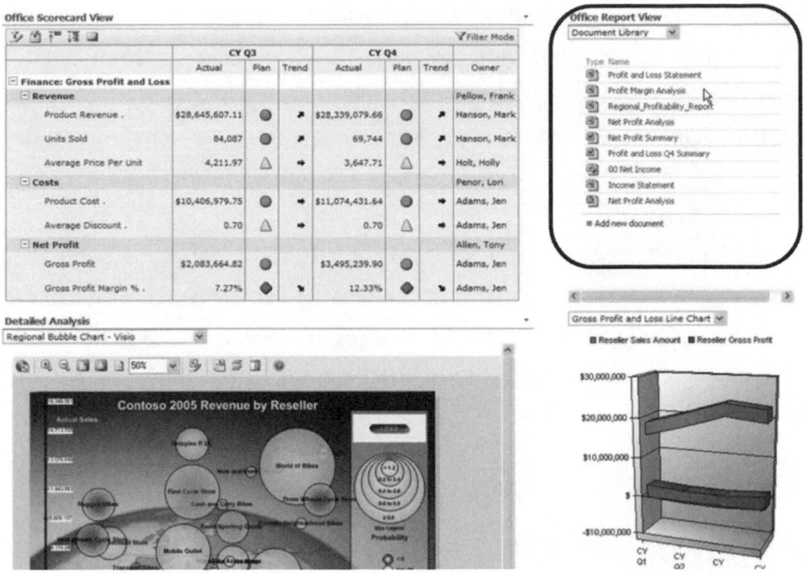

FIGURE 3.11 Document Library

Unstructured data provides context and supporting information rather than data in a structured format, such as a database. A list of documents is the simplest example of unstructured data.

In Figure 3.11, the document list is available right in the employee's dashboard. It displays a document library with different types of documents—spreadsheets, documents, and presentation files.

Each of these documents contains information that will help in understanding more clearly why the KPI results and rankings appear as they do. It is important to incorporate both structured and unstructured sources of information in a performance management solution and to relate them to each other.

Expecting that all the information employees need to make decisions is neatly stored in a database is a costly assumption. Organizations create information faster than their IT organization can or wants to store it. Even further, some of the information created by business groups might not need to be stored at all times—a Board presentation, for example, might be useful once but because its data is not consistent (e.g., doesn't fit the row/column model of a database), its information will rarely end up in a database.

However, the value of the information in the presentation is tremendous to the organization as it provides "soft explanations," the stories behind the numbers, or the context that most decision makers need to be aware of before they can make the right decisions.

When employees across the organization monitor performance, they need to understand the entire picture. Employees should be able easily to tie both structured and unstructured information together to make better-informed decisions. If employees see that a KPI is red, they might want to know why. Employees should be able to click on the given KPI and have additional information beyond the KPI itself. Sometimes this information might be another scorecard or another KPI.

Making structured and unstructured information available in the same decision-making environment allows employees to gain better context of the business situation. When employees gain a more complete view of the business, they develop confidence in their decisions and the information that supports them.

So how can organizations deliver increased integration between structured and unstructured data?

- *Filter across KPIs and documents.* Organizations implement filters that the KPIs and document lists can share so employees have a more consistent view across structured and unstructured information. For instance, an employee in Finance should see Finance-related KPIs in their scorecard as well as Finance-related documents. The same should apply for those in Marketing (i.e., KPIs and document lists should each be relevant to the Marketing domain).

- *Manage and audit documents.* Some companies create a tight integration between their performance management application and a collaborative portal environment they use to share organizational information internally ("intranet") or externally ("extranet"). These portals typically provide document management and auditing capabilities. When coupled with performance management capabilities, they provide a consistent interface and a one-stop shop for employees to find the documents they're looking for, to audit their processes to determine if they're in compliance with policies and procedures, and to manage their performance. This allows organizations to drive consistent behaviors across groups, departments, and divisions.

- *Search unstructured and related information consistently.* Beyond typical document management capabilities, portals should also provide the ability to search for content included in these documents. For instance, imagine that you are looking at a supply metric that is red. It seems there are delivery issues with supplier A. You would like to know what supplier A's history has been, where they are located, and who is their primary contact. Searching for this type of content from within a performance management solution becomes a great way to provide the additional information employees need to make better decisions. Some portals also allow for employees to search for information contained in all data sources available across the company. For example, if an employee were to search for supplier A's information, they might find not only information stored in documents but also information about opportunities in the Customer Relationship Management (CRM) systems or orders in the Enterprise Resource Planning (ERP) system for this supplier. This extends access beyond simple documents, and employees can derive further insights from the combined information.

- *Add information from sources other than documents.* From what system could this "other information" be coming? We talked earlier about databases, documents, CRM, and ERP systems. What else is there? Most companies we have talked to have 10 to 15 systems they rely on for information.

  Some of these "systems" are actually just hard-coded, fixed numbers. A good example might be a target number in a KPI. Say that for a given KPI, you would like the target to equal a specific number, such as 10 units. That number is not intended to change over time. In this case, manually inputting the numbers rather than connecting it from another system data source might be the most efficient way to build the KPI.

In order for employees to effectively monitor performance across the organization, they need to trust that their data and information—despite the source from which it comes or the form it takes—is trustworthy and consistent. To develop the ability to monitor performance, organizations need to ensure consistency not only in their data, information, and their usage of KPIs, they also need to provide consistency between their structured and unstructured data.

ACCOUNTABILITY

Once information is consistent, trusted, and shared across the organization, it needs to be acted upon. If performance management is about action, you have to think about the actor. Action is taken by "actors" of performance, the individual(s) who are performing the tasks required to address particular goals or objectives.

Organizations achieve accountability when individuals and groups agree on and are held responsible for their measured execution against particular initiatives. Alignment plays a big role in accountability because it helps determine who should work on what initiative and how their work will "roll up," or contribute to, the overall corporate goals and objectives.

Accountability brings an additional dimension to performance management, the notion of ownership for execution.

Information Needs to Be Relevant

Say you are in a store shopping, minding your own business, when all of sudden, someone rushes inside and exclaims, "A big truck backed into a car in the parking lot and completely destroyed it."

Understanding the danger of such an incident, the following questions likely come to mind: "Was someone in the car at the time of the accident?" "Was someone hurt?" "Was the truck driver insured?"

Now, what if the person that just rushed into the store added enough information that you realized that the car in question was *your* car. You'd probably drop everything that you were doing and rush to the parking lot to check the damage.

This story exemplifies how relevancy is key to prompting individuals to act. Earlier in this chapter we talked about the concept of information consistency and how it is important that information used to make decisions be trusted and consistent. In this section we discuss the importance of making information relevant to each employee.

Action Is Personal—KPIs Should Be, Too

If we agree that information needs to be personalized in order to be acted upon, then technology needs to support this goal. KPIs are where everything starts—if action is personal, information displayed by a KPI needs to be personal.

Organizations seeking to develop the ability to monitor allow the concept of personalization to persist through all interactions employees have with information.

There are two ways to personalize KPIs: systematic personalization and individual personalization.

1. *Systematic personalization.* This refers to the performance management solution's ability to be aware of the identity of the employee using the information and customize the information on the fly.

   This type of personalization ensures that information is segregated based on automated data filters—for instance, if the employee is from France, present French information; if the employee is from Germany, give German information. Used by itself, however, it becomes quickly very restrictive and inflexible. It assumes that people from both France and Germany care about the same metrics and that the only difference between the French and German business is a data filter. This might not always be true, though. For example, Germany might want to monitor a particular metric, customer satisfaction, for example, more than another. Therefore, organizations seeking to effectively monitor performance need to not only enforce personalization; they also need to give employees the flexibility to customize their views easily.

2. *Individual personalization.* When empowering employees, a company should allow them to monitor performance in their own way, while also ensuring

that they execute in alignment with the company's objectives. Organizations should allow individuals to personalize the metrics they focus on and also the alerts that tell them when performance is off.

To be more specific, imagine that the corporate goal for quantity sold is 12. The countries rolling under Corporate are Germany and France, and they each have individual goals of 6. Performance is checked continuously at the country level, while Corporate checks at mid-year and end-of-year. As a Germany manager, you might want to set an alert when three months into the year you have not reached half of your objective (three units sold). In France, however, they check performance every month and expect that in the first month, they will get half of their yearly orders. In this example, while both countries "roll up" to the same corporate objective, the local requirements for monitoring information are quite different. Obviously, each local manager wants to know when his or her KPI goes red before the corporate KPI goes red.

Personalization means employees can choose to monitor progress in the way that is the most meaningful to them. For example, employees could have an indicator turn red before their manager's does, so they get performance warning signs ahead of their bosses.

Beyond just knowing before their boss does, employees can use personalization to develop a better culture of anticipation. For instance, they can set lower tolerance thresholds so that warning signs can come in earlier than really expected. They can also develop "stretch" goals, which allow teams to see beyond the "minimum" expected results. When these skills are enabled broadly, the whole organization can realize benefits of increased agility.

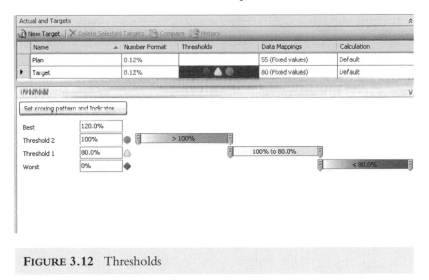

FIGURE 3.12 Thresholds

Green, Yellow ... Green?

Developing this culture of anticipation requires the organization to enable performance to be managed both flexibly and in a highly customizable way by any employee, not just IT.

In order to enable employees to define the "green, yellow, red" logic, you need an intuitive interface such as the sliders shown in Figure 3.12. These sliders allow employees to determine when metrics go green, yellow, and red without having to write any code or conduct complex calculations. We refer to this capability as "thresholds." A threshold is a ratio that defines the relationship between actual and target values to provide a barometer of performance.

Setting threshold logic, both negatively and positively, is also important. For example, as your costs go up, your threshold logic should allow you to reflect that increase with an increasingly negative indicator. This obviously follows different logic than revenue and profit whose increase is a positive.

Building threshold logic is a fairly easy thing to do once; but modifying it in a way that follows the rhythm of a dynamic business is a different story. Some companies might decide that their IT departments can handle the ever-changing requirements driven by new business conditions—acquisitions, changing business models, reorganizations, and so on.

Companies which successfully develop broad monitoring skills, however, trust their employees to modify and customize threshold logic as business requirements change. This allows them the flexibility to monitor their business in real time and more rapidly respond to market conditions. They are not constrained by the laborious work IT would have to do otherwise. By enabling employees to build and manage threshold logic, persistent small changes to customize thresholds do not become the IT department's nightmare. This is particularly relevant if your organization's metrics and their performance thresholds change often, thus making it impossible for your IT department to keep up with the change requests.

Who Do You Call When Something Goes Red?

The best way to drive accountability is to publish ownership at the KPI level. This simple asset, more than any other component of the organization's performance management system, has allowed organizations to develop a culture of responsibility and accountability for results.

Some companies choose to build great looking indicators but forget that what matters is *not* the indicator, but what individuals or groups *do* with the indicator. Including an owner for each KPI has three clear benefits:

1. *KPI ownership makes very clear who owns the results.* If John's name is by a KPI that is red, it ensures that John

knows he needs to find a way to resolve the issue. John might attempt to qualify the "red" or discuss the validity of the number, but luckily you've read our passage on consistency and his argument won't stand a chance.

2. *KPI ownership reflects the individuals' connection to bottom line performance.* Ownership at the KPI level allows for follow-up on execution of specific metrics. Say, for instance, that Germany and France performance are represented by two different KPIs (owned by separate individuals), and they both roll up under Europe (owned by a third employee). Displaying separate owners for each metric (revenue, costs, margin) not only indicates how the metrics themselves roll under each other, but it also provides visibility of how people are performing and how their individual performance, good or bad, is affecting the rest of the metrics.

3. *KPI ownership allows better collaboration.* Imagine if you could communicate directly with the KPI owner (see Figure 3.13). Say you are a COO and you notice that

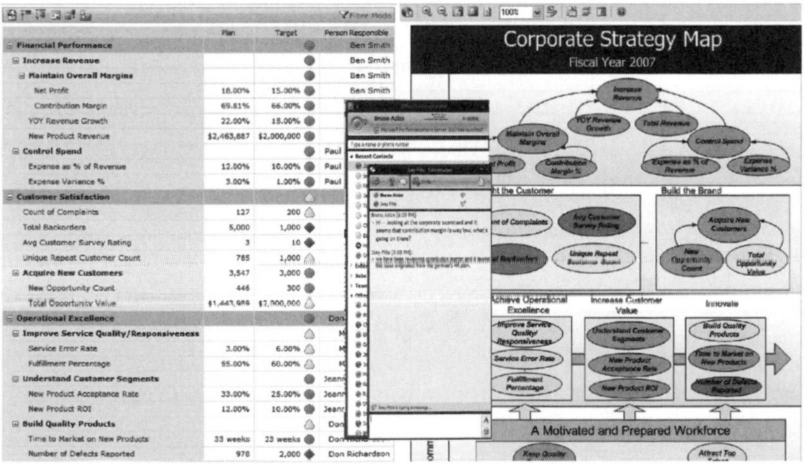

FIGURE 3.13 Communicating Directly with the KPI Owner

a "margin" KPI is yellow and you'd like to talk to the owner of the metric itself. In the old days, you would probably have to:

    ○ *Find who owns the resolution of the problem.* The question would typically go down the hierarchy to find out.

    ○ *Contact the owner.* Once the owner was identified, you would have to contact the owner in some way (e-mail, phone) and ask for an explanation about this performance.

    ○ *Resolve the issue itself.* Once the issue has been discussed, you could finally get to the action of trying to resolve the problem.

Best-practice organizations have shown deep integration between performance management and collaboration capabilities. They manage performance efficiently by allowing employees to talk directly to the owner of the metric, using the method of communication they find most useful (instant messaging, e-mail, phone, text message, etc). While disruptive if abused, collaboration capabilities are essential to the performance management process, which is very iterative and collaborative in nature.

Now that we have explored KPIs and discussed what makes them unique (targets), what makes them flexible (thresholds), and what makes them actionable (ownership), it is important to understand the value of tools like dashboards and scorecards.

Who's Keeping Score?

Previously here, the Big Picture (the CEOs scorecard) was printed out on paper and distributed out through interoffice mail to senior managers. Even before then, most of that number was driven off of month-end numbers. So it was hard for them to see interim month how close they were to meeting their goal. They really didn't see until the second week of the following month if they actually made their goal from the previous month. The data warehouse and our operational data store allowed them to get month to date numbers. That really made a big difference. And then, also, the ability to electronically adjust that information and get it out to everybody's desktop so you can control from the top down what numbers are being displayed to everybody. If someone has the prior month's Big Picture on his desk, he's operating on outdated numbers and can't see areas that need improvement until it's too late. You couldn't control whether he opened the interoffice mail or read the e-mail, but now its updated real time and it appears in their everyday view on their personal dashboard.[25]

Once an organization understands what it wants to measure and has defined meaningful KPIs, where does it put these metrics?

An efficient performance management system simplifies the creation and centralization of the KPIs into dashboards and scorecards. More than just reports, dashboards and scorecards are a way to assemble metrics relating to all types of performance—tactical, operational, and strategic. While KPIs are unique measures of performance, think of dashboards and scorecards as the boxes in which KPIs live.

Dashboards and Scorecards

There have been ongoing discussions about the difference between scorecards and dashboards. On one side, analyst and research firms describe key differences between scorecards and dashboards, while IT and businesspeople at companies often use the terms interchangeably.

In our work with service providers and organizations that use these tools, we notice two key trends:

1. Dashboards are typically used "lightly." They are decision-support applications that anybody in the

company should be able to build. They are often
built quickly and easily and do not follow a particular methodology. They report on performance on a
daily basis and their metrics tend to be more operational.

2. Scorecards tend to follow methodologies, such as the
Balanced Scorecard, which we will review further in
this chapter. There is a rigor and disciplined approach
often implied when referring to scorecards. They are
also often built top-down, to help the executive team
drive alignment and accountability across the company. While dashboards might include many operational metrics, scorecards tend to focus on just a few
KPIs (see Figure 3.14).

Some IT organizations describe dashboards as the containers of scorecards. In other words, a dashboard could be a
portal that the IT department might have used as a platform
to assemble reports and scorecards.

In the end, though, semantics discussions about scorecards and dashboards are less important than the impact
these technologies can deliver. What's necessary is that both

---

FIGURE 3.14 Eckerson's Dashboards versus Scorecards

Dashboards versus Scorecards

	Dashboard	Scorecard
Purpose	Measures performance	Charts progress
Users	Managers, staff	Executives, managers, staff
Updates	Real-time to right-time	Periodic snapshots
Data	Events	Summaries
Top-level display	Charts and tables	Symbols and icons

Source: Deploying Dashboards and Scorecards (Wayne Eckerson, July 2006)

individuals and teams are aligned in their strategy and accountable for their execution.

Dashboards and scorecards present a structured view of the goals and objectives for the organization. We have observed three rules leading companies follow when deploying scorecards and dashboards.

Rule 1: Scorecards or dashboards should not compromise the value of your KPIs. As we discussed earlier, KPIs have key characteristics (actual, targets, ownership). Any scorecard or dashboard that makes it difficult to integrate multiple KPIs easily would be suboptimal. Remember: KPIs are at the heart of performance management.

Rule 2: KPI data should remain portable across scorecards and dashboards. Consider a margin KPI, for instance. Once that KPI is built, then your solution should allow for it to be leveraged in a wide range of other scorecards. For instance, the same KPI could be used in a marketing scorecard as well as in a sales scorecard.

Rule 3: KPI information should remain portable across scorecards and dashboards. Let's go back to the margin KPI for a moment. Imagine if the KPI data could move only from the marketing scorecard to the sales scorecard. You could know what the number is, but you would lose most of the KPI value such as its target or even its owner. Making sure that the entire set of KPI information is portable provides accountability across both scorecards. If Joe is responsible for the margin KPI, both Joe's ownership and his performance against that KPI are consistently indicated wherever the KPI surfaces.

In order to deliver this benefit, an effective performance management solution needs to be flexible and make the KPI independent from scorecards. You can think of scorecards as the "containers" of KPIs. The KPI indicates the specific goal an individual is executing against, while the scorecards provide the context for that performance. For instance, Joe's performance may impact multiple stakeholders, and this KPI may show up in multiple scorecards—Sales, Marketing, Operations, or Finance.

Flexibility is a critical driving force in the design of a performance management solution. This includes flexibility in information presentation capabilities as well as flexibility in accessing, updating, and managing centralized data. Flexibility will allow the organization to guarantee information consistency at a lower cost, making it easier for all employees to understand, use, and align their actions to the right metrics.

ALIGNMENT

Strategy is completely useless unless the results of the strategy process, the position that you choose to occupy, the way you are going to drive your company, is well understood, quite broadly. Because the number one purpose of strategy is alignment, it's really to get all the people in the organization making good choices, re-enforcing each other's choices because everybody is pursuing a common value proposition, a common way of gaining competitive advantage (Professor Michael E. Porter, Harvard University).[26]

A key to executing effectively is to link strategic, operational, and tactical decisions across the organization. Alignment from strategic decisions all the way to tactical decisions is what sets best-practice companies apart from low performers. Many organizations try to create an environment where day-to-day activities support and contribute to corporate objectives. They want to create an environment where employees are like the third bricklayer in the fabled three bricklayers story. In the story, the first bricklayer says, "I'm laying bricks," the second says, "I'm making a wall," and the third says, "I'm building a cathedral." The third bricklayer understands context of the organizational mission and how daily tactics are contributing to the overall goal.

Alignment Requires Context

An example from Drs. Kaplan and Norton further illustrates the benefits of creating line of sight across an organization's decision levels.

> A truck driver for a transportation company that had implemented the Balanced Scorecard provides a good example of "line of sight." While making a delivery to a gas station he recognized that the bathrooms were in poor condition and the service was substandard. Recognizing that service and cleanliness were key metrics for the organization, the truck driver reported the issue because he had "line of sight" to the success objectives of the organization.[27]

The preceding example exemplifies the power of effective communication of strategy from the CEO down to the individual contributor. With contextual information about corporate objectives, individual employees can most effectively impact the company's bottom line.

The example shows that while strategic decisions create a framework for decision making across the corporation, operational and tactical decisions have a strong impact on the company's actual execution and success. Delivering a "line of sight" from strategic to operational to tactical decisions is the discipline that drives aligned execution. Additionally, a better line of sight across all layers of decisions helps corporations drive accountability. Executives build the framework (strategic), managers drive operations (operational), and most employees work toward the corporate objectives (tactical).

There are people in most organizations like the driver in the above example, and while their role might not be viewed as strategic, the number of decisions they make on a daily basis can soon have a detrimental impact if misguided.

Dr. Kaplan has joked about how he learned that a single word could explain so much of the meaning of alignment. As organizations began to formulate and document their strategies, he would ask them what they were trying to accomplish ("You can't measure what you can't describe") by asking, "What are you trying to do?"

> I realized that there were two different meanings for the word *do*. When I asked executives what they were trying to do, they would explain the organization's overarching objectives —raise the stock by 3%, increase profitability or cut costs, etc. Whereas when I asked the line managers what they were trying to do, they explained the tactics they were going to execute to reach their particular contribution to this goal.[28]

In strategy formulation, it's important to have the leaders set overall direction and allow the managers to sign up for their contribution to this goal and determine the tactics they want to implement to deliver their contribution—they know best how they want to "do" it. This process allows alignment and "line of sight," or visibility from the tactical things that are being done to the organization's overall objectives (see Figure 3.15).

This also allows for metric alignment between the organization's overarching objectives and tactical metrics that managers own to contribute to the mission. This can be thought of as an org chart for metrics, indicating how the various levels of the organization's metrics relate to one another. Mine roll up to my boss, my boss's roll up to the Director's, the Director's roll up to the VP's, which finally roll up to the CEO's.

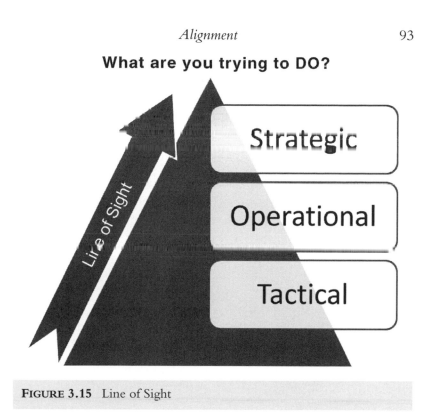

FIGURE 3.15 Line of Sight

The Balanced Scorecard

Business leaders often first learn about performance management from our friends at the Balanced Scorecard Collaborative. As they seek to formulate and communicate their strategies, they read the sage and now famous advice from Drs. Kaplan and Norton, "You can't manage what you can't measure, and you can't measure what you can't describe." The last part of this guidance—". . . you can't measure what you can't describe"—is often the starting point for most organizations in improving their performance management capabilities. It is the description of strategy that is the primary step that must be taken.

> The use of measurement as a language helps translate complex and frequently nebulous concepts into more precise ideas that align and mobilize all individuals into actions directed at attaining organizational objectives.[29]

The Balanced Scorecard methodology provides a framework for companies to answer questions such as "How do you want to describe success?," "What are the measures that matter?," and "How do we align and execute strategy?"

The Balanced Scorecard was created by Harvard Business School professors Drs. Robert S. Kaplan and David P. Norton in 1992 and is now a globally recognized and popular performance management methodology. The Balanced Scorecard Collaborative Hall of Fame for Strategy Execution—a community of 90+ organizations (as of October 2007) that experience significant returns from using the methodology to execute their strategies—is comprised of some of the largest companies and public-sector organizations in the world. A sampling of "breakthrough results" from the Balanced Scorecard Collaborative's Hall of Fame companies includes:

- $637 million loss to $1.9 billion operating profit in three years
- 100% increase in shareholder value in two years
- 21% revenue growth *and* 14 percent decrease in operating expenses in two years
- 450% growth in customer base in three years[30]

The Balanced Scorecard methodology is specific in its descriptions of the four key perspectives for managing performance across an organization. These four focus perspectives of the business allow an organization to keep a balanced view of the organization's performance:

- Financial
- Customer
- Operational
- Learning and Growth

In the example shown in Figure 3.16, notice how the KPI categories reflect the Balanced Scorecard perspectives.

Each area of the Balanced Scorecard provides a framework for identifying underlying objectives, for example, "Maintain Overall Margins" in the area of Financial Performance or "Improve Service Quality/Responsiveness" in the area of Operational Excellence. The next level of the Scorecard aligns appropriate KPIs to measure performance for each of the objectives. These underlying KPIs are specified by unique business drivers and can be expanded or extended to suit the measurement requirements of an organization.

In this case, the objective to Improve Service Quality/ Responsiveness is measured by Average Call Wait time in minutes, Service Error Rate measured as a percentage, and Fulfillment Percentage, which, obviously, is also measured as a percentage. Notice that each objective and key area also has a KPI, so information can roll up to higher levels to display performance measures by objective and key area. The CEO may want to view performance for key areas, while the call center manager is most interested in the details of

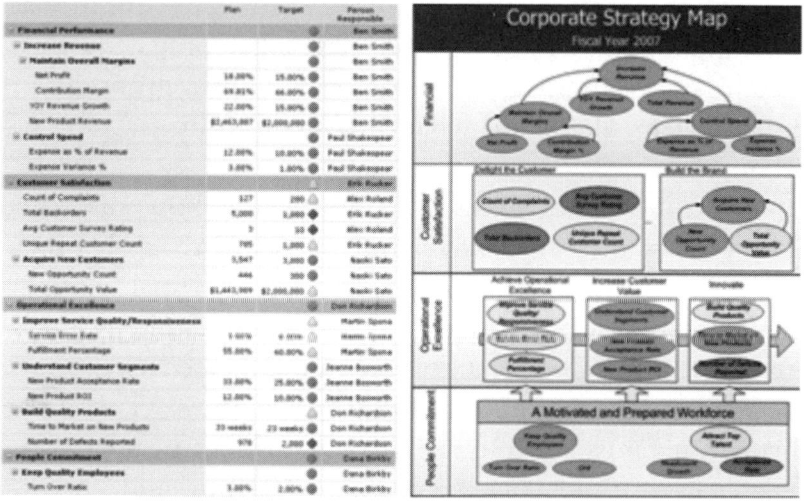

FIGURE 3.16 Balanced Scorecard Perspectives

the metric found under Improve Service Quality/ Responsiveness. This information alerts the manager to the fact that action must be taken to change the unacceptably long call wait time.

Strategic Context

Once organizations have defined their strategy, they need to communicate it. The way companies think about communicating strategy has changed drastically over the years, as Michael Porter aptly describes: "Many people believed that strategy documents should be locked in the safe at night and should not be made available to the 'rank and file' and there was a concern that some competitor would find some secret. Well, we've actually learned now that it's the opposite. Employees have to know your strategy, channels have to know your strategy, your suppliers have to know your strategy."[31] So how can companies effectively communicate strategy?

As we have discussed, KPIs, dashboards, and scorecards are tools that organizations can use to create organizational goals and cascade these down and across the company—thus helping to ensure that the metrics owned by a group or an individual are aligned to what the organization is trying to accomplish.

A great way to visually communicate how different components of a company's strategy relate to each other is with strategy maps. Strategy maps are visual displays of an organization's strategy and objectives. Strategy maps are central to Kaplan and Norton's Balanced Scorecard methodology as they provide a visual and concise view of information across the four major management perspectives: financial, customer, operational, and learning and growth (people).

A strategy map adds additional information to typical scorecards, as it allows employees to quickly see relationships between objectives and how metrics impact each other within the context of their own perspectives. For example, in the screenshot above, employees can see that " Total Back Orders" fit under the "Customer Satisfaction" perspective, and that they have impacted the financial perspective, particularly the "Contribution Margin" metrics. Armed with more contextual information from the scorecard and the strategy map, employees are better informed and can execute with more relevancy.

When done well, a strategy map clearly:

- *Communicates the end goal.* At the top of the strategy map should be the overall corporate objective, for example, "Increase Shareholder Value."
- *Identifies the business levers and drivers.* Individuals and groups throughout the business can easily identify how this objective is affected by other initiatives or metrics. For instance, customer satisfaction performance affects shareholder value. This helps employees better understand which concrete initiatives might impact the corporate goal.
- *Isolates areas of most impact.* Looking at a strategy map, employees can see what impacts performance directly and indirectly (e.g., "Operational Excellence" impacts "Shareholder Value" through "Customer Satisfaction"). This clear insight can provide better focus for execution.

Developing strategy maps involves a great deal of introspection and collaboration within an organization. From a technology perspective, what does this typically look like? At any company today, the process of building strategy maps is mostly manual:

- Business analysts might check with various people throughout the organization to get consensus around the strategy map's metrics, and they might use Excel, Word, Visio, or even a notepad to capture the information that will ultimately end up in the scorecard and strategy map.

- Once they have gathered all business input, they communicate back to IT what their requirements are for creating mock-ups of the end results.

- Then IT will implement the business specification. This process is very interactive, and when IT shares their first prototype with the business, they likely will be asked to make additional changes, some minimal, some significant, some flat-out impossible.

- In most cases, though, the resulting solution ends up being fairly inflexible, requiring the intervention of the IT group whenever change is required. Change might be needed in multiple places: new KPIs, new targets and thresholds, or maybe even new strategy map layout.

Strategic Now

A performance management solution should simplify this process. Employees should be able to build strategy maps, whether they already have scorecards or they're starting fresh in formulating their strategy. Let's look at each of two scenarios for strategy map development:

- *To provide strategic context to existing scorecards or dashboards.* If the organization has already deployed scorecards, business analysts empowered to use the performance management system should be able to simply add existing metrics from scorecards into a

strategy map. As discussed previously, KPIs can often be reused for multiple performance management
scenarios and views—this is another example. The
metrics may be coming from multiple scorecards and
are likely connected to multiple data sources. Because
the performance management solution manages these
metrics, when employees build strategy maps, they
will not only drag over the KPI name to their strategy
map, but they also will take with it the metadata of that
KPI—meaning its name, it color, its associated shape,
and other attributes. Essentially, this results in creating a strategy map that is connected to the back-end
information the same way the scorecard is—so when
any of the KPIs turns red in the scorecard, it will also
turn red in the strategy map. This helps guarantee
consistency of information.

This ease of use is important, as it empowers employees across the organization to add strategic context
to their performance management initiatives and help
ensure alignment to objectives. By pushing this capability out to employees, it has the added benefit of not
taxing IT or delaying the strategy map development
process, which means greater agility for the organization to go along with the increased alignment in
execution.

- *To formulate and communicate strategy.* Sometimes the
  strategy map is the starting point for an organization's
  performance management journey. If the organization has not yet built scorecards but wants to start
  with building a strategy map, they should be able to
  do that fairly easily within their performance management solution. Even if you're not using the Balanced
  Scorecard methodology, having technology that is capable of building strategy maps will give you peace of
  mind that you can use it to create your own strategy

maps aligned to whatever perspectives or methodology you choose.

Another effective practice to help ensure strategic alignment is to allow teams to use the tools with which they're familiar to develop their strategy maps. Employees should be able to use standard visualization applications like Visio or whatever they are accustomed to using to create workflows, org charts, or floor plans—these applications should work for strategy maps as well.

By drawing their own picture of how their performance contributes to organizational success, groups and teams feel more bought into the process, have a better understanding of how their actions relate to organizational objectives, and take greater ownership of their contribution.

Some practical guidance for those pursuing this path:

- Create a template that indicates the areas different teams are being asked to fill in.
- Once the teams have documented their shapes and KPIs, they should be able to turn this file over to their IT department, who will literally take the diagram as the source for creating the scorecards.
- IT will "hook up" the strategy map metrics by adding connection information, calculations, and other necessary attributes, therefore creating a "live" strategy map.
- As a by-product of this process, IT will have not only ensured consistency, but also created KPIs through the strategy map, which can be used anywhere in the organization's dashboards and scorecards.

As more people around the organization are empowered to use performance management tools, innovative approaches to managing performance surface. Using everyday visualization tools to create strategy maps, some teams have

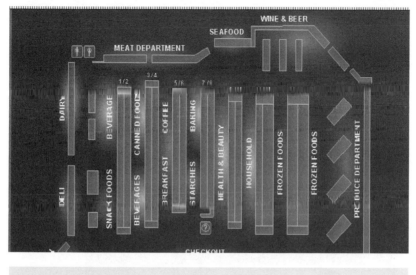

FIGURE 3.17 Retail Floor Display

become very creative in managing their performance more effectively. For instance, retail companies have created floor plan displays that show how their store shelves are measuring against specific plans. (see Figure 3.17—although this is in black and white, note the store sections—such as Snack Foods, Health & Beauty and Produce Department. On the display, these are colored according to the KPI status—red, yellow or green).

IT shops can monitor server rooms and monitor them against Service Level Agreement (SLA) targets by layering KPIs on top of server room displays. When teams have the flexibility to create management tools to help them monitor performance, the options seem endless (see Figure 3.18; the circles are shaded to indicate the status of SLA performance)

Organizations that have enabled their people to link their tactics to strategy can "roll" scorecards up, down, and across the organization and orchestrate the display of various scorecards to reflect the hierarchical structure of the organization. With this hierarchical alignment, these scorecards are often called "cascading scorecards."

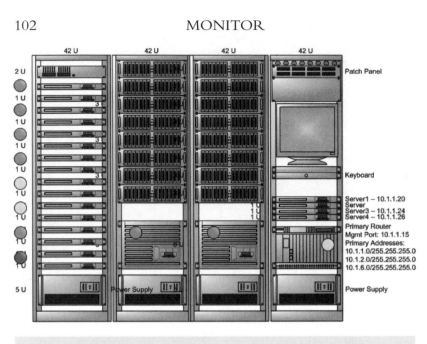

FIGURE 3.18 Server Room Display

Cascading Scorecards Deliver
Metrics to the Masses

Cascading scorecards provide accountability and alignment—
they hold the value of the company and credit cards at a high level.
Collections keeps people from charging off, customer service
maintains satisfaction, and the correspondence team responds to
letters and requests. We drive accountability down across management . . . to the customer facing and tactical roles, the area of
the company that is the agile part of the company. Those are
the people moving around the floors, making the decisions and
affecting the workflow of the credit card applications and service
through our system. They know they're being watched and that
they are a part of the bigger number—it helps everybody understand what their goals are and helps us to trust each other and
execute with confidence.[32]

With cascading scorecards, organizations can distribute
critical business information throughout all levels of an organization in ways that are meaningful for individuals based
on their roles and responsibilities. By delivering this metric

alignment, organizations are able to more effectively drive execution that is aligned to the overall corporate objectives.

Let's take the example of a large manufacturing com pany. Their CEO and other senior managers review an Executive Scorecard that utilizes the Balanced Scorecard methodology, so it shows the four key metric areas of finance, customer, operations, and people. They may review this summary scorecard daily, weekly, or monthly. Depending on management styles, they may review the KPIs for key areas and objectives, or they may drill down into the KPIs that measure each objective in detail.

Whereas the CEO looking at an Executive Scorecard may review only the KPIs for the four key areas and see that targets and trends are all where they should be, the line manager in charge of customer relations will want to drill down on the Customer Satisfaction KPI. While overall customer satisfaction is on target, the line manager still needs to know the details. He may see that customer retention and acquisition are on target, but customer satisfaction needs corrective action.

Meanwhile, a CFO, looking at the Executive Scorecard from the financial perspective, will want to drill down into the financial indicators to understand the financial status of the organization in greater detail. His responsibilities are in the financial sector, and he needs a more detailed picture of the financial health of the organization than what the Executive Scorecard offers. How can he get this information?

This is where cascading scorecards come into play. By cascading scorecards, additional scorecards are linked to the top level to provide detailed information tailored to various management requirements. In this case, the CFO can view financial data available at the Executive Scorecard level knowing that he is only one click away from a Finance Scorecard built around his concerns and responsibilities within the organization. It's important to note that security settings must be applied and carried through each of

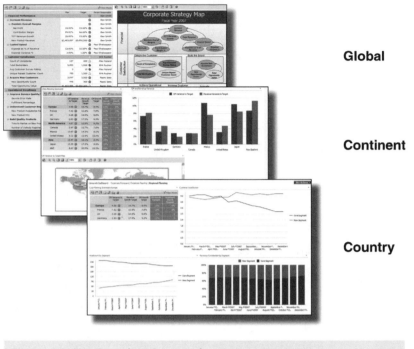

FIGURE 3.19 Cascading Scorecards

these cascading scorecards to protect sensitive information from being distributed inappropriately, so that, for instance, early indications of financial performance are communicated only to the executive audiences who need to know about them (see Figure 3.20).

The Finance Scorecard provides detailed information on Revenue, Costs, and Net Profit, giving the CFO a clear picture of the financial health of the organization. In this case, the CFO sees from the Executive Scorecard that the financial indicators are on target, but in the Finance Scorecard he can see that the specific objective Gross Profit Margin % is not on target. The problem has not yet reached a level where it impacts the overall financial objective. By using the Finance Scorecard, the CFO is able to pinpoint a potential problem in its early stages when it is easier to take corrective action (see Figure 3.21).

Finance: Gross Profit and Loss								▾

Product Category: [Accessories ▼]

🔳 🗒 📋 🗂 🔊 📇 🖳   ▼ Filter Mode

	All Periods ⊟ 03 Actual	Plan	Trend	⊟ 04 Actual	Plan	Trend	Person Responsible
⊟ Gross Profit and Loss							
⊟ Revenue							Pellow, Frank
Units Sold	16,878	●	✈	15,746	●	✈	Hanson, Mark
Average Price Per Unit	$81	◆	➡	$67	◆	➡	Holt, Holly
⊟ Costs							Penor, Lori
Product Costs	$80,183.83	●	➡	$83,463.34	●	➡	Adams, Jen
Average Discount .	0.01	△	➡	0.01	△	➡	Adams, Jen
⊟ Net Profit							Allen, Tony
Net Profit .	$156,800.29	●	➡	$163,114.88	●	➡	Adams, Jen
Net Profit Margin % .	45.37%	◆	↘	49.96%	◆	↘	Adams, Jen

Tasks						▾
Type	Title	◔ Assigned To		% Complete	Priority	Due Date
🗋	Build action plan on margins	Kim Ralls		20%	(2) Normal	9/30/2007
🗋	Board Meeting Briefing Book	Kim Ralls		75%	(1) High	10/12/2007
🗋	4th Quarter earnings production	Kim Ralls		50%	(2) Normal	10/18/2007

FIGURE 3.20 CFO Scorecard

Notice that the Finance Scorecard has a different look and feel than the Executive Scorecard and that the information has also been changed to match the CFO's key areas of concern. In this case, the CFO may want to further explore the Revenue category to analyze the yellow indicator. By applying a filter to the scorecard, the perspective can once again change to a highly targeted and granular view appropriate for the CFO.

Meanwhile, the CIO also needs a scorecard to monitor her area of responsibility. Technology is rolled up to the top-level Operational Excellence indicator. In the Executive Scorecard, the top-level Operational Excellence KPI is on target, but drilling down to the Technology Scorecard alerts the CIO to potential issues with Global Technology Services and Enterprise Services (see Figure 3.21).

Drilling down further into the Technology Scorecard, the CIO will see that even though the Messaging indicator

IT Health Scorecard

	Actual	Target/Score	Trend
▭ Summary - CIO IT Health		△	
▭ Global Technology Services		△	
▭ WNIS		△	
(10) First Time RAS Connection Success	0.73	0.75 △	↗
▭ Manageability		△	
(12) % of All Servers Patched At Deadline	0.97	1.00 △	↘
(13) IT Configuration Accuracy	0.96	0.98 △	↗
(14) Tickets from Monitoring	0.90	0.80 ●	↘
▭ IT Utility		△	
(07) Backup Data: % HA/DC b/u jobs successful	0.99	0.99 △	↘
(08) Restore Success Rate at DC & HA sites	1.00	1.00 ●	→
▭ Data Center		△	
(06) Production Server IPAK Compliance	0.65	0.95 ◆	↘
(05) Data Center Availability	1.00	1.00 ●	→
▭ Remote IT		●	
(04) P1&2 Telecom IRs Closed w/in SLA	0.97	0.80 ●	↗

FIGURE 3.21 CIO Scorecard

is green, the Exchange Server Availability is in the yellow zone. As she drills down to this problem area, the scorecard also changes to picture a chart of Server Availability by region, allowing the CIO to pinpoint which office in her organization needs to take action.

Together, Balanced Scorecards and cascading scorecards create a monitoring environment that is horizontally and vertically aligned with your organization.

Once Aligned, Incent

> Reward the results that matter most. Many companies have archaic incentive plans that do not directly link rewards with the contributions that matter most. Review your company's incentive plans to insure that payouts are directly linked to the precise results that will make the most difference.[33]

Having identified the measures that matter most and cascaded this to be understood and aligned across the organization, leading organizations understand how to leverage incentives and compensation to increase the positive actions and amplify the impact of their employees. Particularly effective organizations that have successfully aligned their employees' activities with the organization's strategy take an additional step to drive increased results. They incent intelligent execution.

Hilton Hotels has realized the benefits of tying incentives to aligned objectives. Hilton cascaded their scorecards across the organization—from executives all the way down to the front desk clerk —and identified and linked objectives across the organization. They tied everyday activities to the targeted results and tied compensation to the performance as indicated by the KPIs. To ensure that the relationship was clear, employees could even tell how their bonus was affected by their performance in their scorecard. So not only did they know how they were performing, but also how this would impact their pay.

Hilton went a step further, however. They decided to offer an additional incentive program called the Million$ Team Pride Award: $1 million to be shared equally by all employees of each property that achieved all green status across eight KPIs. Employees were encouraged to "Go for the Green." In the first year they ran the incentive, only one property out of 330 hit the objective and split the $1 million. Within 5 years, they had 33 properties that were performing at all green status. You might wonder if there was some sandbagging going on here. Actually, because the company was providing this as an additional incentive on top of the regular pay employees received, they had in fact become more strict in defining the type of performance that was required to count as green. They raised their standards. And they raised their performance and competitive advantage.[34]

Expedia has followed a similar course. "We have the entire company now using strategy maps. We found a lot of people at review time asking, 'Well, how do I link my goals to my manager's goals?' We worked with HR and now can cascade goal linkages using strategy maps to show top to bottom goal linkages to allow people to track their own performance."[35]

Yet another example of successfully tying metrics to rewards is Whole Foods. As Gary Hamel describes in his enlightening book *The Future of Management*, "Whole Foods calculates the profit per labor hour for every team in every store. Teams that exceed a certain threshold get a bonus in their next paycheck." This leads to important cultural drivers for positive team building and collaboration. Given the importance placed on team performance and how this impacts individual compensation, team members are encouraged to hire the best team members possible who will help them reach their team goals. As Hamel well notes, "frontline employees at Whole Foods have both the *freedom* to do the right thing for customers and the *incentive* to do the right thing for profits."[36]

CONCLUSION

In review, we have discussed how organizations strive for consistency to develop their Monitor capability. We have explained the fundamental need for organizations to first get their data to a state that it can be trusted and is consistent. Further, we have explained that importance of information consistency. The critical role of KPIs has been discussed, as has the need to leverage both structured and unstructured data to inform decision making.

We have also discussed how organizations need to drive accountability by personalizing performance management, setting thresholds, and delivering this broadly through aligned dashboards and scorecards. Finally, we've discussed how methodologies like the Balanced Scorecard and utilizing strategy maps can help drive alignment execution.

How to Know If You Have the Ability to Monitor

We have discussed the three guiding principles to which an organization needs to adhere to monitor effectively:

1. *Consistency* of data and information, utilizing both structured and unstructured information and how to effectively use KPIs.
2. *Accountability* through personalized KPIs that are portable across scorecards and dashboards and through the effective use of thresholds to anticipate issues before they become problems.
3. *Alignment* using methodologies like the Balanced Scorecard and strategy maps to line up individual and team execution to organizational goals.

The following test may prove helpful in assessing your organization's capabilities. Think about it as a framework to organize a conversation around the subject of performance management with your teams across divisions and groups within your organization.

Take the Test

Some of the statements below are multifaceted, and you may find you have stronger agreement with some parts of the statement than other parts. Answer "True" if you find that the statement is generally true and "False" if you find the statement is generally false in describing your organization.

1. Our organization has standard definitions of goals and objectives across the company. Across Finance, Sales, Marketing, and Operations departments, we all agree on the definitions of success and how we measure it.

2. Our organization has dependable and relevant data. We can rely on the numbers we each may look at as being common and trustworthy—we have "one version of the truth" across the organization.

3. People across the organization have the relevant information for their specific role to make well-informed decisions, when and where they need to make them. Employees not only have the numbers they need, but they also have additional relevant information about the numbers that provides them context. When we refer to this information—what we call a customer, product, or service; how we measure profit; and so on—we know we're all working from the same, consistent information.

4. Employees have a complete picture of company performance. Information from all sources—both structured and unstructured—is captured and provides employees with the necessary context they need to make the best decisions.

5. Goals are publicly known and communicated broadly across the organization. They are assigned, bought in to, and owned by individuals. People understand that they are held accountable for results and trust that their counterparts across the organization (above, below, and beside them) are as well.

6. We have visibility as to what factors impact our business, and we are measuring proactively. We can apply thresholds to anticipate issues before they become problems.

7. The people in our organization have dashboards and scorecards in their everyday work environments that

provide them with personal, team, and/or group performance information about customers, partners, markets, products, or services they need, to do their jobs most effectively.

8 Individuals, teams, and groups execute in a coordinated fashion such that achievement of their individual goals contributes to the achievement of the organization's goals. Teams trust each other to work toward common and mutually beneficial goals.

9. Our execution is more predictable as we are able to monitor throughout the execution process—from strategy formulation to actual results delivered. The framework for execution we have created allows us to obtain the results we are looking for with increased accuracy.

10. We are able to understand how performance against one initiative or goal area impacts performance against another (e.g., how customer satisfaction relates to revenue). The relationship between metrics and objectives is communicated clearly, and teams and groups are working on the right things and are able to understand how their goals relate to corporate objectives.

Your Score

When reviewing your score, note that the score should not be viewed as an outcome ("How did we do?"), but rather as a starting point ("Where are we starting from?"). The purpose of the test is not just to give you a number, but to provide a framework for driving performance excellence.

Add up the number of "True" answers you provided above. If you have answered all of the above "True," the people in your organization are equipped with the ability to monitor, and management has its finger on the pulse of the organization. For the rest of us, refer to the following:

0–2 True answers = limited Monitor strength; your score is 1.

3–5 True answers = moderate Monitor strength; your score is 2.

6–8 True answers = major Monitor strength; your score is 3.

9–10 True answers = superior Monitor strength; your score is 4.

Note your score, as you will need it to determine your stage in Chapter 6. Further guidance on how to improve your monitoring skills is also provided below.

Improve Your Results

If you answered "False" to any of the above questions, note the number of the question and review the corresponding suggested remedy below to help move you to a "True" answer—and, more importantly, provide your organization with competitive advantage.

1. Remember the three rules of effective KPIs: KPIs, like people, need goals. They need to reflect actual performance and specific individuals or groups need to be accountable for them. They also need to be portable across scorecards and dashboards so they can be shared throughout multiple departments without losing consistency.

2. If your organization does not yet have trustworthy and relevant data upon which your employees can rely, you need to start by implementing a Data Warehouse. This is the first step to develop "one version of the truth" across the organization.

3. If you answered False to this question, you lack consistent information. Your performance management system should not only allow for the data to be reliable and consistent, but also for employees to monitor their business objectives in a personalized way.

4. Provide your employees with the information they need by including related unstructured information like documents, presentations and reports in your employee's personal scorecards and dashboards.

5. If your organization is deficient in this area, increase accountability by personalizing metrics, allowing for personal adoption and ownership of goals and commitments, promoting transparency, publicizing performance and strictly sticking to policies around accountability—no matter what the title.

6. In order to anticipate issues, incorporate multiple thresholds to the same KPI so you can proactively monitor the status of initiatives as they progress and take action before the issues become problems.

7. Provide your people with the information they need where they need it by incorporating scorecards and dashboards in their everyday work environments where they work and make decisions. Remember the example of bank tellers and customer service representatives who know how to recognize opportunities to up-sell, which promotions to offer and how to identify and avoid problem customer scenarios.

Use a familiar interface and make it intuitive so they will actually adopt and use the information effectively. Be sure to personalize the information to their specific role and provide additional information so they understand context.

- In order to better ensure goal alignment, agree first on the perspectives by which you will drive your business (e.g., financial, operational, customer, people). Then ensure that your scorecards map to your organizational structure so that people can clearly understand how their individual performance relates to the organizational goals.

- In order to drive more predictable results, you first need to more effectively formulate and communicate strategy. Leverage methodologies like the Balanced Scorecard, Six Sigma, LEAN, Total Quality Management—whichever relate best to the particular type of success you're trying to achieve. These methodologies will help you define success and figure out the specific drivers to attain your desired results— which metrics in which departments are critical for attaining the results that are desired.

- Communicate your framework for success so that everyone across the organization understands how he or she contributes to individual, team, and organizational objectives.

- Because you have an understood framework, you can more easily adjust the relevant levers to take corrective action while the strategy is executed. As your performance management capabilities mature—and as your organization's execution becomes more aligned and coordinated—you can more predictably deliver the results you planned.

- Communicate clearly how the relationship between metrics and objectives can be accomplished by using a strategy map. Strategy maps allow employees to quickly visualize relationships between objectives and understand how metrics impact each other within the context of their own perspectives. Armed with more contextual information from scorecards and the strategy maps, employees are better informed and can execute with more relevancy.

When done well, a strategy map clearly:

- *Communicates the end goal.* At the top of the strategy map should be the overall corporate objective, for example, "increase shareholder value."

- *Identifies the business levers and drivers.* Individuals and groups throughout the business can easily identify how this objective is affected by other initiatives or metrics. For example, customer satisfaction performance affects shareholder value. This helps employees better understand which concrete initiatives might impact the corporate goal.

- *Isolates areas of most impact.* By looking at a strategy map, employees can see what impacts performance directly and indirectly. It may show that "operational excellence" impacts "shareholder value" through "customer satisfaction." This clear insight can provide better focus for execution.

NOTES

1. Discussion with Laura Gibbons, November 2007.
2. *Ibid.*
3. *Ibid.*
4. *Ibid.*
5. *Ibid.*
6. *Ibid.*
7. *Ibid.*
8. *Ibid.*
9. *USA Today,* January 2006.
10. Q&A with Jeanne G. Harris, coauthor of *Competing on Analytics* (Boston: Harvard Business School, 2007).
11. Discussion with Peter Klein, corporate VP and CFO, Microsoft Business Division, Microsoft, September 2007.
12. Discussion with Bill Baker, September 2007.
13. Marianne Kolbasuk McGee "Managers Have Too Much Information, Do Too Little Sharing, Says Study", *Information Week,* January 3, 2007, http://www.informationweek.com/news/showArticle. jhtml?articleID=196800921.

14. Paul Hamerman, "Business Performance Solutions: The Competition Heats Up," Figure 3. Forrester Research, February 7, 2007.

15. Discussion with Randy Benz, CIO of Enegizer, September 2007.

16. Discussion with Allen Emerick, December 2007.

17. Kathleen Melymuka, "Harrah's: Betting on IT Value," *Computerworld,* May 3, 2004.

18. Discussion with Scott Farr, Former VP–Performance Management, Hilton Hotels, November 2007.

19. Jonathan Low and Pam Cohen Kalafut, *Invisible Advantage* (New York: Perseus Press, 2002).

20. Report on the Intangible Economy to the European Commission, October 2000.

21. Discussion with Scott Farr, former VP–Performance Management for Hilton Hotels, December 2007.

22. Discussion with Laura Gibbons, November 2007.

23. Discussion with Christophe Couturier, VP Corporate Planning and Strategy Management, Millipore, December 2007.

24. Capgemini Intelligent Enterprise CXO Survey, December 2007.

25. Discussion with Ron Van Zanten, Premier Bankcard, November 2007.

26. Professor Michael E. Porter, Harvard University, HBR Interview, The Five Competitive Forces That Shape Strategy, http:// harvard businessonline.hbsp.harvard.edu/flatmm/hbrextras/200801/ porter/index.html?cm_mmc=npv- _ -hbopostcard- _ -Jan2008- _ -5 CompetitiveForces.

27. Dr. Robert Kaplan, keynote address at the Performance Measurement Association Annual Conference, Boston, 2003.

28. *Ibid.*

29. Robert S. Kaplan and David P. Norton, *The Balanced Scorecard* (Boston: Harvard Business School Press, 1996).

30. Randy Russell, *Leveraging Information Assets to Execute Strategy* (Boston, MA: Palladium, November 2007).

31. Professor Michael E. Porter, Harvard University, HBR Interview, The Five Competitive Forces That Shape Strategy, http:// harvardbusinessonline.hbsp.harvard.edu/flatmm/hbrextras/ 200801/porter/index.html?cm_mmc=npv-_-hbopostcard-_- Jan2008-_-5CompetitiveForces.

32. Discussion with Ron Van Zanten, Premier Bankcard, November 2007.

33. Jack Welch, from Jeffrey A. Krames, *Jack Welch and the Four E's of Leadership* (New York: McGraw-Hill, 2005).

34. Discussion with Scott Farr, former VP Performance Management for Hilton Hotels, December 2007.

35. Discussion with Laura Gibbons, November 2007.

36. Gary Hamel, *The Future of Management*, (Boston: Harvard Business School Press, 2007) 73.

4

Analyze

If the only tool you have is a hammer, you tend to
see every problem as a nail.

Abraham Maslow

THE U.S. DEPARTMENT OF VETERANS
AFFAIRS STORY

The Veterans Health Administration's (VHA, and also
known as the VA) health care system, a department within
the Department of Veterans Affairs, was once considered
to be one of the worst health care providers in the United
States. The entire VHA health care system had deteriorated
so much by the early 1990s that Congress even considered
disbanding it.

"The VA of today is not your father's VA," explains Jack
Bates, Director of BI and Performance Management at the
Veteran's Health Administration. The VHA is now considered to be one of the highest-quality health care systems in
the nation and a leader in almost every health care performance metric. Performance management has enabled the
VHA to go through a dramatic transformation over the last
decade. "Today, we serve twice as many veterans as we did
in the mid-1990s and are delivering the best quality-of-care

119

scores in the industry. Developing our performance management capabilities drove that change."[1]

Challenges of Scale

The VHA has tremendous demands as it serves over 5 million patients each year. Comprised of over 254,000 employees, the VHA runs 153 medical centers, 724 outpatient clinics, and over 200 VHA "Vet Centers" with a budget of over $36 billion. Managing performance is exceedingly complex with so many people to serve and facilities to administer and such a large budget.

Commitment to Performance

In 1994, Dr. Kenneth Kizer was brought in as the VHA's Under Secretary for Health. He saw that the VHA needed to reinvent itself if it were going to survive. He believed the VHA could become a model of health care in the United States, and he set out to have the organization accomplish exactly that. He promoted the use of information technology, instituted a performance measurement and reporting system, and realigned services to achieve high-quality, effective, and timely care. As an example, he reorganized the VHA, creating a new category of employees called regional managers, who were held accountable for performance in their respective regions by the use of performance contracts.

Awarding Quality

"We've completely done a 180-degree change. The VA today is a leader in performance and a model of health care in the United States. It's an exemplary organization, and that's directly attributable to the performance management program," says Bates.

The Institute of Medicine (IOM) noted that "VHA's integrated health information system, including its framework for using performance measures to improve quality, is considered one of the best in the nation." The VHA has developed a world-class electronic health record (EHR) system called VistA. The American College of Physician Executives found that while many physician executives and doctors "loathe" clinical information systems, VHA clinicians provided a "notable outlier from the nexus of negativity."[2]

Harvard agrees, granting two separate awards as testimony to the VHA's capabilities. First, in 2006, Harvard's Kennedy School of Government awarded the VHA an "Innovations in American Government" award for its advanced electronic health records and performance measurement system. Second, Harvard Medical School concluded that "federal hospitals, including those run by the VHA, provide the best care available anywhere for some of the most common life-threatening illnesses." Their performance management capabilities were again identified as the reason for their superior results. "This study further demonstrates that VHA is providing high-quality health care to veterans," Dr. Kussman said. "Our computerized system of electronic health records and performance measurement means that veterans are getting the top-level care and treatment they have earned through service to our country."

"VHA prescribes medication to patients with an accuracy rate of 99.993%, a standard that simply does not exist anywhere else in American health care. And we maintained this standard of excellence while filling 231 million prescriptions in 2005," says Jim Nicholson, Secretary, U.S. Department of Veterans Affairs.[3]

Developing a Culture of Performance

"We're not there yet, but we're moving to a Culture of Performance. We see it as a journey, not a destination," says Bates.

Realizing the Six Stages of Performance Management Value
So how have VHA's capabilities helped them? Let's review how the VA is realizing the six stages of performance management value:

1. *Increase Visibility:* By providing access to information that you simply didn't have before. A regional director's compensation package is based on how well he or she performs against performance measures. "Without visibility to performance, we can't understand how we are doing and how to feel about it," explains Bates. They use external benchmarks (such as from the Centers for Medicare and Medicaid) to understand the quality of care they are providing relative to others. They also utilize internal benchmarks of performance called "floors," which are minimal levels of performance that are acceptable. All the facilities (like local clinics) that roll up to a medical center must meet the floor requirements or the entire performance of the medical center is deemed as underperforming.

2. *Move Beyond Gut Feel:* In the past, information was often not available—and what was available was often not digital. As an institution, the VA has told its employees, "We're going to hold you accountable, and we're going to provide you the information to monitor these measures, and then it's up to you to utilize that information and make adjustments as necessary." The VHA demonstrates strong commitment to developing a fact-based culture, whether information is readily available or not. While other companies might hide behind typical excuses—"the data is not available" or "this is too hard to measure"—the VHA conducts manual chart reviews when information is not available electronically.

3. *Plan for Success:* "Planning for Success" at the VHA means focusing on the metrics that make a difference. Every year, the Undersecretary of Health (the CEO of VHA) publishes the strategic goals for the upcoming year based on an in-depth strategic planning process. Many factors are taken into account to establish the strategic goals. These factors include any unforeseen issues related to war, anticipated conditions of the aging veteran population, known areas of improvement from previous years, and Congressionally mandated issues, just to name a few. The VHA's performance management system revolves around these strategic objectives. Goals of the performance measurement program include decreasing variation in practice (consistent care across the organization), increasing consistent outcomes of care across the organization, improving quality of care delivery, and continuous process improvement. The measures themselves revolve around six domains of value: quality, access, function, satisfaction, cost effectiveness, and healthy communities. "There are hundreds of candidate measures submitted to a special working group that is charged with developing the performance measures for the upcoming year. Once the measures are evaluated, there are usually 125 to 175 measures across the above domains of value that are accepted as the performance measures for the upcoming year," explains Bates, underscoring the importance of identifying key metrics to keep an eye on.

4. *Execute on Strategy:* Once the performance measures are ratified, execution is in motion. To facilitate communication of objectives and strategy, an intense marketing effort takes place to make sure the performance measures are publicized. Many people have to understand the nuances of the performance

measures to be able to execute on them. Therefore, there is also an education program to make sure key personnel know and understand the details of the measures. Once the measures are implemented, reports are made available to track adherence to the measures. Regions and facilities across the organization are then empowered to monitor their performance, as well as that of their peers, creating internal and healthy competition.

5. *Power to Compete:* Competing effectively requires the use of external benchmarks, and the VHA provides a great example. As noted in the *National Journal,* "The VA health system embraced outside scrutiny to reinforce a revolution it had already begun. 'We were doing [other] customer satisfaction surveys as early as 1994,' recalled Dr. Kenneth Kizer, VA Undersecretary for Health from 1995 to 1999, but the American Customer Satisfaction Index (ACSI) was arguably 'a better instrument. . . . I thought it was important that we could compare ourselves to the private sector: Is the American taxpayer getting a good return on investment? Let's see what customers think.'"[4]

So, as a public-sector organization, what is the most important competitive advantage the VA realizes from their performance management initiatives? Bates explains:

Quality. Quality of care. We basically went from the back of the pack to the front of the pack. And that's a public, evidence-based statistic. Quality is at the forefront. Cost is another. Our patient population has doubled in the last ten years and our budget has shrunk in real dollar terms. So we're serving twice as many people, at the best quality standards, with no budget increase. The Centers for Medicare and Medicaid studies comparison of a number of private and public health care systems across a number of performance metrics proves this out.[5]

6. *Culture of Performance:* Close to 100 % of the employee population know of the existence of the performance measurement program—and it starts at the top. Many know of the specific measures, especially as they relate to their specific work area or specialization. Most, if not all, local facilities and regions have staff dedicated to the program to monitor performance and assist in reaching performance goals. A combination of communication, personalization of performance metrics, and commitment from the top of the organization allows them to deliver on strategy.

Conclusion

The VA has been able to transform itself from a struggling organization at risk of being dissolved to a world-class organization that sets standards others aspire to achieve. Their diligent development of performance management capabilities and commitment to honest and public analysis of their performance was a key component of their success.

IN THIS CHAPTER

In this chapter, we focus on the three guiding principles that organizations follow in order to effectively analyze their performance, as well as the specific skills and assets needed to implement this capability. At the end of the chapter, we invite organizations to test their Analyze capability and provide guidance on how they can improve their results.

The three guiding principles organizations follow to implement the Analyze capability are:

1. *Agility*: Driven by delivering analytic capabilities to all employees to allow them to easily ask questions and get answers more quickly.

Analyze Capability

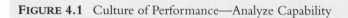

Principles to follow	Agility	Relevancy	Efficiency
⬇ Skills and assets needed	• Web-based analytics • Deep and broad analytics	• Filtering (simple and smart) • Guided analytics	• Drilling (up and down) • Cross-drilling • Data mining • Predictive analytics • Advanced analytics

FIGURE 4.1 Culture of Performance—Analyze Capability

2. *Relevancy*: Enabling greater focus by tailoring information to employees' roles and responsibilities.

3. *Efficiency*: With faster decision making and greater organizational impact.

Figure 4.1 illustrates the guiding principles organizations follow, as well as the specific skills and assets they develop to analyze performance.

AGILITY

What does the ability to analyze have to do with organizational agility? How does it enable companies to respond quicker to market conditions and competitive pressures? How does analysis drive agility?

Dr. Santosh Mohanty, Global Director and Head of the Business Intelligence and Performance Management practice at Tata Consultancy Services Ltd., describes increased agility as one of the benefits of being able to "experience certainty": "Organizations who have developed their analytic capabilities have the ability to experience certainty. When an organization can experience certainty, it becomes more agile and can respond to market challenges more quickly and with greater effectiveness." So who all needs to be able to experience certainty within the organization?

Analytics have historically been designed for the "guru" analysts in the company that have the time and skill set required to understand how to use the analytic technologies to investigate answers to business questions. It has historically been the opinion that typical business users would not have the skills or bandwidth to think beyond the quick insights their "cockpits" would give them . . . *if* these managers even had "cockpits."

The role and needs of management have changed, however. Information creation, collaboration, and reporting have all increased—and thus the importance of effectively using and managing information has increased as well. We are more accustomed to seeing visualizations of information as they have become more broadly available—on web sites, within reports, and embedded in documents. Generally speaking, analysis and context for information is more a part of our everyday lives. We have become more aware of information and accustomed to seeing our world explained in charts and graphs.

Technology has changed as well. We now have the tools to generate and understand analytic information right on our desktops. The visual displays that used to require a handful of analysts to develop can now be developed by a student on a home computer. Depending on how this is managed, this can be part of the short-term problem or long-term solution. It's a short-term problem if it means just a few employees understand how to effectively create, communicate, and read this information. It's a long-term solution if the organization can institutionalize effective use of the tools.

With the ability to analyze information more seamlessly across the organization, previous performance management solutions that favored a few highly skilled analysts and didn't empower the many across the organization no longer provide the competitive advantage they may have even as recently as five years ago.

Analytical Paradox

Deeply empowering a few analysts is a good starting point but doesn't solve the problem of organizational agility. The reason for this is something we call the Analytical Paradox. While analysts have the analytic capabilities to derive insights, they lack the ability to directly act upon these insights. Conversely, while decision makers have the ability to take action, they often lack the ability to derive insights by themselves. The result is that business analysts' request queues are overloaded on a daily basis, and decision makers end up making decisions which lack insight, timeliness, or both. This situation makes it impossible for organizations to quickly recognize and act upon changing market conditions—to be agile.

Information Couriers

Whenever there is a breakthrough technology, the first stage of adoption consists of a few experts who must manage access and management of the technology for others who seek to use it. This was true for shared access to massive computers prior to the advent of personal computers—a few experts split time managing the queue. With the birth of telecommunications, a switchboard operator could manage a few connections at a time to connect conversations for those seeking to use the technology. Another example was recounted to us by a dear friend of ours who is from a small town in rural Brazil that didn't get home phones until the 1990s—they all relied on a single public phone for the town to use, and those who knew how to use the phone served as the experts and would help place calls on behalf of others. That all changed, of course, when the town's residents were set up to have their own phones and, through practice, learned how to use the phones themselves.

A similar environment exists with analytics today. Analysts are the couriers of information and insights. They are equipped to understand how to derive insights from masses of data. They have specialized skills and understand the complex tools of inquiry.

However, in order to compete in today's world, organizations need to understand and react to competitive pressure more quickly. As Gary Hamel explains, "In a more hierarchical company, top management only sees problems once they've become pervasive and, therefore, expensive to fix. At Whole Foods, tight linkage between business intelligence and decision-making authority ensures that little problems don't have to compound into big problems before action is taken."[6] How long does it take your organization to realize that there's a competitive program, pressure, or threat and respond?

We were recently impressed to see a multibillion-dollar international organization have the visbility to recognize that a competitor had launched a directly competitive customer education program attacking their licensing strategy for certain products in Europe and the United States. They had their finger on the pulse of the organization and could detect a competitive threat. An organization needs to have its feelers out there to understand market conditions in the present, before they become future problems, while they are changing and when risks can be mitigated and opportunities seized.

This organization's response was informed and rapid. They didn't just cut prices across all accounts, which would have likely eroded their margins, nor did they delay their response and wait to see the damage. They were able to analyze past market trends and determine that this was indeed a competitive program and not just a typical quarterly trend. They were also able to analyze the types of customers who licensed specific products in a particular way which were at risk. This enabled them to develop a customer education program and change field engagement practices in accounts which were subject to risk from this competitor. The end result was that they were able to effectively mitigate the competitor's success with the program before it cost them customer accounts. And it was time for the competitor to go back to the drawing board.

More Couriers?

So if an organization wants to increase its analytic capabilities to realize this type of agility, should it simply hire more analysts? This is certainly a popular approach, and it can deliver some benefits for some types of analysis (as we shall see). However, it is very costly and does not solve the problem of enabling increased agility en masse. An army of analysts can't be deployed to assist the bank teller in making better decisions or to help the emergency room administrating nurse get the most people who need treatment most urgently in to hospital beds. Not only does a company need to have its feelers extended to the front line to detect changes in market conditions early, it also needs to empower action at the edge, so early detectors can be first responders.

Hiring more analysts doesn't solve the agility problem—it maintains the old paradigm of centralized thinking and slowed action.

We're All Couriers?

A transition from just informing the few executives at the center to also empowering the many at the front line, is needed. Jeremy Hope, coauthor of *Beyond Budgeting* (Boston: Harvard Business School, 2003), calls this transition a "cultural climate change":

When I think we are all trying to move from a an organization where it is accepted that information knowledge and strategy gravitates to the corporate center, and that the guys on the twenty-first floor are the only ones that have the insight and the understanding of where we need to go, what we need to do. Companies have realized that they simply cannot respond, react and drive innovation from the corporate center alone [7]

In addition to cultural challenges, companies might experience technical ones. As they try to expand the footprint of their analytical capabilities, the complexity of analytical tools could limit the broad deployment of these capabilities.

Only analysts, who are typically very tolerant of complex environments, have historically been taking advantage of analytics. While organizations may not want to hire an army of analysts, they also don't want to make everyone become a PhD in statistics to do their jobs.

So, if neither hiring an army of analysts nor making everyone an analyst is the solution, what should organization's do? Again, Hope provides clear guidance:

The way to do this is through an information system that is far more open and transparent than people were used to before. Most importantly, organizations must transfer accountability from the corporate center to the front line teams in, for example, the supply chain, sales, and marketing business units, etc.—in fact, all over the place! We need to give them much more scope; much more freedom to use information to make decisions very quickly.[8]

Change the Model

To fully understand this suggestion to "give the people what they need," we need to explore what employees need. What are the types of analytical capabilities a company requires in order to achieve competitive advantage through analytics? What types of decisions are being made across the organization?

Analytics Based on Need   A primary function of analysis is investigation: discovering what the data means for an organization.

An analyst in the energy industry may investigate the most effective ways to increase capacity, improve plant efficiency, or react to changing environmental conditions. An analyst in the insurance industry may investigate how rising crime rates in a city affect profitably or which claims require the greatest amount of resources to resolve. And a telecommunications analyst may investigate which points in their network are the most susceptible to failure or downtime. These investigations may require evaluating structured and unstructured data from multiple sources, finding correlations, validating assumptions, and tracking conclusions over time. Most importantly, these investigations result in action. In the preceding cases, the actions may be to implement a new quality control process to reduce manufacturing defects, to hire additional employees to reduce call-wait time, or to invest in additional research and development to diversify product offerings.

Analytical capabilities need to align with organizational objectives and be based on the actions that need to be taken. In some cases, a team of analysts needs to develop statistical models. In other cases, employees just need to glance at analytics and take action right away.

Three Analytic Needs   Just as with the three types of decisions we discussed previously, we also recognize three needs that analysis is intended to meet: tactical, operational, and strategic objectives.

1. *Tactical*: Analytics that happen on the spot, in customer environments, typically by the customer facing individual contributor. These analyses must be highly intuitive and fast.

2. *Operational*: Analytics typically run by management, but still in close proximity of customer environments. These analyses typically take a bit longer and have greater scope and impact.

3. *Strategic*: Advanced analyses typically performed by analysts for significantly impactful considerations and decisions such as mergers and acquisitions, investments, intellectual property decisions, and so on.

Tactical Needs   Depending on its objective, the process of performing analysis may have different scopes and occur at different time intervals. When monitoring performance against plan, tactical analysis is relevant within a short time frame: daily, weekly, or monthly. This type of analysis is about responding to issues in the day-to-day operations of the business. For example, a wait time at a call center is too long or the number of defects in a manufacturing line spikes. The turnaround time for action is quick: Additional support staff is called in or equipment is serviced. To do this type of analysis well, users need the following:

- Continual access to updated data
- Clearly defined targets
- The ability to quickly identify the scope and root cause of the issue
- An identified action plan for exception conditions

Companies need to enable this type of analysis primarily through scorecards and interactive analytic grids and charts. What does this look like in real life? Refer to Figure 4.2 for an example.

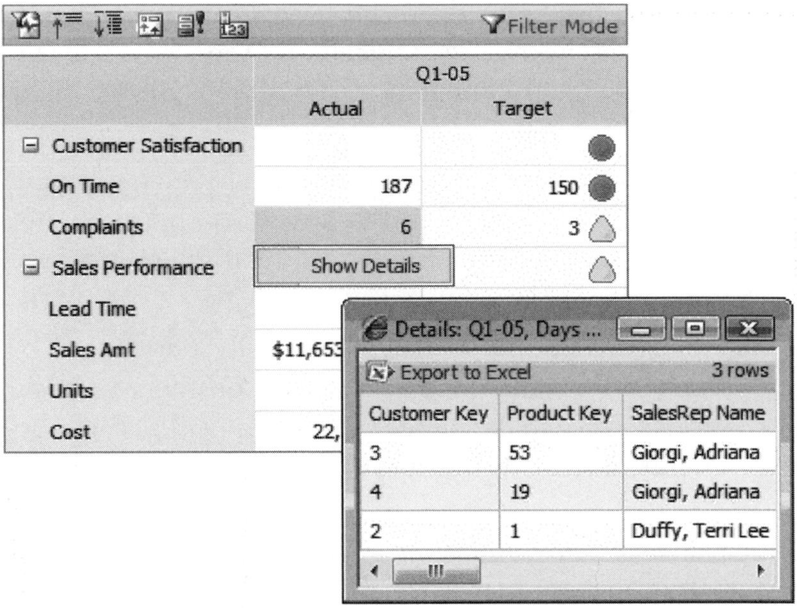

FIGURE 4.2 Scorecard Details

Let's look at a retail example. Assume that a store manager is responsible for ensuring high customer satisfaction rates. The "Customer Satisfaction" objective is broken down into two measurable metrics: "On Time" delivery and "Complaints." When the store manager realizes customer complaints are higher than the goal, she quickly investigates by having the performance management system "Show Details," which displays the detailed transactions contributing to the "Complaints" value.

In the detailed report, she finds that complaints by two different customers have been filed against the same sales rep, John Doe. With this information, she can meet with John to understand the background for these complaints and determine whether additional training or other action is merited. Because the data is near real time and delivered directly to the front-line user in a simple, web-based interface, the store manager is empowered to make an immediate course correction to ensure her store's performance goals are achieved.

More importantly, notice that the analytical functionality was tied to the objective being followed through a score card. Whether to meet tactical, operational, or strategic needs, analysis is a function that should be tightly coupled with the monitoring capability (dashboards or scorecards) to ensure alignment with strategic objectives and allow for appropriate context for the role of the person doing the analysis. In this case, it is the store manager who monitors her scorecard, in the store, and analyzes factors impacting her store's performance.

A large number of tactical decisions are made on a daily basis, therefore making it very important for those decisions to be aligned with the corporate objectives. Each tactical decision may individually have a minor impact on the bottom line, but the collection of tactical decisions has a critical effect on business results. Whether analysis is informative (relevant to the employee's role), timely, understood, and acted upon determines whether competitive advantage is attained or inferior results are delivered.

Operational Needs

> Our performance management environment has support for operational decisions in addition to strategic decisions. There are an awful lot of bills paid by operational decisions. We strive to find inefficiencies and automate how those different departments work—in terms of number of letters per representatives, number of phone calls per customer service rep, dollars collected per collector—these are all operational things which add value to the bottom line. As these become more efficient, then our number of full-time employees (FTEs) per credit card account goes down. The lift that you get from these things can be justified in real dollars, in real savings. They can help you quantify the return of hiring 100 representatives. They are much more quantifiable.[9]

In addition to analysis done to meet tactical needs, analysis is also conducted to meet operational needs. Operational analysis may occur over an extended period of time, especially when seeking to improve processes or systems. For example, a manufacturer's yearlong study on plant efficiencies reveals that one plant performs measurably better in two key areas: output and cost control. By analyzing and understanding the processes at the high-performing plant, an analyst can recommend improvements to other plants to achieve similar performance. Or a manager discovers that a sales team has been particularly successful selling one product family to a targeted segment of buyers. By training other sales teams on the same sales approach, the manager can help improve sales of the product across the entire organization.

To do this type of analysis well, employees need access to navigation and visualizations that can reveal relationships in the information that may not be apparent otherwise. As in tactical decisions, operational decisions are typically made by employees in the front line—those closer to customers. Analysis done to meet operational needs may start by investigating a hunch or a trend they might notice. Information needs to not only be available, but it also needs to be consumable quickly and intuitively so employees can easily spot trends and readily identify opportunities.

Organizations that realize competitive advantage think about analytical capabilities that reach all kinds of employees—whether trained analysts or managers making operational decisions. Most employees neither have the time nor energy to learn a complex system in order to analyze something.

Analyzing is a part of their work—they need the analytic tools to be a useful part of their work environment. Focus on simplicity and intuitiveness and make it easy for all to understand information faster.

Take the example of Clalit, the world's second largest health maintenance organization (HMO), which employs 7,500 physicians, 11,500 nurses, 1,300 pharmacists, 4,400 paramedics and laboratory/imaging technicians, and 9,400 administrative personnel. With such a varied set of employees, Clalit focused on its number one resource: time.

"We have created a new working environment for our caregivers," explains Gadi Gilon, Clalit's Chief Information Officer. "The most valuable thing to a doctor is time. Our physicians can now get all the relevant information about a client in one place at one time, without having to reinvestigate."

Your organization might also need to revisit its employees' working environment and design it to enhance its employees' productivity.

Take a look at Figure 4.3 to give you an idea of some of the analytical capability you could enable. The figure represents a time-folded analysis showing peaks and valleys in sales over the past three years.

In each of the past three years, the lowest sales have occurred in February and the highest sales in October or November. This information is very useful and can help employees more effectively manage inventory levels throughout the year.

However, this alone is not enough. In this situation, an employee will probably want more information about 2004,

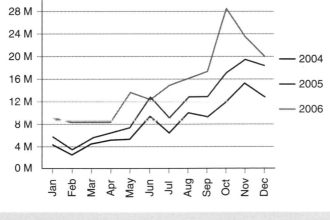

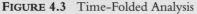

FIGURE 4.3 Time-Folded Analysis

for example, which is the year showing the most sales. What products were sold in 2004, what geographies sold the most in 2004, what day did they sell the most? And so forth.

These questions will come naturally to any employee looking at analytical views like the preceding one (Figure 4.3). Performance management solutions need to accommodate the ability to interact richly with information so employees can drill up, down, and across their information to get to the answers they're seeking.

This brings up a key concept called "cross-drilling." Cross-drilling allows employees to navigate across multiple business dimensions to answer such questions as "How do my product sales break down across geographies?" or "What products are my most valuable customers buying?" Employees can discover relationships among the different dimensions, hierarchies, and levels of information simply by navigating from one item to the next. Cross-drilling will be discussed in more detail later in the chapter as an analysis capability used by business executives, analysts, and IT staff.

As we see with this example, operational needs are met with more detailed analysis typically performed by management. These analyses require more time and have broader implications than on-the-spot, tactical analytics performed by individuals in a short amount of time.

Strategic Needs   When determining a strategic direction for the organization, analysis may occur over months or years. This is often a highly collaborative process that includes multiple teams or people, data from inside and outside the organization, and continual iterations and validation. For example, an organization identifies potential mergers or acquisitions to strengthen the company's competitive advantage. Or an organization evaluates products that have exceeded growth expectations to identify innovative directions in their product lines.

Strategy analytics can be used to support long-term planning decisions, such as long-term margin goal metrics set for management. Imagine that the CEO of ABC Company wants to set a 15 % margin growth objective for the next five years. Information to back up the feasibility of the goal prior to making that commitment to the Board will be critical. Additionally, information to figure out how to achieve the goal after having made the commitment is equally critical.

In order to support these types of decisions, employees need access to broad and diverse sets of structured and unstructured data, the ability to simulate scenarios (also known as "What If" analysis), and advanced ways of navigating and visualizing the data. For example, the bicycle retailer's chart in Figure 4.4 compares three bike types using two metrics: sales amount (on the left axis, identified by the height of the bar) and gross profit margin (on the right axis, identified by the line).

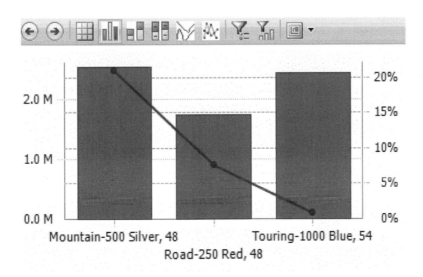

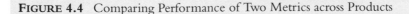

FIGURE 4.4 Comparing Performance of Two Metrics across Products

Although both the mountain bike and the touring bike generate nearly the same amount of sales (about $2.5 million), the mountain bike has a much higher gross profit margin (22% compared to 1% for touring bikes). Thus, the mountain bike is much more profitable for the company. If a product planner were to simply evaluate the sales amount in determining which products to expand, he may choose to invest more in mountain bikes and touring bikes. However, focusing the investments on mountain bikes may actually lead to greater revenue for the company over time (see Figure 4.4).

With these types of visualizations, employees can conduct better and more complete analysis to meet organizational needs: tactical, operational, or strategic. They can perform the analyses that are most appropriate for the information they are seeking, using a variety of navigation techniques and visualizations. For example, they can show further details to discover specific, actionable records or they can find relationships between multiple sets of information. Regardless of their goal, with such analytics, all employees can gain insight into the data that can help drive improved performance across the organization.

Analytics for All   The need to deploy these applications to more users across the organization pushed organizations (software vendors as well as organizations themselves) to create what are called "thin client" applications. Thin client applications are accessed over the web and enable broader visibility and distribution of analytic information, such as through a portal or intranet.

Most decision makers are looking for analytics that they can jump to directly from their performance dashboard. They are driven to use analytics to answer the "why" of an issue they see on their dashboard. They might see, for example, an issue with "Total Backorders" and they would like to quickly get access to the reasons why. Employees gain better insight when they are looking at analytics in the context of their dashboard and thus thin access has become critical to delivering agility.

An effective performance management system allows for the organization's scorecards, dashboards, and analytics to take advantage of the same performance information (metric definitions, thresholds, personalized information, security settings, etc.). This allows employees to stay focused on the speficic area that they are investigating. When they use analytics, they are consuming the information in the analytics in the same context as the information they have in their scorecards. They can monitor their performance, analyze and derive insights in the same environment and with the same context. They can understand "with what products?," "in what geographies?," and "since when?" the total backorders have occurred. Delivering this integrated context to employees helps greatly to drive organizational agility.

Depth Based on Need   While boundaries between monitoring, planning, and analysis should be removed, the latter has a distinguishing characteristic: It goes deep, in terms of both functionality and information access.

Analysis is about drilling into data (up, down, and across), sorting and filtering data to uncover pertinent information, and synthesizing the results into meaningful information on which good business decisions can be made. Above all, analysis is an iterative process in which data is continually examined and questioned in search of the patterns and anomalies that reveal the underlying health of an organization.

The definition of depth will depend on the employees you want to serve. For highly trained analysts, depth might mean drilling up, down, and across the applications, building calculations, and the like. For most employees, "depth" is likely to mean using analytics in a broader context—making analytical functionality available within the context of the environment with which they are familiar. Providing analytics in the context of already familiar portals and dashboards will make it easier for employees to use analytics on a daily basis. In addition, providing analytics as a support for scorecards, dashboards, and "non-performance-related" applications such as documents, will make the end-user experience much more complete, providing employees with further context for their analysis.

Whether very deep for analysts or less deep for business users, employees will most likely expect that either functionality be available in a web environment. A web analytic environment has become the standard and for just reasons— it enables more employees to gain access to better insights without making your IT environment more complicated. Web analytics are integral to making analytics more "approachable."

Organizations that do not understand that the new standards for analytics is to deliver them both "thin" *and* "deep" often respond to the need for data analysis by generating reports—predefined, highly formatted static sets of data. Reports are efficient tools for revealing answers to explicit questions: "What was last year's revenue?" "What is the highest selling product?" "Which region had the highest sales?" However, reports are less effective at addressing the inevitable follow-up questions: "*Why* was revenue so low last year?" "*Why* did one product sell better than another?" "*Why* did sales drop in the Southeast region?" These "Why?" questions are at the heart of analysis and this minimum amount of inquiry must be enabled to enable analysis and agility.

Empowering Broad Analysis When analytics are deployed "thinly," decision makers can work with it right from their web browser and get answers more quickly. All they have to do is click on any analytical graph or grid and the answer to their questions is a few clicks away. Examples of the simplicity afforded by analytics in this environment include:

- *Perform analysis easily in a web browser.* Analytics integration with the browser delivers the analytics capabilities you hope to empower employees with in an environment in which they are comfortable working. This provides flexibility for users who may decide they've gone down the wrong path of analysis and want to backtrack or start a new path of investigation. They can simply click forward and back in their browser, browsing the info as conveniently as they browse the web. This ease-of-use spurs adoption and impact.

- *Know the details of the information being viewed.* For example, while hovering over graphs and charts, underlined information about the data should appear (if a user is hovering over "margins," the underlying information about "margins" will appear such as percentage, number, etc). This clarity of what's being viewed makes it very easy for any user to navigate through the analytics themselves—users should be able to drill up, down and across from virtually anywhere in the analytics—if they have questions about a legend item, they should be able to click to drill from there as well.

- *Launch reports from a metric online.* Users should have the ability to generate adhoc reports from a given metric they are viewing online, so if a given metric looks interesting, they can have the report run on the spot.

- *Don't restrict to online or offline work alone—enable both.* In addition to performing analysis online in a web browser, employees should be able to export their view into Excel or PowerPoint if they want the convenience of the spreadsheet or presentation environment. This is quite useful for the folks who need to bring the analysis with them on trips or whenever they still want to be productive but do not have an Internet connection—this flexibility is central to organizational agility.

Personal Change   Finally, it is important to recognize the significance that personal applications have in the life of most employees. Office applications, such as Excel and PowerPoint, are quite familiar to most employees and they are also very flexible.

They allow any employee to quickly analyze their information or even create their own presentations to communicate their findings without having to ask for additional support or assistance. Thus, these applications can be a great place for people to collect their thoughts, analyze information and formulate plans. In order for agility to be realized, there must be broad adoption of analytic tools. To do this, it is critically important to leverage environments with which employees feel this level of familiarity and comfort. The simple guidance is to leverage these environments as much as possible.

However, we do offer a few words of caution. When leveraging personal applications to support analytics, three key situations should be avoided:

1. *Using personal applications as databases.* Imagine that you are a marketing executive trying to drive customer demand through marketing events. The way your group can prove its value to the organization is by showing the clear impact it has to the bottom line. Here's a process often used to deliver that value: Your group purchases prospects' names and you invite these contacts to events (in marketing speak, programs and campaigns). Your sales organization talks

to these contacts and further qualifies them in or out of their pipeline (in sales speak, opportunities) and some of the selected prospects end up buying your products or services (sales speak, "deals"; in fi-

〃〃〃 〈〃 〃, "〃〃〃〃〃〃〃〃 〃〃〃 〃〃〃") 〃〃 〃〃〃〃〃〃 〃〃

your prospects ("leads") is what allows them to move through the process seamlessly. The more targeted the list and the more compelling your message, the more likely these leads will turn into deals.

Now, let's suppose that in order to measure the quality of this process, you are using a Customer Relationship Management system (CRM) which offers some performance management capabilities, such as reports and dashboards. You notice that the West region has an incredibly high rate of conversion (from leads to opportunities). You find that with 50 leads, the West region can generate twice the amount of revenue of the East region. Excited by this discovery, you'd like to find out more information about these leads and replicate your learnings to all other regions.

However, the CRM system you are using just records counts of leads but not lead details. Investigating further into the issue, you find out that most of the contact information was stored in a spreadsheet that the local marketing manager was maintaining. While the CRM system could have enforced information consistency and made this information shared easily, the list stored in the spreadsheet cannot. The spreadsheet contains inconsistent data and doesn't have the information you would need in order to take this best practice and expand it to other groups and regions.

Best-practice companies understand the role and place of personal productivity applications. While productivity applications should be used for their great flexibility, they shouldn't be used to host the

"the source of truth." Personal productivity applications are personal and their flexibility allows individuals to customize the information they contain for their singular use, making it hard for the rest of the organization to take advantage of them.

2. *Using personal applications as aggregators of information.* Imagine that you run a service group and that you report on the health of your business on a weekly basis. You have created a weekly scorecard that reports on key metrics for your business—sales numbers, number of incidents, and a few other metrics that are derived calculations of the numbers coming from the various systems from which you collect information. Most of the information in the scorecard is stored inside a few spreadsheets, and calculations are the results of linked cells across tabs and spreadsheets. Each week, one of your analysts spends two days collecting the information from the various systems, plugs them into the spreadsheets to finally collect all the information needed to create the consolidated view that you desire. Each step of the process is documented, and although each mouse click from this analyst makes it more likely you are looking at erroneous data, you have not so far uncovered data that "looked odd." Now, your analyst leaves the company but you still need the information. The new analyst realizes that some of the data you had been looking at in the past actually was erroneous. All of a sudden, you find out that your analytical instincts and your sense of what was right had been shaped all along to look at reality a different way. You had become so accustomed to looking at erroneous numbers as valid that erroneous information didn't "look odd." Your new analyst struggles to get information that, when you present it, will have to be explained in the light of the perception of truth that had been created with the previous, erroneous information.

3. *Using personal applications as a disconnected, rapidly stale view of information.* To further extend the example of the service executive above, imagine that you now need information in a format that was not collected originally. Assume that you were looking at metrics on a weekly basis, and now you would like to report the information based on quarters. Your analyst has two options: Either go back through all the spreadsheets and aggregate the numbers manually or go back to the source systems where the original information came from and just change the query. Being a good analyst, she relies on the systems and opts for modifying her query at the source system. Once she gets the results, she cross-references her "spreadsheet numbers" with the "system numbers." She quickly realizes that the numbers from the systems do not amount to the aggregation of the numbers in her spreadsheets! This solution can mean one of three things: Her spreadsheets have an error, the systems have an error, or both! As she investigates the situation further, she finds out that the system definitions of certain types of incidents had changed over time—she has no way of comparing her spreadsheet numbers with the system numbers!

Best-practice companies drive agility by making analytic functionality available to all employees in an easy-to-get-to manner. They have figured out a way to provide the right level of depth to the right audiences and have done so by using personal productivity applications in the right ways.

They enable their employees to gain insight and understand information faster and in a way that relates to the corporate goals and objectives. Fewer of their employees starve for information or spend hours collecting data that will take them days to understand or that they won't be able to *do* anything with.

RELEVANCY

We emphasize "do" because action is the end goal of analytics. You don't analyze for the sake of analysis, you analyze to determine how to make things better and take action.

Organizations that provide employees with the ability to rank performance based on effectiveness and results achieved can replicate effective practices. They can do more of what works, less of what doesn't. Some organizations utilize analytics to go beyond just ranking areas of best performance. They have developed sophisticated ways of benchmarking performance so they can understand the factors which make top-performing groups succeed so that best practices can be captured and replicated.

How can best practices be captured when you have large and diverse communities of employees or business groups? Two examples can be instructive:

1. *Hilton came up with a concept of peer groups.* Benchmarks are meant to drive focused execution and better accountability regardless of who you are in the organization. Given the diversity of properties and brands we managed, providing accurate and fair benchmarks might seem like an impossible task to take on. It all depends on the quality of the peer group that you define: We had devised a method by which we could assess the performance of a particular property against a pool of peers, whether you were a food and beverage department in an airport Hilton, or a totally different brand hotel in a nonurban environment for example. The accuracy of the peer group allowed us to not only better compare performance, but provided better plans across the various properties, brands, and the business models provided by the Hilton Group.[10]

2. *Clalit reviewed clinical demographics.* We can compare every clinic's performance against all other clinics.

But more specifically, we have developed a way to compare similar clinics by characteristics such as size (small/medium/large clinics), demographics (high elderly populations, many children), etc. Using these criteria, we create small benchmark groups, which allow us to truly assess performance across very similar clinics. This eliminates political discussions and discourages people from coming up with the wrong excuses for why they are unique. This method makes it easier for us to determine best practices of how others faced with similar challenges are approaching and better addressing these challenges.[11]

Analytics should be designed to focus employees on execution. In order to do this well, organizations need to go beyond providing access to information. The best analytics are not only easy to get to, they are also easy to understand and act on—they are relevant to the audience who needs to use them. While employees need to understand overall corporate performance, they particularly need to be focused on the slice of information that they can truly impact, that which is relevant to them.

When Does Information Democracy Become Anarchy?

In the past seven years more new data and information has been created than was created in all of history prior to 1999.[12] As noted by Forrester, information in corporations has been growing at an almost unmanageable pace for IT departments to manage:

The information revolution is producing mountains of digital data that are becoming more and more challenging to process and analyze. Not only are businesses generating more data every day, but our approach to data analysis (structured databases, indexes, and distributed data architectures) generates even more data. Furthermore, the volume of unstructured content is also increasing, adding to the proliferation.[13]

This has created information management headaches for employees who have had to sift through immense amounts of information, which is sometimes even duplicated across systems and applications. While the management of information is an increasing problem, the access to it is an increasing need.

You might have heard the concept of "information democracy." It refers to the pervasive access to information throughout the organization, based on the premise that this broader access enables greater impact.

The concept of political democracy rests on two ideas: rights and responsibilities. Information democracy follows by suggesting that the right to information is tied to responsibility. Employees should have the right to access information they need to perform their jobs—to deliver on those things for which they are responsible.

While achieving broad-based knowledge throughout the organization is a trait of best practice companies— "information democracy" must not be mistaken for "information anarchy."

In our definition, information democracy is about making each employee closer to his or her numbers, his or her obligations, and this concept is differentiated from "access to everything for all."

Access for all can become "information anarchy" quickly if mismanaged. Information anarchy occurs when employees have access to all types of information and consequently lose the ability to discern the relative importance of any of the information. It happens when employees are deluged with information that is not related to their responsibilities. We have encountered cases where managers, after hours of working with volumes of irrelevant reports, have learned more about their reporting systems than they have about the actual problems they were trying to solve.

Lost in Analysis

Information anarchy is fueled with the perception that if IT groups make all employees "super analysts" by empowering them with more, they will analyze more and perform better. This is purely a technological, binary approach that rarely yields the desired results. Instead, employees become lost in analysis. Employees who are overwhelmed with information and analytic functionality spend hours analyzing information that might not be pertinent to their business at all. More importantly, they can spend time learning more about the analytical application than doing their jobs and getting the answers they need.

Best-practice companies like Clalit drive efficiency for their employees and help them focus on what matters.

> We have developed a methodology for how people interact with information. We have doctors who are doctors most of the time and they have limited time to spend in the manager's role. So we have to adjust the system to make it very simple and acceptable for them so they will be able to use it for whatever decision they have to make. We strive to help doctors focus to get answers they need. For example, if they want to see what's going on right now in their environment, they can quickly compare between periods, see trends, or specific strategies for dealing with an issue.[14]

Fooled By Randomness

When organizations lose perspective of what employees' roles and specific needs are, they may enable all employees with analytics in the same way. In so doing, they run the risk of randomizing their employees with irrelevant analytical capabilities. Employees, in turn, run the risk of becoming fooled by the randomness of their analytic insights.[15]

While analysts come to work to do analysis, a sales rep, marketer, or operations manager comes to work to sell, market, or manage operational logistics. Also, while analysts need to focus on a particular issue very deeply—and need to be enabled to analyze with great depth, a business manager needs to make business decisions across a broad range of sales, marketing or HR issues for example, and does not need to spend the day analyzing deeply. In short, a business manager needs to make decisions.

> We have a methodology for defining business needs. We are working with a limited number of reference users who understand how the business works. They help us understand the business needs of every population of users. We provide different solutions for different users—for analysts, very complex querying tools with a lot of flexibility and we give them a lot of data and they can do a lot of difficult analysis. Whereas for the managers, who have very little time and they are not experts with computers, we developed a very simplified system that is easy to use.[16]

Analytics for business analysts, however, should give them depth, more information, and more functionality—allow them to analyze to their heart's content. Analysts always tend to investigate at deeper levels than middle managers or executives.

Wayne Eckerson from The Data Warehousing Institute (TDWI) underscores this point in his research:

> An executive, once they see a red light in their scorecard, typically only drills down one or two levels before picking up the phone and calling an analyst. Middle managers, on the other hand, drill down three or four levels. So you need a performance management system that supports the needs of the executive who wants to drill down one or two levels, the manager who wants to drill down three or four levels and the analyst who wants to drill down to the details.[17]

Just What Matters, Please

So how do you provide employees the information they need to be more empowered without randomizing them? In order to enable role based relevancy, information needs to be:

- Based on things that people care about
- Based on who people are

Information Based on Things that People Care About We discussed earlier the difference between data consistency and information consistency. In summary, data consistency guarantees that your organization has the right numbers—that numbers are consistent, reliable, and trusted. Information consistency means that the understanding of what these numbers mean is universal across the organization.

Performance management solutions should understand and utilize data and information for what each is—whereas data can be things like numbers, information is the understanding of these numbers. Information, is a layer of abstraction above the data. Performance management solutions allow the organization to shape the information in a way that is both germane to the data and essential to driving better business performance.

Let's suppose that you want to determine your organization's revenue per employee in Italy. You know that your company's total revenue is $10 million. That number is a global number; it is the "one version of the truth." The first question you might ask is, "How many employees work for the company?" so you can evaluate "revenue per employee," which is the metric you really care about. Next, you realize that the total number of employees is global but you just need that number in Italy. Also, you'll need to know the revenues in Italy. Finally, you'll want to know what a

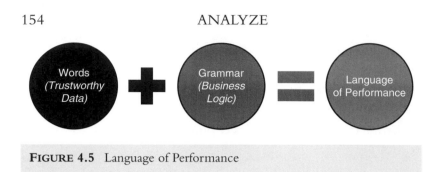

FIGURE 4.5 Language of Performance

"good" number is—how do you evaluate whether this ratio represents good performance?

This very simple example describes the importance of "business logic." Business logic is essentially the abstracted layer of thinking used above the crude data. Business logic is the "grammar" that allows individuals to formulate their thinking about a piece of data, and thereby gets employees much closer to acting on the information. Remember the Language of Performance formula, shown in Figure 4.5.

In the preceding example, business logic is the way an individual would think about the $10 million number. To break it up more specifically in five easy steps:

Step 1: Determine the revenue number for Italy.

Step 2: Figure out how many employees are in Italy.

Step 3: Divide Italian revenues by Italian employees.

Step 4: Assign a number for what "good performance" should be.

Step 5: Compare the revenues per Italian employee to your target.

Information Based on Who People Are   In addition to showing information that you care about, your information should be presented to you with an understanding of the person you are. The information should be relevant to your role and responsibilities. Imagine that you are the employee in the example above. At what step would you have preferred to start your analysis? At step 1 or step 4? Hopefully many of you responded step 4.

Securing the information is a first step, but guided analytics that understand what people will be reviewing at a particular time of the year for the particular role should be your aspiration. The goal of analytics is not to let employees wander around reports, but rather to help them solve specific problems that their specific roles are chartered to solve.

Providing employees with relevant information is different from merely providing information access. To improve results, allow the employee's experience with information to be as relevant and as actionable as possible.

An example of that would be to examine how information can be filtered in your performance management solution.

Filters: From Simple to Smart   Without the ability to filter, employees are left to interpret unrelated information by themselves, and retrieving the information that they really need is time consuming. The information needs to be filtered to cut down on this time and deliver agility.

For this reason, "dashboard filters" are very popular tools for analysis. Companies use them to allow an individual to have personalized views of their entire dashboard (i.e., having the ability to filter all entities of a dashboard—scorecards, analytics, and even a list of unstructured documents).

A great example of automation is "enforced filtering." This means that dashboards and scorecards are automatically filtered when employees open them for the first time. Companies may also let employees have a say in the degree of relevance and specificity of their view by giving them the ability to use multiple filtering options that they can pass through all dashboard views. For instance, an employee could filter a dashboard based on time, geography, and product line all at the same time, depending on what they want to see.

Sometimes, filtering can be very difficult to implement because the various views of a dashboard might not necessarily share the same filtering options. This is when you will need capabilities such as "smart filtering" to guarantee information consistency.

Smart Filtering   Smart filters contain additional logic that can drive more compelling views such as the top ten products for a selected region or performance over the past year for a selected manager. By simply applying a filter to a view, employees can make the view relevant and personal to them.

Imagine that your dashboard is composed of two views: One is a scorecard showing information by quarter; the second is an analytical view but showing that same information by month. The current filter for both shows Q2 (see Figure 4.6—dashboard on top, analytic at the bottom).

However, if you would like to see the scorecard and analytics information for Q1 and you use the drop-down menu to select Q1, what would you expect to happen?

- *Option 1*: Everything breaks. The scorecard has a filter set to accept quarter values. The analytic is set to accept month values. You either have to rely on two filters or decide not to filter one of the views.

- *Option 2*: The view returns the information desired. Although the analytic didn't display quarter, it "understood" the relationship of Q1 in months and retrieved the information desired to make the right decisions.

Clearly, we'd all hope to experience option 2, which provides the flexibility which should be enabled for employees.

Filtering can be very powerful when it can contain sophisticated logic such as the example discussed above.

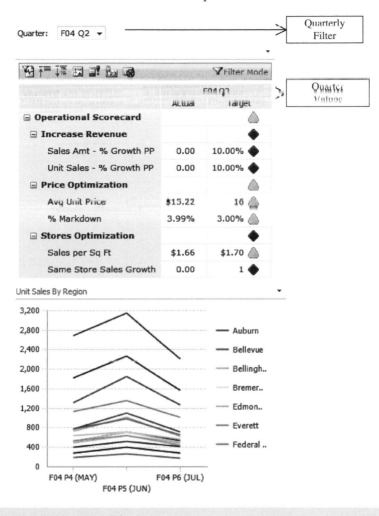

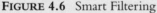

FIGURE 4.6 Smart Filtering

Filtering frames the employees' universe and delivers them the information in a way that is relevant to them. This provides them with focus, which is one step closer to relevant action.

The VHA provides a good example of how smart filters deliver focus:

> Our employees click on a button in their toolbar and launch a dashboard that already knows who they are. So it pulls up their

relevant information and has the time frames already set up. The four quadrants may be things like Quality, Access, Cost, and Patient Satisfaction, for instance. They just have to pull it up and that's it. They know what their current state is and they're off going about their business. The application even tells them the causes for performance. When something is red, the dashboard provides more detailed information, such as which patients need attention. This makes information truly actionable.[18]

From Information to Action

Employees today find themselves bombarded with information. Reports and additional numbers, no matter how relevant, might not always be the best way to encourage employees to focus on what matters and to act. Sometimes, so many reports and information are provided that it is easier for employees to just "shut down" rather than engage, thinking, "If it's important, the person will send it again or mark it urgent." Rather than more noise, actionable e-mails are preferred and appreciated. Simple suggestions or instructions can go a long way to not only delivering the message, but achieving the desired outcome.

Consider the following scenario: You run a brokerage house and you make money on securities transactions. Your employees are paid on sell and buy actions for your clients. Naturally, compensation drives behavior so a large part of the employees' days might be spent trying to better prompt their clients to either buy or sell. How could analytics better condition clients to act appropriately to the broker's goal? Would more reports do it? More statements and proxy vote requests, sent via email or snail mail? Most clients typically ignore those.

A look at how Scottrade addresses this particular issue is instructive. Figure 4.7 describes the performance of a stock (graph on the left) and additionally proposes possible actions clients could take.

Scottrade SmartText™

If you find yourself buried in complex stock research and charts, Scottrade SmartTextT can summarize complicated information into a plain English explanation that's easy for you to understand.

You'll spend less time deciphering extensive data and more time finding your ideal investment opportunities!

See how it works...

Your Personal **Stock Market** *Interpreter*

Start using SmartText.

[Open a Scottrade Account]

| Symbol: ABC | Duration: 3 Months | Type: Moving Average | * Submit |

ABC

ABC closed below its 13 minute moving average. This is generally considered to be an indication of a bearish trend.

Complex data in plain English!

* In addition to spotlighting Moving Average, Bollinger Bands and MACD, your Scottrade account also gives you access to the following indicators: Parabolic Sar, Price Channel, Slow Stochastics, Relative Strength, On Balance Volume, Williams % R, Directional Movement Indicator and Ultimate Oscillator.

SmartText is integrated into three areas of Scottrade's Quotes & Research section:

FIGURE 4.7   Scottrade

This analytical use eloquently demonstrates the deep understanding this brokerage company has of its business and its audience. To attract more clients and grow its revenue out of its existing customer base, Scottrade must provide more than just information. Pretty charts and graphs don't do it anymore with clients—most leading vendors have them. Interpretations, however, are different. They are more valuable to the audience primarily because the audience doesn't always understand the whole picture, or because the audience doesn't have the time to interpret; rather, if the audience has time, Scottrade would prefer that they use it buying or selling stock!

In a way, this situation is very similar to that of an organization that tries to get its employees to act consistently with company objectives in mind. Analysis is an essential component of better decisions, but as more and more information is available, organizations need to find better ways to encourage employees to act, and to act in accordance to the company's objectives.

An effective performance management solution needs to enable analytics "a la Scottrade." These types of analytics have two major benefits:

1. *It doesn't assume the audience knows everything.* This is a key enabler to make analytics "stick" with your audience. Assuming that employees know more than the information presented to them is not always wise. This is why presenting simple and clear analytical views to your employees is key in making sure that they can understand them without having to perform extra mental work or interpretation of jargon. For instance, if you present information on margins in a graph, your analytic better help inform employees on where the information comes from and what it means. Note how the Scottrade SmartText application helps clients understand what they are looking at via filters and a legend. Further, the "interpret" text spells out exactly the meaning of the numbers they see in the graph.

2. *It doesn't confine the decision to the prescribed action.* The Scottrade analytics do not just provide the interpreted text. Rather, it still provides the original graph. This increases its credibility with the audience. As a client of Scottrade, if you do not agree with the interpretation, you still have the opportunity to analyze the information your way and act on it the way you think is most appropriate. This is a key consideration when providing interpretations to employees. The interpretation by itself does not override the analytics. In some cases, employees might know more than just the analytics or its interpretation. Employees should

have the option to draw their own conclusion based on the information.

To conclude, there is one thing that the Scottrade analytics is missing: a suggestion on what to do next. Once you have provided your employees with the logical interpretation of the information, it is good to provide a way to take action. For instance, a button taking the employee to the next graph or maybe to an e-mail that needs to be sent. Take a look at the top right of the page. This is exactly where Scottrade has put such a button.

There are companies already implementing this type of intelligent analytics. Let's consider Clalit, for example:

> Our performance management system is an operational system. It helps doctors focus on the population they are treating, especially those who need medical treatment but have not yet been treated. The system provides doctors with knowledge that the patient is waiting for a particular test result but more importantly displays the phone number where the patient can be reached. This allows doctors to know to take action right away because they know that if they wait until next week, it may be too late.[19]

In short, providing information that is relevant is essential in having every employee's world make sense more rapidly. When analytics succeed, they enable more people to understand information faster and take action on relevant insight. Clalit is able to move from reactive to proactive management using advanced analytics:

> We have gone from looking backwards at what happened yesterday to foresee what is going to happen tomorrow. We have developed a way to forecast which patients have a higher risk of medical status deterioration. We want to understand why some people have moved from being relatively healthy to becoming much sicker. We are now able to provide a list of people at high risk to doctors so the doctors can decide ahead of time how best to treat the patients (change their medication, change their diet, etc). When we built this system there was concern that the

doctors would resist the assistant informing them of the likely progression of their patients. But instead they've really embraced it and like how it has helped them focus. This is particularly true as our culture has moved to measuring and managing everything—every sector, every clinic, every doctor—against targets.[20]

Clalit's focus is on how best to serve patients and prevent health deterioration before it happens. They agree to respect the accuracy of the predictions based on the data, rather than battling over intuition and expertise.

However, their concern on whether these systems would be adopted was justified. As it turns out, Clalit's culture was surprisingly mature. Cultures with experts sometimes resist a different approach than their expertise dictates. It is understandably the case that experts are often reticent to change to a culture where data can override their judgment. Companies often experience pushback when introducing predictive analytics, particularly in cultures in which:

- Expertise is highly revered and not doubted.
- A premium is placed on gut feel and intuition.

Ian Ayres speaks in depth about this transition from individual trial and error based on experience to using data mining and predictive analytics to improve decision making:

> We are in a historical moment of horse-versus-locomotive competition, where intuitive and experiential expertise is losing out time and time again to number crunching. In the old days, many decisions were simply based on experience and intuition. Experts were ordained because of their decades of individual trial-and-error experience. We could trust that they knew the best way to do things because they had done it hundreds of times in the past.[21]

In the next section, we take a look at efficiencies that can be gained by providing highly interactive and intuitive analytical functionalities to increase your employees' efficiency.

EFFICIENCY

The concept of efficiency is critical when it comes to analytics because rich analytics are not just analytics that have a lot to offer; they are also analytics that allow employees to understand information, see trends, and act, faster.

Focused Insights Drive Faster Decisions

Throughout this book, we have been referring to efficient and effective performance management solutions. If effective means that you can "do more things better," efficient means that you can "do more of these things faster."

Learning from Experience

As our personal and work lives are more and more intertwined, so is our interaction with information. Whether on a computer, online, or on a mobile device, we are constantly able to find, use, and share information. In each of these environments, the need to work efficiently with information persists. Thankfully, today we have the ability to manage and utilize this information efficiently in each of these environments.

Perhaps the best example of efficiency is when information appears as we are thinking about it. As we are seeking information about people, products, or places, using a personal computer or mobile device, software assists us with getting to the relevant information faster. As soon as we start thinking about what we need and start typing it in, the information starts surfacing; sometimes search suggestions may even appear as we are typing. For example, if we are looking for market information in Japan, we can start typing "market info" in our computer, and various e-mails, documents, files, and information from all over start being suggested. This relationship with information is based on our preferences, experiences, and specific needs at a given point in time.

This is the type of relationship that best-practice companies enable their employees to have when using analytics. Great analytics not only guide employees with the relevant information, but also anticipate their needs.

With such pervasive access to information, employees have come to expect to find what they need, when they need it. This has created something we call the "twitching finger."

The Twitching Finger

"Twitching finger" refers to the need employees have when discovering an issue and wanting to click on the problem to know what is causing the issue, why it is happening, and what it means. As soon as they see the red metric in their scorecard or the downward trend in their analytics, their finger twitches with anticipation to click and know more.

A common example of exercising the twitching finger is drilling. Simply put, drilling is the ability to get to the bottom of an issue, to start from the red metric and dig deeper all the way to its root cause.

A good way to think about drilling is with a nature analogy. Consider a tall, healthy oak tree. What if you want to find out what makes this tree so big? What if you want to know how old it is or maybe understand what has nourished this tree to become what it is today?

You would probably start digging to find out how long the tree's roots are, how deep they have grown, how wide they span or where their source of water might be. The ability to rapidly get to the answers is enabled by drilling capabilities.

There are two types of drilling: drilling up and drilling down. Drilling down starts at a high-level (the tree) and then gets down to details (the root). Drilling up involves moving from a low level (a particular root) to a higher level (a root cluster, or even all the way back to the tree).

Employees need to drill into information at any level of the information hierachy. In applying the concept of the tree to a business, you can imagine the geographic information comprised of the following levels: Global, Country, State, County, City. Working within the right environment, employees should be able to execute the following easily:

- *Drilling down* to lower level information, as in going from Country information to City information.
- *Drilling up* to higher level information, as in going from City information to Country information.

It is important to be able to drill back up. Why? Because employees are not machines. They might click through steps to test a theory, and if this theory is not confirmed, they will need to drill back up to test other assumptions.

While the ability to drill up and down is a great asset, your employees will rapidly find themselves limited by the simple up-and-down pattern of their analysis. Analyzing information up and down might be useful, but it is not enough to accommodate the needs of inquiry.

Employees should be able to work with data in a way that makes sense based on their business needs at a given point in time. And they should be able to do this on their own—it's costly and inefficient otherwise. Constantly modifying your data architecture to adapt to ongoing business requests is an expensive and time-consuming approach that kills agility. At some point, organizations need to enable employees to manage information to meet their own needs. A good example of this is cross-drilling.

Analysis at the Speed of Thought

Let's go back to the tree example shown in Figure 4.8. Let's say at the top of the root structure of the tree, you identify a big root that you think may explain the tree's primary source of water. You start digging and digging, following that root to lower levels underground. At a certain point, you encounter a fork. You can either go down to the left or to the right. The root on the left side of the fork is bigger so you are thinking that's the way to go. You then continue left a few levels below. As you are digging down, you can still see the right side of the fork and it has not deviated a lot from your digging pattern, although it points away from the other root now. Continuing on with the left root, you finally get to a rock a few levels below. The direction you had chosen didn't take you where you thought it would. You can still see the other root, though—how can you get to it? You could dig back up to the area where both roots forked (drilling up) or you could potentially drill sideways to that other root (drilling across).

Which option will be more efficient for your employees to get to the information they need? Cross-drilling can be

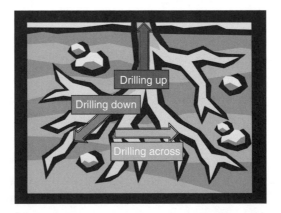

FIGURE 4.8 Tree Roots

immensely efficient because it better follows the way the human brain investigates issues. While drilling up and down is great and a "must-have" to drive efficient analysis, it is limited because it is more appropriate for simple, up/down, yes/no types of analytical patterns.

Cross-drilling provides the ability to drill across data hierarchies to allow decision makers to answer a much wider variety of questions and will likely apply more frequently to your daily business needs. Beyond the botanical example discussed earlier, let's take an example that might be closer to your daily challenges (see Figure 4.9).

Jack owns a retail bicycle chain. He notices that margins have been low but does not know what could be the cause of the issue. He opens up his analytical application and loads the margins information across all of his 150 retail stores. The dimensions of his analysis allow him to drill up and down margin dollars by country and product lines. He starts at the global level, which shows all products, all countries and margin information. He drills down to Europe, where he can now see margin numbers for all products. He drills down Europe again and now can see the Germany, France,

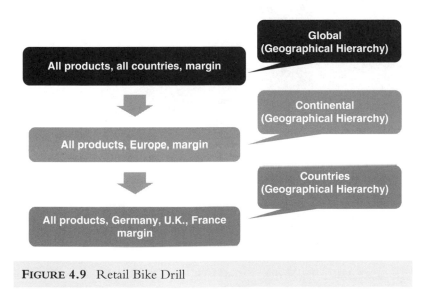

FIGURE 4.9 Retail Bike Drill

and U.K. margin information. At this point, he can compare how these countries are doing on margin numbers against each other and he can go up and down this path as much as needed. By drilling down, Jack has been able to find out that France was losing money on all bikes.

While the above analysis can be useful, Jack really hasn't used his analytics as an interactive information tool. By strictly drilling down the data hierachy defined by his IT department, Jack hasn't been able to ask the data the questions that he really wants to answer. For instance, what products is Jack's company making money on? Where are these products primarily sold? Of these locations, when were the high margin products in particular sold? What day of the week? That's what cross-drilling enables—almost limitless questions to help deliver the answers people need to make informed decisions (see Figure 4.10).

Cross-drilling allows employees to:

- Use more of the available information. As you can see, cross-drilling really is differentiated from simply

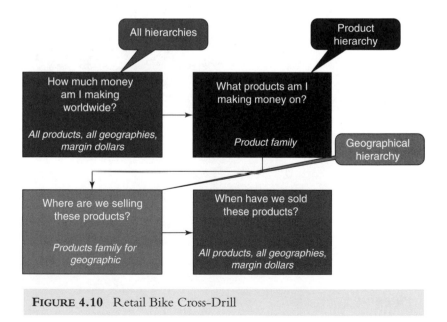

FIGURE 4.10 Retail Bike Cross-Drill

drilling up and down. While drilling up and down is a necessary and good start to efficient analysis, cross-drilling allows decision makers to use all the information available to fully answer their questions.

• Investigate with Flexibility. Cross-drilling takes into account that a typical analytical path cannot be defined ahead of time. Rather than being restricted to predefined paths of inquiry (such as Bikes in France for 2005), with cross-drilling, employees can define their own paths of analysis, across all available data hierarchies. As analysis is performed, analysts can answer the questions as they arise: One day the data might prompt them to investigate where products are sold in Germany, the next day it might be when products are sold across Europe.

Many organizations create performance management systems, especially tactical and strategic dashboards, using spreadsheet, presentation, and advanced charting packages. However Wayne Eckerson advises that these dashboards are too "flat": "Although these applications often look fancy, they generally do not provide enough data or analytical capabilities to let users explore the root cause of problems highlighted in the fancy graphical indicators."[22] They don't allow drilling or further investigation. This is why we underscore the value of being able to drill from *anywhere* . . . even the legend. Let those twitching fingers click.

See Better, Do Better

We could have called this section "advanced capabilities." However, that title would have been deceptive. In the following section, we discuss the type of functionality that empowers all employees to do more with the information, not their applications. "Advanced" would have implied that we advocated more functionality. As you might have picked up from this book so far, our research shows that companies that win are not the ones that focus just on analysis, but instead they are the ones that focus on executing, doing more with the information.

Technology is only as good as the quality and timeliness of the decisions it fosters. As a consequence the meaning of "advanced" in this passage is more about allowing more employees to see better, so they can do better.

What do we mean by that—how does sight relate to performance? The subject of visualization has been explored many times over by experts such as Edward Tufte. He cautions to avoid overpowering and complicating the viewer of the visualizations. Use only as much as is necessary and carries meaning. If a line doesn't add clarity, don't use it. He guides creators of information visualizations to resist the urge to layer unnecessary formatting of bolds, italics, and underlines. He admonishes to refrain from layering colors for the sake of having colors—use them if they convey information; avoid unnecessary graphics that do not impart meaning.

Tufte's research on information visualization advocates the use of rich visuals that are not only complete but also present the audience with an easy-to-understand framework. Complete means that a good visualization stays true to the original information—it retains and delivers the core information to make its point. These visuals should be very graphic and use visual forms that the human eye can recognize and use to draw quick conclusions.

He talks further about the power of what we call "prepared" analytics. By "prepared," we mean that these analytics are used by analysts to share an understanding of their findings to an audience that knows very little about them. Professor Tufte suggests shying away from dry tables or stale presentation slides because they rarely engage the audience or retain their attention. On the contrary, colorful analytics are effective because they draw attention and are easy to quickly interpret.

What can we learn from Edward Tufte's lessons when it comes to performance management? Clearly, it is easier to customize a graph or a visual if you know ahead of time the information you'd like to convey. In the performance management context, however, where data is accessed and displayed in live situations, there is less opportunity to massage and prepare the information for display—it just happens, and the visual might not always make sense.

So, when it comes to "advanced visualizations" for analytics, two concepts are key: simplicity and flexibility. Both concepts are intertwined, so instead of reviewing each separately, we will provide a few specific examples to show the importance of these concepts.

Getting to the Core, Regardless of the Amount of Data   Imagine that you are a bookseller and that your company sells millions of books on a daily basis. Your business business is driven by three key metrics:

1. Number of books sold
2. Revenue from books sold
3. Margin driven from books sold

The obvious objective of your business is to sell the highest number of books for the highest margin. The issue is more complex than just focusing on margin numbers, as the cost of selling books is impacted by your inventory—your stock management efficiencies are tested on a daily basis across your numerous stores. The longer your retail stores stock "unpopular" books, the higher their chances to sell them at a discount, thus reducing your margin. As you are looking at store performance, you must then understand margins, number of books sold, inventory, and buying patterns. That's a lot of information to understand concurrently.

The analysis of store performance becomes a lot more sophisticated, and the sample of data that you need to get access to can become dangerously big. Take a look at the screen shot below. This "performance map" is derived from the tree map conceived by Ben Shneiderman, a computer scientist and professor at the University of Maryland, College Park. It allows you to see data patterns among a group of items using the size and color of boxes arranged together in a small space. Figure 4.11 compares sales and percent markdown among history books.

Although the figure below is in black in white, you may be able to picture the visual indicators at play. The size of the box represents the gross sales for the book (bigger is better) and the color of the box represents how much the book price has been marked down (greener is better). Ideally, books with the highest sales would have the lowest percent markdown; that is, the largest boxes would be the brightest green. This view indicates a serious problem in the

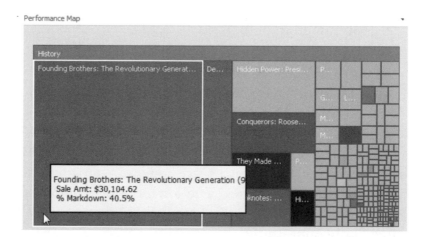

FIGURE 4.11 Performance Map

top-selling book *Founding Brothers* because it has the highest markdown percent of all books in this category. Reducing the markdown on this book may improve overall revenue and margin for the company.

You'll notice that this type of analytic is simple to understand by any employee, not just analysts. Furthermore, it surfaces patterns from large amounts of data, which as we discussed in our example, is a requirement that many employees will run into as soon as they want to investigate their key business drivers. This analytic is simple because it encapsulates a key point in a very visual fashion. It is also very flexible as it allows employees to click through the different boxes in order to find out more. Even better, notice that by simply putting your pointer on the red box, you can find out the name of the item which is underperforming as well as the percent markdown and revenue numbers.

Simplicity and flexibility are paramount analytic attributes that allow employees to understand information faster and encourages them to use information more throughout the day without apprehension. The goal of analytics is not to scare away decision makers with complexity. The performance map highlighted in Figure 4.11 is becoming increasingly familiar as more and more of us use these advanced analytics to review portfolios online as shown in Figure 4.12 (which can be viewed in color online at http://www.smartmoney.com/marketmap).

Look familiar? Include visualization assets like these in your performance management solution to drive efficiency. If individuals already know how to monitor their own financial performance on the web for free, there is no reason that they couldn't utilize them for the benefit of your company's profit, too!

All Employees Are Different Making analytics mainstream is also about recognizing that each individual is different in the way they analyze information. Suppose, for instance,

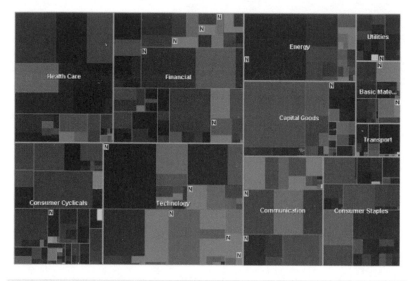

FIGURE 4.12 SmartMoney Market Map

that an employee gets the following view in their dashboard (see Figure 4.13). This is a great example of accommodating employee preferences for how they want to view analytics. Beyond the fact that these views can help employees uncover trends much easier, they also allow greater flexibility of interaction.

Figure 4.14 shows performance of particular types of books over time. While this type of visual might be useful, it makes it difficult to recognize any kind of trend. The view below shows the same information, but in a line chart.

Item By Category	⊞ January	⊞ February	⊞ March	⊞ April	⊞ May
⊞ Business	$310,575.59	$304,412.76	$291,066.65	$229,297.08	$209,812.01
⊞ Graphic Novels	$4,228.40	$3,865.46	$4,273.55	$3,717.60	$4,596.43
⊞ Literature	$110,729.17	$117,196.90	$111,901.44	$100,820.88	$115,332.33
⊞ Military History	$71,114.83	$62,689.33	$55,404.27	$46,434.01	$44,621.09
⊞ Reference	$224,846.49	$173,318.92	$160,729.49	$185,479.26	$180,889.83

FIGURE 4.13 Types of Books Table

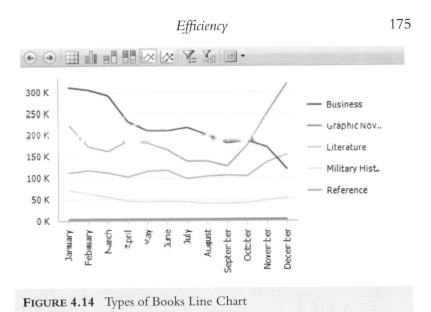

FIGURE 4.14 Types of Books Line Chart

Notice the type of insights you can draw from the graph. You can see that the Reference section has been booming since September, while the Graphic Novels have been flat over time.

To be particularly effective, these sets of information should be separated by only a click—the twitching finger should be able to get from the table view to the graph view easily (see Figure 4.13).

While this example is a simple one, it indicates the flexibility required to facilitate analytics that are accepted widely by your employees. Here are some additional guidelines to consider:

- *Easy.* Analytics are easy when they are web based and when most of the functionality employees need is simple to access and requires very little specific skills. Making analytics web based makes them easy to integrate to web portals, which contributes greatly to adoption throughout the company.

- *Interactive.* Making analytics web enabled shouldn't be a trade-off to functionality. All the functionally we discussed earlier should be available without the need to download software because this type of functionality is essential to helping all employees to understand information faster.

- *Flexible and relevant.* In order to make better decisions, employees need to have flexible analytics. Their first view of the data might not be the one that provides the most insight. Organizations that win are the ones that allow more of their employees to work seamlessly with information that is relevant to them in an environment that gets them to the answers they want without having to call IT.

In an increasingly competitive environment, companies that develop a Culture of Performance are not the ones that force their employees to become "super-analysts." They don't report on information that is both irrelevant (because it's out of date or not tailored for the audience) and non-actionable (because it can't be interacted with and incite a decision). Analytics that provide agility, relevancy, and efficiency deliver competitive advantage for the organization. And they do so while providing the most value for both IT and for the business communities.

CONCLUSION

In this chapter, we've discussed the guiding principles organizations follow to develop the Analyze capability (see Figure 4.1 at the beginning of the Chapter). We've talked about how they follow the principle of agility as they develop web-based analytics that are both deep and broad. We've underscored the importance of getting the right amount of analytic capability to people based on their analytic needs. We've also discussed how filters and guided analytics can help provide focus and relevancy for the people in your organization. Finally, in order to drive efficiency, organizations develop skills and assets like drilling (up, down, and across) as well as incorporate advanced analytics to enable more intuitive understanding and faster decision making.

We've now covered two-thirds of the capabilities you need to begin realizing the benefits of managing performance—monitor and analzye. We now need to add the third leg of the stool. In Chapter 5, we review the role of planning, budgeting, and forecasting (collectively, the Plan capability) in driving performance.

HOW TO KNOW IF YOU HAVE THE ABILITY TO ANALYZE

We have discussed the three guiding principles to which an organization must adhere to Analyze effectively:

1. *Agility* to respond quickly to changing market conditions and enabled by allowing more people to leverage analytics via web-based analytics; delivering depth where needed, depending on the types of decisions being made (tactical, operational, or strategic).

2. *Relevancy* of information enabled by delivering information that is based on the things people care about while filtering the irrelevant and unnecessary information; delivering it in a way that makes sense to them by tailoring it for their roles; making it intuitive and extremely easy to use.

3. *Efficiency* by allowing people to follow their path of inquiry by drilling and cross-drilling to get the answers they need without delay; making complex sets of information quickly comprehensible through advanced analytics such as performance maps; enabling trends and patterns to be intuitively recognizable.

The following test may prove helpful in assessing your organization's capabilities. Think about it as a framework to organize a conversation around the subject of performance management with your teams across divisions and groups within your organization.

Take the Test

Some of the statements below are multifaceted and you may find you have stronger agreement with some parts of the statement than other parts. Answer "True" if you find that the statement is generally true and "False" if you find the statement is generally false in describing your organization.

1. When our employees have a need for information, regardless of where they are, they are able to get to it by themselves without making additional calls, downloads, or special requests.

2. Analytics is part of our employees' everyday work life and environments. They do not consider analytics as a different set of capabilities that they either need to get special help with, need to download or get training to use. Analytics has become second nature, like e-mail, and all employees can produce the analysis they need, with no inhibitions.

3. Our analytics are appropriate for each of our employees' roles. We have a mechanism that allows us to understand how to best serve their analytical needs. For instance, managers may start with a global view of the business while business analysts may go straight to their area of expertise—Finance, Operations, Marketing, or others. We don't overwhelm employees with deep information they wouldn't understand, nor do we underwhelm others with information that doesn't help them.

4. Our analytics can be filtered in context of the rest of the dashboard they are part of. For instance, if our dashboard is filtered for a specific country or product, the scorecard and the analytics will be filtered in context so that employees look at consistent picture of performance.

5. Our information filters understand the underlying information our analytics are based on. For instance, if an analytical view can be viewed by months, while another one, in the same dashboard, can be viewed only by quarter, the filter will adapt intelligently. Employees do not have to second-guess information, but rather trust they still work with a consistent set of information, regardless of the technical difficulties involved in getting the right information.

6. As soon as our employees see a metric or a trend they want to investigate, they can drill into the information tree to know what is causing the issue, why it is happening, and what it means.

7. Our employees are not restricted in their pursuit of answers. As they start asking questions and build further insight, they can drill in a way that follows their thinking path. This could mean drilling down or up, but also drilling across the information.

8. When faced with a large set of information, our employees are able to quickly identify trends and patterns. Employees are able to understand complex information faster through visual and intuitive analytics.

9. Our employees can easily take action based on the recommendations made by our analytics. Rather than giving information for information's sake, our analytics orient employees toward the solutions to the problems they are faced with.

10. We are able to identify and replicate effective practices and discontinue ineffective practices. We know which customers, partners and sales representatives are most effective and which are least effective.

When reviewing your score, note that the score should not be viewed as an outcome ("How did we do?"), but rather as a starting point ("Where are we starting from?"). The purpose of the test is not just to give you a number, but to provide a framework for driving performance excellence.

Add up the number of "True" answers you provided above. If you have answered all of the above "True," the people in your organization are equipped with the ability to analyze, and management has its finger on the pulse of the organization. For the rest of us, refer to the following:

0–2 True answers = limited Analyze strength; your score is 1.

3–5 True answers = moderate Analyze strength; your score is 2.

6–8 True answers = major Analyze strength; your score is 3.

9–10 True answers = superior Analyze strength; your score is 4.

Note your score, as you will need it to determine your stage in Chapter 6. Further guidance on how to improve your analytical skills is also provided below.

Improve Your Results

If you answered "False" to any of the above questions, note the number of the question and review the corresponding suggested remedy below to help move you to a "True" answer—and, more importantly, provide your organization with competitive advantage.

1. When employees are not able to get to the information they need by themselves, they not only make less informed decisions but they also make them slower. Understand that your employees may need information throughout their day, regardless if they are at their desk or visiting a customer. Consider using the web as a way for employees to get to the analytics they need on their own.

2. When analytics are hard to get to, they aren't used and their benefits aren't realized. The scope of impact is also limited to a small community. While some might be informed, few make fact-based decisions daily. The best way to foster an analytical culture amongst your employee base is to provide them with a simple and intuitive way to get to the answers they need. When employees can use analytics as part of their daily environment, they will adopt and leverage analytic capabilities faster. Use technologies such as portal or other productivity applications to encourage your employees to use analytics within trusted and familiar environments.

3. Agility and competitiveness are lost when employees can't quickly develop insights for their areas of ownership. When employees are blasted with information to which they can't relate, don't understand or think is not relevant, they give up on analysis. They either ask others to go find answers for them or make decisions based on hunches, sound bites or gut feeling. Consider employees' roles before you provide them with a "one-size-fit-all" analytical answer. While analysts may need deep functionality and information access, other employees may prefer simple but broader analytics.

4. Lack of focus diminishes the impact your employees can have. When they can't see a consistent picture of

performance, they take more time understanding the information than they do by taking action. Consider integrating common filters across all your analytics, so that employees develop faster insight.

5. Impact is delayed when employees second-guess information. Consider smart filters that understand the underlying information on which your analytics are based so that when they are looking for information across multiple analytics that share different products, times or geographies, they don't have to guess how that information is structured in the various data sources the analytics are based upon. Instead, the analytical application caters to their needs and presents the information in a way they can use it. For instance, if an employee is looking for Q2 information while one of the views can only be filtered by months, your performance management solution can translate "Q2" into the appropriate months.

6. Efficiencies are lost when dashboards are "flat" and employees cannot get to the root cause of issues by themselves. Without deeper knowledge of root cause, business insight and actions are delayed. Organizations should enable employees to investigate metrics by drilling down to understand what is causing the issue, why it is happening and what it means.

7. Employees should be able to follow a logical path of inquiry to get their answers. By enabling them to ask questions as they arise, the acquisition of answers is more efficient. Cross-drilling, the ability to navigate information across multiple dimensions—products, time, geographies, etc—facilitates efficient analysis and also delivers better answers.

8. Some organizations have to sort through literally millions of lines of information to try to derive higher level insights. This is a slow, costly and error prone

approach. By making this information more visual and leveraging technologies like performance maps, companies enable their employees to see trends and patterns, and take action more quickly

9. Employees who are overwhelmed with information and lack focus are inefficient and less effective. Analytics should guide them toward their goals—keep them in close proximity to the answers they can use. Organizations seeking this result should look at delivering guided analytics to their employees.

10. Organizations that provide employees with the ability to rank performance based on effectiveness and results achieved can replicate effective practices—do more of what works, less of what doesn't. The best analytics can help employees to go beyond just ranking best areas of best performance, such as "most profitable customers," "top margin products," "best achieving geographies." This helps not only to target these attractive sets but also to understand the factors which makes them "high performers" so that best practices can be captured and replicated.

NOTES

1. Discussion with Jack Bates, U.S. Department of Veterans Affairs, December 2007.

2. David O. Weber, "Survey Reveals Physicians' Love/Hate Relationship with Technology," *The Physician Executive,* March/April 2004.

3. "VA Blazes Path to Preventing Drug Errors," *USA Today,* July 2006 (www.usatoday.com/news/opinion/editorials/2006-07-31-letters-va_x.htm).

4. "VA Medical System Earns High Customer Satisfaction ratings." *National Journal,* February 2006 (www.govexec.com/story_page.cfm?articleid=33377&ref=rellink).

5. Discussion with Jack Bates, U.S. Department of Veterans Affairs, December 2007.

6. Gary Hamel, *The Future of Management* (Boston, MA: Harvard Business School Publishing, 2007).

7. Discussion with Jeremy Hope, December 2007.

8. *Ibid.*

9. Discussion with Ron Van Zanten, Premier Bankcard, November 2007.

10. Discussion with Scott Farr, former VP-Performance Management, Hilton Hotels December 2007.

11. Discussion with Mazal Tuchler, BI Project Manager, Clalit, December 2007.

12. Jeff Raikes, Microsoft BI Conference, May 2007.

13. Boris Evelson with Erica Driver, Noel Yuhanna, Rob Karel, J. Paul Kirby, Jamie Barnett, *Data Data Everywhere!* (Forrester Research, Inc., July 2007).

14. Discussion with Mazal Tuchler, BI Project Manager, Clalit, December 2007.

15. Credit for the phrase "Fooled by Randomness" goes to Nassim Nicholas Taleb, *Fooled by Randomness: The Hidden Role of Chance in Life and in the Markets* (New York: Random House, 2005).

16. Discussion with Mazal Tuchler, BI Project Manager, Clalit, December 2007.

17. Interview with Wayne Eckerson, video online at www.cultureofperformance.com.

18. Discussion with Jack Bates, U.S. Department of Veterans Affairs, December 2007.

19. Discussion with Mazal Tuchler, BI Project Manager, Clalit, December 2007.

20. *Ibid.*

21. Ian Ayres, *Super Crunchers: Why Thinking-by-Numbers Is the New Way to Be Smart,* (New York: Bantam Books, 2007).

22. Wayne W. Eckerson, *Performance Dashboards: Measuring, Monitoring, and Managing Your Business*, (Hoboken, NJ: John Wiley and Sons, Inc., 2005).

— 5 —

Plan

> The right budgeting process can change how a
> company functions—and reinventing the ritual
> makes winning so much easier, you can't afford
> not to try.
>
> *Jack Welch, from his book* Winning[1]

We begin this chapter with the Energizer story. Energizer's transformation to a culture that recognizes and enables decision makers across the organization is inspiring and instructive.

Following the Energizer story, the focus of this chapter is on the Plan capability and includes detailed descriptions of the skills and assets organizations need to develop in order to mimic the results of organizations like Energizer.

THE ENERGIZER STORY

"I used to be one of those," said Randy Benz of Energizer, the world's largest producers of batteries. "We all were command and control management types. We used to have a view that only the top management members could deliver significant impact—we called these folks the 'difference makers' and our IT efforts were geared toward getting information only to this select few. But not anymore. Now, we're aiming our efforts towards the hundreds of people across the organization who make the thousands of day-to-day decisions that really make the difference in business performance. We're getting new capabilities out to these "difference makers" across the enterprise—and recognizing wide scale increases in our effectiveness and impact."[2] This is central to Energizer's strategy of empowering employees and decentralizing decision making throughout the company.

The Challenges of Multibrand Leadership

Energizer has a variety of leading brands across a breadth of markets—from being a leading provider of batteries and flashlights (Energizer and Eveready brands) to being the second largest manufacturer of wet-shaving products (Schick and Wilkinson Sword brands). With the acquisition of Playtex Products, Inc. in October 2007, Energizer is now also a leading manufacturer and distributor of a diversified portfolio of skin care, feminine care, and infant care products, including brands such as Banana Boat, Hawaiian Tropic, Wet Ones, Playtex gloves, Playtex tampons, Playtex infant-feeding products, and Diaper Genie.

Describing the breadth of Energizer's product offerings is difficult on its own. Even without counting the latest Playtex additions, Energizer has a broad scope of business to manage: 28 product groups with over 10,000 stock-keeping units (SKUs), conducting business in 150 markets, and distribution through multiple channels (direct, indirect) in each market. Additionally, there are thousands of commercial and consumer usages of the products to understand across all socioeconomic segments.

Setting the Stage for Change

When Energizer spun off from prior parent Ralston Purina in the spring of 2000, they faced a tough competitive landscape and a difficult global economic situation. In the months that followed, Energizer struggled to get on track, and business performance floundered. Late in 2001, Energizer took the hard steps of deep cost cuts to provide an immediate lift to results, but it was clear that deeper cultural changes would be required in order to provide sustained improvements in business performance going forward.

Lessons from the Shop Floor

The earliest signs of this cultural change were visible on the manufacturing shop floor. The manufacturing management team had a novel idea—let the people who work on the shop floor determine how to run the shop floor to improve results instead of sending an engineer from headquarters to analyze the situation and tell them what to do to improve efficiency. What began with some simple empowerment programs grew to be a far-reaching LEAN program across the manufacturing facilities that connected each colleague with their role in delivering value to the customer and delivering business results. "The impact was immediately visible, but more importantly the cycle of setting and achieving shared goals for improvement became integral to the workplace culture."

A New Idea Catches On

The culture of performance ownership did not end in manufacturing. To optimize margin, Energizer empowered the field sales force with complete access to customer profitability and worked to establish goals for improving not only sales volumes but also the bottom line performance. Beginning with a pilot group and ultimately extending across the field sales force, Energizer provided basic analytic tools and related training to equip the field force to handle these new responsibilities. Again, the results were immediate. "Setting goals and making decisions 'close to the action' proved once again to be the most effective route to real performance gains."

The Untapped Opportunity

Energizer's historical approach to performance management had focused on enabling the executive decision makers and information analysts at the top of the pyramid. At the bottom of the pyramid, transactional systems and processes automated as much as possible. Benz explains the recognition of untapped opportunity, "There's this huge middle area—the majority of the organization's decisions—which we had left virtually untapped. Thousands of day-to-day, week-to-week decisions that ultimately shape results. We recognized an opportunity to create an organization of 'difference makers.'"

The Empowered Organization

The end result of this cultural change clearly demonstrated that every employee had the potential to make a difference—and, in fact, many already were. But equipping a broad organization of "difference makers" with the right tools was a challenge for the information technology function at Energizer. Benz provides guidance on the fundamental requirements of performance management tools aimed at an empowered organization:

- *Must "fit in."* Performance management must not be a separate set of processes that employees are forced to execute. The act of monitoring, analyzing, and planning business performance must fit in employees' work habits and the rhythm of their jobs.

- *Must be intuitive*: The applications employees use to manage performance must be intuitive. Many "difference makers" are *not* technology experts. They need a solution that has a familiar look and feel so that they can focus on execution, rather than learning how to use the application.

- *Must be focused.* There is a natural tendency to simply provide more information to more people to help them perform better. However, difference makers do not have time to look at a lot of information. Meeting their needs requires more forethought than simply providing more information; it requires an understanding of what specific information is relevant to them to help them make the decisions they need to make. If they are to be effective, they need to be provided with information that is relevant to them, their roles and what is expected of them.

- *Must be scalable.* Organizations must think about the scale of their solution to ensure it can empower the entire organization. This requires thinking broadly to meet the various needs of difference makers across the organization. Understanding how a solution scales to meet these needs—in terms of resources required to purchase, implement, train, support, and adapt to the various needs across the organization are important factors that organizations should consider and address prior to scaling broadly.

Developing a Culture of Performance

Creating a culture of performance and empowering people to deliver has had a significant impact on Energizer's results that has reflected in their stock price. Benz explains, "We're up over fivefold in the last five years. People have made that happen."

Realizing the Six Stages of Performance Management Value
Let's review how Energizer is realizing the six stages of performance management value:

1. *Increase Visibility*: Performance metrics and improvement goals have been made clearly visible to employees throughout the organization to allow them to effectively participate in the improvement process.

2. *Move Beyond Gut Feel*: Employees have been given full access to the details that they need to make performance driven decisions. They are equipped with tools and techniques to allow them to model the impact before they act.

3. *Plan for Success*: Planning and goal setting are deeply ingrained across all levels of the organization.

4. *Execute on Strategy*: Top-line strategic goals provide the umbrella under which the organization operates to ensure that short-term actions are appropriately balanced with the long-term growth goals of the business.

5. *Power to Compete*: Energizer has incorporated a wide range of customer scorecards and competitive benchmarks into the performance management process to avoid goals that are irrelevant to the market.

6. *Culture of Performance*: Energizer began by creating a culture in which colleagues realized their connection to performance, rather than attempting to force actions through autocratic process and edict.

IN THIS CHAPTER

This chapter will describe how leading companies achieve alignment, accountability, and agility by developing world-class planning capabilities. We will discuss pitfalls to avoid

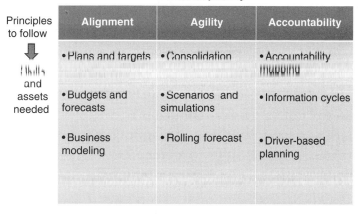

FIGURE 5.1 Culture of Performance Model—Plan Capability

and best practices to follow to implement these assets within your organization. We particularly focus the three guiding principles that best practice companies follow in order to effectively plan their performance as well as the specific skills and assets needed to implement the Plan capability (Figure 5.1). At the end of the chapter, we also provide a test to assess your Plan capabilities as well as guidance on how to improve your results.

ALIGNMENT

In Chapter 3, we discussed how alignment can be accomplished by better formulating, communicating, and executing on strategy and how scorecards and dashboards can help to deliver alignment. In order to better align with scorecards and dashboards, a company needs a process that allows it to clearly set its strategy and design a plan to execute against that strategy—planning is that process.

The Planning Cycle

The term *planning* is often used to refer to plans, budgets, forecasts or other finance-driven performance exercises.

All successful companies have plans. As the adage says, "Failing to plan is planning to fail." It is the way companies conduct planning that differentiates them.

In this chapter, we think of planning as the exercise that a company goes through to determine what its goals are and, more importantly, what its actions are to make the plan a reality.

The section that follows describes what a generic set of planning activities might look like. It is not meant to be used as a "how to plan" guide. Planning activities are specific to each company. While these activities may be different at your company, for most these common processes will apply.

Know What You Want

Assume that your company wants to be number one in its space and, in order to do so, it has to show profitability and growth in a major business over the next 5 years. Strategic planning defines what the strategic direction of the company is, why it wants to get there, and how to get there. The strategic planning exercise is typically intense because it is determining the major focus areas for the company's long-term success. It requires a lot of thoughtful analysis, well-reported historical information and the ability to project business in the future—often for three to five years ahead. This is not a trivial exercise and the pressure of doing the right things is high. Decisions made during the strategic planning exercise have repercussions throughout the rest of the planning cycle, so starting right is important for the success of the overall planning process.

There are two key guiding principles to enable a world-class strategic planning exercise:

1. *Provide a clear and accurate picture of the business.* The executive team needs to have the right information about not only where the business is today, but also where it has been in the past and where it can be in the future. Given the importance of the strategic planning process and what is at stake, influence and pressure from the board or other stakeholders is often high. When a management team's decision is more informed, their strategy is often more defensible and actionable. The nature of the information can make this a difficult task. Internal information alone is not enough; often industry information, demographics in markets, government forecasts, and competitors' performance are needed. A performance management solution needs to provide organizations with the ability to share the plan across the management team in a format that is easy to analyze and allows them to get a quick understanding of where their company has been, why it is where it is today, and where it can be.

2. *Get to what you want faster.* There are many ways to "be number one." Options might include broadening your offering to new markets, focusing on your core business, restructuring your organization, or even acquiring competitors to capture customers and growth. The ability to simulate all plausible scenarios to chart out the consequences of major changes can make or break strategies. Organizations may need to consider reorganizations, acquisitions, and other organizational changes to optimize the structure of the company to achieve its goals. Organizations should be able to easily create and compare these scenarios. Business drivers need to be clearly understood

so the team can focus their attention on what moves the business faster. Without the context of multiple scenarios and drivers, you may not know the best possible route. It is good to know what you want, but isn't it better to get the best you can get?

Christophe Couturier is Vice President, Corporate Planning and Strategy Management for Millipore Corporation. Millipore is a leading global supplier of products and expertise that span research, development, and production stages in the life science research and biologic drug manufacturing fields. Couturier explains specifically how planning helped the company get on the right track:

> In order to continue to be what we are, a leader in our space, we developed a very strong "execution culture." We started in 2005, with the use of methodologies such as the Balanced Scorecard and Beyond Budgeting, as we identified them as good tools to implement our strategy. We customized them very heavily for our company and deployed strategy maps and scorecards that we tied to our planning process. In the end though, there is a very simple secret in the world of planning: What you measure is what you get, and what you want to get has to be tied to reward and compensation. So we set out a very clear strategy, which we communicated heavily. Then, we tied the performance of our goals to each individual's compensation.[3]

Be Specific

Once strategic direction has been agreed upon, specific targets need to be determined. For instance, if we know that being number one means generating a certain amount of revenue or margin, the organization should be able to set specific targets for the business. Targets are sometimes set at a five- to ten-year horizon, then translated into one- to three-year objectives, and then more specifically translated into shorter-term milestones that allow management to monitor the progress the team is making towards the identified strategic goals.

The executive team is often involved in the review of targets, which often originate from the finance organization and its analysts. Target setting is an exercise of translation: "How do we take strategic objectives and craft operational or tactical objectives that are realistic, attainable, and utilize the organization at its best?"

Effective target-setting exercises provide the ability to:

- Translate top-line objectives into specific and realistic guidance based on the company's organizational structure and capabilities.
- Work across different, sometimes complex business models without losing sight of the end goal. Benchmark across very different businesses (perhaps one part of the business specializes in retailing products, while another delivers intangible services).

Both of these factors are often affected by a company's ability to accurately represent—or model—the key drivers of the business (where the company does business, how it makes money, how it spends money, etc.).

What Drives Your Business?

Just as Kaplan and Norton said of strategy formulation: "You can't manage what you can't measure, you can't measure what you can't describe," a similar axiom holds true for business modeling: "You can't drive plans you can't model; you can't model what you can't describe." If you can't understand what drives your business, then you can't drive results.

The model represents the way business occurs. The more the model reflects the true drivers of outcomes, the more effective you can be achieving desired business results. As a consequence, it is critical to create a model and create it well. By "modeling," we are not describing the data modeling that you might find in an IT environment. Rather, we are talking about the modeling of a business: where the company does business, how it makes money, how it spends money. This is the content employees and managers use to evaluate and interpret information which feeds their decision-making process.

The quality of a model will impact the effectiveness of downstream management activities such as monthly management reporting, weekly operational flash reporting, or financial results consolidation.

There are three attributes of an effective model:

1. *Accurate*: Although it might seem like an obvious expectation, the need to drive accurate models is the single most important requirement in developing plans. A model needs to accurately represent how the business is run, the organization's key drivers and how they relate to overall performance. This is often not a trivial task. An accurate representation of the business requires access to the right information and the ability to model this information in light of the organization's business objectives. In order to create accurate plans, organizations need flexibility in the way information is sourced and in the way it can be used to reflect objectives.

2. *Simple but sophisticated*: In any performance management exercise, there are at least two types of employees being supported: those who build and manage the models used by the organization and those who utilize the models as a tool to get their job done and report performance. Both types of employees have very different expectations of a performance management model.

a. The model creators are often business or finance analysts. They are typically the administrators of the models and expect performance management to be sophisticated enough to include the specifics of the business (e.g., the types of products, geographies, markets, and currencies they want to measure). They use the model to understand performance results and as such are interested in the supporting algorithms and structure of the model so they can fully understand how the information they are managing is being consolidated.

b. Those who are executing other processes within which they utilize the models to plan, budget, or forecast are the executors. They may include the line of business managers and employees closer to the front lines of interaction with customers and partners. They expect performance management to be simple so they can understand how best to utilize it to meet their business needs. Although the executors' job is to execute on strategy, they rarely wish to be lost in the details behind complicated models.

Understanding these audiences' respective sophisticated and simple needs will affect the organization's quality of execution. Your performance management system needs to be relevant and useful to the audience which is interacting with it at any given time.

3. *Shared*: Performance management is conducted at its best when it spans across all business units. Although planning might start within the finance department, successful companies are those that have taken performance management outside the office of the CFO

and made it a key initiative across all business units. Organizations execute and impact performance at a larger scale when performance management moves beyond the office of finance. By extending broader participation across business units, the office of the CFO can truly become the agent of change and enable the rest of the business to do their job better.

Think Globally, Act Locally

Once strategic direction has been defined ("be number one in five years") and management expectations have been expressed in specific guidance ("Europe needs to grow 10%, the United States 25 %, and Asia 40%"), then the targets are submitted to the individuals and groups who are ultimately in charge of making it happen.

At that point, forecasting comes into play. Forecasting requires thinking globally ("be number one in five years") while still enabling local stakeholders to plan how that objective can be accomplished (e.g., does being number one mean being number one, across all geographies and products in Europe, the United States, and Asia?).

Forecasting is the process by which the organizational, functional, and geographical units of a company determine what their anticipated results are going to be and evaluate them in the context of the objectives set in the corporate planning and target-setting exercise.

The forecasting process is one that involves the largest amount of flexibility. It is also the process that most employees relate to easily as a complete forecast is one that involves many participants across the organization—finance, sales, operations, and other functions of the business. Forecasts are a great way for business units to communicate up the hierarchy what they think they can accomplish in consideration of corporate requirements and perceived market conditions.

A forecast is most effective when:

1. *Corporate objectives have been communicated clearly throughout the company*—using cascading scorecards, dashboards, or strategy maps that clearly represent the objectives of a business globally.

2. *Corporate objectives can be translated into local expectations, actions and plans*—10% global growth might mean that Germany produces 15%, while France would produce 9%.

3. *Each local group can analyze corporate objectives and work with their information locally to relate global objectives and local requirements*—a local manager is able to explore multiple scenarios before committing to a particular course of action.

4. *Corporate and local entities can collaborate and communicate throughout the process with high efficiency and agility*—local forecast contributors can iterate versions of their forecasts and work with the corporate process owner to refine their inputs.

5. *Local information can be entered in local terms and translated into global results*—enter information in euros but have them consolidated in U.S. dollars.

6. *A global view has been created without losing accuracy or the ability to drill to relevant details when necessary*—navigate from global numbers down to SKU-level information for a specific geography.

As Ron van Zanten of Premier Bankcard notes, forecasting requires flexibility but its collaborative aspect reinforces the need for the process to be precise and accountable:

Every department is accountable for the profit number they put forward in their plan or budget. This includes plans for how to be more effective with expenses associated with mailings and marketing, as well as the plan for revenue in terms of late fees and over limit charges. All those numbers are incorporated in

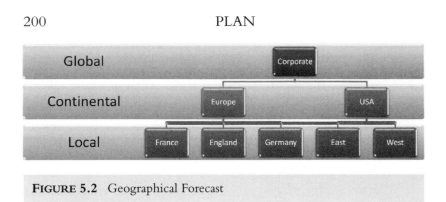

FIGURE 5.2 Geographical Forecast

the planning system. This system really organizes the negatives and the positives to come up with that final number, in this case determining how best to impact profit. Some things you're saving money on, others you're raising income, both are increasing profit—but it's in finding the right balance that you determine that final profit number.[4]

We mentioned simple scenarios when geographical complexities occur, such as entering forecasts in Germany and consolidating it up to Western Europe, Total Europe, and Worldwide. However, most companies experience much more complex scenarios where both geography and functions intertwine. Consider the following financial function in Germany as an example:

Your company might work in a simple geographical model, maybe a functional or even a matrix model. The ability to forecast to relevant drivers for a business is the most important (see Figures 5.2 and 5.3).

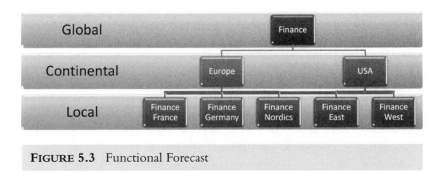

FIGURE 5.3 Functional Forecast

Suppose that your company is composed of two primary businesses. The first one resells tangible products (computers) while the second business provides services for these products. Each business has different drivers and ways of measuring success:

- The retail business' main drivers are cost of acquired goods, margin drawn from reselling and inventory churn.
- The services business might measure length and profitability of each engagement.

Each business has different targets for success and forecasts will have to represent the various factors that impact that success. Furthermore, each business monitors different metrics in order to drive and reward desired behaviors. For instance, the service business monitors travel expenses of their consultants—a metric that would be irrelevant to track in the retail business.

In the end, though, revenues and expenses for the business will have to be accounted for globally, but their origin needs to be understood at the local level. For instance, if a global expense such as travel has reached an unacceptable level, we will know how much the service or retail business drove that number locally.

More explicitly, take a look at the business model in Figure 5.4 to see the various factors that could affect the accuracy of forecasts. At the local level, the retail and service business both use the term *custom* to describe two different and distinct expense categories.

The complexity of forecasts can be exacerbated both by the structure of the business and also by the frequency of forecasts. The timing of forecasts needs to be taken into account while the other processes of the planning cycle could happen during different time frames (monthly, quarterly). In addition, forecasts often lose accuracy as time goes

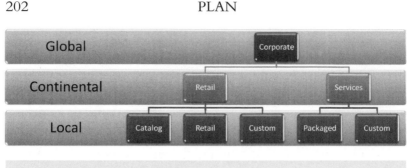

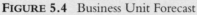

FIGURE 5.4 Business Unit Forecast

by. For instance, a three-month forecast might be very accurate while a three-year forecast might be very inaccurate.

Inefficient forecast models are the most important point of failure for many companies. While strategic planning and target-setting exercises are crucial in setting up direction, the validity of forecasts determine the predictability of the business.

Fortis, a leading provider of banking and insurance services, has seen tremendous performance benefits due to its ability to better predict its business. Fortis' CEO, Jean Paul Votron, who was elected as "The Business Leader of the Year" by *BusinessWeek* in January 2007,[5] has led the company to set and achieve its 5 year net profit goal in less than 3 years.[6]

The bank's approach to performance management shows its dedication to developing the right processes for maximum predictability. Jean-Francois Gigot of Fortis explains:

> Sometimes—having better processes matters more than the results they might produce at first. Better processes provide your organization with better control and predictability. This has tremendous value by itself. First, better predictability means you can act earlier and more appropriately. Secondly, better predictability instills better confidence. When you are trying to change cultures towards better performance, confidence is extremely powerful—because everyone wants to be in control of their future. Finally, confidence has an external benefit, especially with analysts and investors. Regardless of the company's

performance, observers tend to reward companies that "know what they are doing.[7]

In summary, predictability matters. The validity and reliability of forecasts are tested by:

- *Business models.* Make sure that your approach is flexible enough to accommodate different business models and drivers. Understand the model appropriate for planning versus the model driven by actual reporting systems (and how they can be related at the correct levels and appropriate time). In other words, your forecast input model should not be a profit and loss (P&L). Think of the retail and service example

- *Hierarchy.* Make sure that you can map your various models back to the global business regardless of the complexity of the various disparate models. A common challenge is accommodating forecasts results in multiple currencies locally but then reporting globally in U.S. dollars.

- *Cycle.* Make sure that you can sync forecast cycles with the rest of your planning activities. Forecast cycles need to be completed and communicated during the window of time in which they are relevant.

- *Time frame.* Understand that forecasts are most accurate when they are used to predict short-term business results. A three-month forecast needs to be considered differently from a two-year forecast unless the business is extremely stable and predictable.

- *Inclusion.* Don't let people "disown" their plans. The value of forecasts comes from the people who own and enter the numbers. Too many groups delegate forecast contribution because it is too difficult for employees or their solution is so inflexible that letting more business owners enter their numbers would delay the forecast process. Beyond the obvious issues related to compliance and errors linked to double entry, lack of inclusion leads to poor alignment. Forecasts are used to drive accountability and alignment of businesses to the corporate goals. It is important to enable business owners to contribute to their forecast in a manner that is efficient and doesn't disturb their daily activities. Driver-based planning forecasts or prepopulated forecasts might make it easier for forecast owners to facilitate information entry. In any case, forecasts need to be targeted to the right audience and reflect the things they control. Have a consultant forecast expected billable hours not their quarterly net revenue, for example.

Well-run forecasts are the ultimate tool for accountability and alignment across the company. When they are flexible and accurate they can lead to quality conversations about business objectives, and can be used as great frameworks, not only for business execution but also to better predict business results by taking advantage of local input. Think globally, forecast locally!

Closing the Loop

Once forecasts are submitted, most negotiation ends and execution begins. Budgets and plans are now finalized, and they represent the way performance will be measured ongoing.

Note that reforecasting might occur three to four times a year based on the business rhythm, so renegotiation of targets might happen throughout the year. Most companies do this as a "stop-and-start" process building budgets just a few times a year. Best practices suggest that enabling constant reforecasting at the business unit level increases decision making and improves performance. Jeremy Hope, author of

Beyond Budgeting (Boston: Harvard Business School, 2003), suggests that the forecast system should not enable the best negotiators to become the best performers based on their negotiations, but instead enable employees to constantly revise their numbers so they get closer to the maximum potential achievable.

In other words, do not let budgets simply be driven to a minimum negotiated number, but rather focus on the opportunity that's attainable. Use constant reforecasting to challenge the organization to achieve optimal results. Hope cites Unilever's capabilities in this regard, and we hear this consistently from other leaders like Energizer and Millipore as well. We discuss this in more detail in the "Rolling Forecasts" section later in this chapter.

There are two key concepts for maintaining budgets:

1. *Managing the final process.* Defining clear time frames and process owners, and holding every stakeholder to a calendar, will help close the loop and close it in time. The exercise of setting the strategy and goals and forecasting expected results typically takes a very long time. The budgeting cycle is the last mile of this exercise. Timeline and process efficiencies will be rewarded here. Look for solutions that have great calendaring and automation ability, as they will help you to rely less on manual intervention to get the budgets closed.

2. *Refining the truth.* Budgets also include the numbers that are submitted back to management for a final analysis of expected revenue and expenses. The corporate budget will not be concluded until the local budgets have been reviewed and accepted. In the end, while the forecast is the operational prediction of where the business is likely to land, the budgets are often more conservative and more strategic— they are modified less often and their scope typically

spreads further out than forecasts. Forecasts can look out three to six months or a year. Budgets will likely align to the strategic plans and then be broken up in smaller increments (quarters and half years). The ability to refine the models behind these budgets is key. Very much like the strategic planning exercise, the budgeting exercise at a corporate level is one that management practices a few times a year, but one that bears tremendous consequences to the business.

It is important to note the relationship of all these various processes and how, when done well, they can better allow your organization to align groups and individuals across the company. As we take a look at the entire planning cycle, we note that companies that run planning the best are the ones that have technology that adapts the best to the way the organization plans.

What Did We Learn Here?

There are four attributes to running efficient planning processes.

1. *Iteration*: As you might have noticed through the processes described above, planning is extremely iterative. The process could take multiple tries before it can be considered final. A good performance management solution is one that can accommodate iterations while making it easy to keep track of changes made throughout the various iterations.

2. *Collaboration*: Planning requires people to be measured and participate efficiently in the exercise. For this reason, consider a solution that can easily be adopted and understood by all types of roles across the organization, not just the business analysts. A large part of forecasts' or budgets' validity will hinge on

the ability of forecast and budget owners themselves to participate. If the solution is not collaborative or easy to use, owners will quickly find "workarounds."

3. *Partnership*: Performance management scenarios require strong partnerships between corporate and the various business units as well as partnerships between IT and the business. These partnerships help reduce internal resistance factors and deploy a solution in which everyone feels an ownership.

4. *Integration*. Planning rarely happens in isolation from all other performance management activities. Monitoring and analysis are not only integral parts of the process, but better monitoring and analysis make better planning. When information is continuously monitored and analyzed, accountability is better enforced. Best-practice companies understand that monitoring, analysis, and planning must live together and should not be segregated (i.e., be deployed as isolated, "point" solutions that target only a single capability—Monitor, Analyze, *or* Plan—rather than enabling all three).

This last point of integration is particularly important. As Hope discusses, if you want to enable an agile planning capability at your company, you have to think about the integration of systems, processes, and people before thinking about the deep technical ability of each isolated performance management system:

> As you think about increasing the value of your planning processes, you have to realize that constant monitoring and analysis of planning information needs to be performed. For instance, how are we doing year-to-date? Can we invest in a tactical initiative to increase revenue? These tactical decisions need to happen at any level throughout the company. It may be at the corporate center, it might be at the business unit level.[8]

The implementation of specific "point" solutions that could be very good at doing the monitoring, analysis, and planning processes in isolation might not lead to more collaborative planning. By implementing point solutions, the organization not only increases costs to support varied solutions but also increases its risk of isolating people and processes even further.

This is not solely a technological problem. It's difficult enough to get different departments to work on a plan together; this becomes all the more difficult when they use different systems as well. Finance may have a planning system that meets their budgeting and forecasting needs quite well, while marketing uses a different system to perform analytics. Their business functions are further isolated as they specialize in different systems—and we're back to the Tower of Babel. Not only do the people not talk the same language, their systems don't either.

AGILITY

We talked above about the exercises that companies go through in order to align plans and execution. Each step from strategic planning to budgeting relies on the core concept of "the model."

As introduced previously, a model is a way for companies to define objectives and goals around a common framework. A model describes the drivers of the business and allows management to develop a culture of discipline around that framework, corporate-wide.

An efficient model embraces a company's culture and allows the organization to execute within the framework of that culture. Suppose your company strategy is to provide world-class services to your customers. Enabling that strategy is a set of attitudes and traits that will be embodied by all employees. These core traits drive how the company hires new talent and communicates about performance. For instance, if "world-class customer service" is a core value, the measurement of performance might be different than if the strategy dictates to compete on price.

A company's culture is a key factor in a company's strategy. Your performance management solution needs to embrace both the culture and strategy. Further, it needs to allow the organization to manage to the framework that drives execution. That framework is the model. Let's take a closer look at how effective models drive agility.

Independent but Related

Models are important from strategic planning to budgeting because they provide consistency and help with alignment across the organization.

One model, however, cannot fit all business problems throughout various business units. Business units and departments have their own way to look at their specific business. A "one-model-fits-all" approach rarely works if it requires the inclusion of everyone's specific factors in one place. In order to guarantee alignment while still allowing business groups to run with high agility, multiple models will be required. In this case, there are two major principles to observe:

1. *Independent models.* Let's assume your company sells jeans and the product line "jeans" is broken down into three items: "straight-leg," "boot-cut," and "acid-washed." While these definitions work for revenue recognition for each category, they don't work for the supply-chain manager who needs to manufacture and ship jeans from 11 different locations worldwide. A supply-chain manager may want to know where each type of jeans is being sold per region.

She also wants to track production cost and inventory levels at the 11 manufacturing locations. Further, she wants to take a look at the relationship between manufacturing sites and sales regions to evaluate distribution costs. Each of these needs reminds us that building models is not simply the vehicle of an exercise that flows through the organization vertically (i.e., from corporate to subsidiary). These needs must also be considered across departments. In the example above, it is useful to break down the model into a sales model and a supply chain model. These two models could have different structures. The sales model could have products, whereas the supply chain model would have products, manufacturing locations, and sales regions. An effective performance management solution allows modeling this business into multiple models that can be shared across departments and that are specific and unique to answer the needs of the specific units.

2. *Related models*. As soon as models can be built across the organization, groups can drive their local business more effectively. However, the need to compare results across divisions and the need to analyze and plan across multiple business units rely on the ability of the organization to relate one model to the other. Imagine that you want supply-chain information to be related to revenue information for the same item. The revenue model might look at a pair of jeans a certain way, while production is captured a different way by the supply-chain group model. Management may then decide to assess viability of a particular type of jeans and would like to understand the impact of changes. Most companies are not able to bridge the gap between each model. They often attempt to link spreadsheet models to one another, hoping that the links will not break or turn out to be inaccurate.

Agility is obtained when the transfer of information across business units and information is made easier. The ability to "associate" between models allows organizations to not only be more efficient at the individual model level, but also across the multiple models (supply chain and revenue).

While acknowledging that each business unit deserves its own model, it will become equally powerful that information can be associated across the models. The ability to create independent models across the company but still relate them to one another with high agility allows businesses to plan with greater attention to detail without compromising the way the business is run.

For many years, companies have designed models to the companies' technical limitations rather than their true desired outcome. Living with ineffective models and investing more money, time, and resources to maintain them has proven ineffective. Performance management solutions have evolved tremendously over the last decade and companies no longer need to compromise flexibility and agility.

Business Is about Change

Agility is important because business is about change. A company can build the best plan in the world, take all possible factors that would impact performance at the time of the plan, but still fail at execution of the plan.

In their book, *Made to Stick,* the Heath brothers give a great example of how "building a plan to build a plan" can not only be very myopic but can also lead to complete disaster.

The Army is used as an example, as it has great experience at building plans that work. Over many years of experience, Generals have learned that "no plan survives contact with the enemy."[9] In short, you can build the best plan in the world, but after the plan has been crafted, it needs to be executed even in situations of great duress. Unforeseen events occur, new information surfaces, competitors change tactics—execution needs to be dynamic and responsive while maintaining alignment to the mission.

In business, the same rules apply. Plans do not always properly assess competitive pressure or internal market stress. Customers, suppliers, and others can create an environment that might have been quite different from what you anticipated when crafting the plan.

Companies need agility to respond to changing business conditions—their models need to reflect that agility.

Agility requires two key components: consolidation and scenarios. Consolidation provides a place to begin reviewing forecasted activities. The trick with consolidation is to automate much of it because, if done well, consolidation can bring you the base numbers you need to analyze and plan business performance. If you are lucky, consolidation alone will be enough in providing you the numbers you are looking to achieve globally. In most cases, though, the corporate center and the various units will need to adjust particular factors and assumptions to get closer to a number that is realistically achievable. This is when scenarios come into play.

Scenarios allow you to adjust business levers to get to the target you want. Often, companies will start by slashing expenses or increasing revenue targets, or maybe even both. As Christophe Couturier of Millipore explains, "The truth is that scenarios should not be thought of simply in terms of increasing revenues and limiting expenses. They also describe what appropriate action to take based on the action's alignment with corporate objectives."[10]

To define the best scenario you need the ability to analyze the impact of changes. So there are a lot of cultural issues associated with this, such as egos, historical reasons ("the way it's always been done"). Couturier continues,

"Good scenarios can be used as a tool to bring everyone back to what matters for the business overall, almost like a reminder of what specific actions and plans align to the bigger picture."[11]

The integration of monitoring, analysis and planning capabilities are key to developing scenarios. Instead of focusing solely on tactical maneuvers such as increasing revenues or cutting expenses, organizations should be able to monitor and analyze what initiatives are best aligned with company objectives and therefore prioritize them in the plan. Consolidation gives you the base; scenarios allow you to customize it.

Interestingly, indoor plumbing might provide the best analogy to explain these two concepts. Consider when the various members of a family need to take a bath. While children may enjoy cooler waters, parents may prefer a relaxing hot bath. In order to deliver this to each, two things are required: plumbing and faucets.

1. *Plumbing*. Before anyone can take a bath, the infrastructure needs to be in place, ready to go. When you are ready, it is ready to quickly deliver the water. It just needs to be turned on.

2. *Faucets*. With plumbing available to deliver the water, it needs to be flexible to give us the water the way we want it. Some like it cooler, and others like it hot. Faucets just need to be adjusted to respective needs. The ones who like it cold don't want to get scalded, while those who like it hot don't want to freeze—some amount of testing is needed before jumping in!

Consolidation and scenarios work the same way. Consolidation is like plumbing—it provides a framework and the parameters that allow for expected functions to be run. Scenarios are like faucets. They enable flexibility and can be adjusted and tested based on meeting changing needs. Both of these components deliver agility.

Consolidation—The Plumbing

Models need to enforce a set of rules that are recurrent and reliable and can be applied repetitively without incurring too much effort for the organization. Consolidation can cause issues for companies that struggle with combining and reconciling the disparate but needed information across their company into one view that makes sense for financial reporting, statements, analytics, and other planning processes.

There are three primary types of consolidation that organizations conduct:

1. *Simple aggregation or summarization of information.* Imagine 200 departments planning operating expenses for the coming year. These expenses are summarized to 20 business units and then to 5 major divisions. Finally, they are added up to a company-wide, consolidated total.

2. *Management consolidation.* It could still apply to budgets, but may also apply to actual results. In a management consolidation, additional financial operations are performed to prepare a complete view to management—typically in the form of balance sheets, income statements, cash flow statements, and so on. In these types of consolidations, the process might address things like multiple reporting currencies, allocations of overhead costs to operating units, and eliminations of internal transactions between operating units.

3. *Legal and statutory reporting.* This type of consolidation extends concepts used in management

consolidation, but is constrained and guided by regulations such as U.S. Generally Accepted Accounting Principles (GAAP) and International Financial Reporting Standards (IFRS). Many of the regulations may be proprietary, and local consolidation requirements may be different from corporate consolidation requirements.

The rules of consolidation are constantly put to test by changing business conditions. Over time, teams reorganize, operations are moved across countries of diverse currencies, and businesses are bought and sold.

Juggling with constant change creates inefficiencies for companies that are not able to set rules, calculations, and processes that automate the consolidation of their key performance information. Companies that succeed not only gain time-to-decision, but also become leaner in their execution. Jean-Francois Gigot from Fortis explains:

> "Without an efficient way to consolidate information and easily run scenarios, companies might feel that they are not in control of their own future. Automating the critical steps of consolidation allowed us to spend more time thinking about our future, and therefore better prepare for it."[12]

When deployed well, consolidation rules provide great flexibility. Consider the example of Oticon A/S, a global supplier of hearing-aid devices based in Denmark with offices in Europe, North and South America, and Asia Pacific.

Oticon A/S looked to improve its financial operations holistically, including consolidation, reporting, planning, budgeting, and forecasting. Oticon A/S recognized that its consolidation and calculation capabilities were essential to increasing accuracy and agility. Worldwide, there were more than 50 local operating units that would provide information to corporate, in their own terms, such as in different currencies. The issue then would be to consolidate the information in a format that makes sense for the corporate management team. To consolidate this information, finance employees at the corporate headquarters in Denmark would export the locally entered data to their spreadsheets, make calculations and adjustments, and prepare reports on the consolidated results.

One of the more complex calculations involved the elimination of intercompany transactions. The collection system didn't easily identify such transactions so corporate finance personnel had to manually identify and reconcile them.

> This also created uncertainty about the accuracy of the work since users had to translate data between the local and central models.[13]

When building models, companies need to consider more than just their corporate model. There are implications to each piece of models up- and downstream. Consolidation rules are a key component of what runs a business, and they should be a key efficiency enabler of business models. Over time, consolidation rules may need to change, and these changes can be driven by mandate or changing business conditions. Rebuilding consolidation rules is typically a very lengthy process. The flexibility to build and manage consolidation rules and calculations should be the second point of your inquiry, after model flexibility.

Scenarios—The Faucets

If consolidation is plumbing (the infrastructure that you can rely on to run your business), scenarios allow organizations to adjust to changing conditions. They are the faucets that can be adjusted to accomplish the various results. How can a company easily react to changes by simply adjusting factors? What's a "good" scenario capability?

There are four key rules to developing good scenarios:

1. *Time scenarios need to be built into your models early on.* The ability to incorporate flexible scenarios as an integral part of your model needs to be considered early on so your company can become much more agile. For instance, let's assume that you need to plan for a special six-month promotion as well as a three-week promotion program. How would you report the impact of these promotions that are running in different time cycles? Would you track the first one every three weeks and the second one monthly? Would you wait for results in your standard review process? Maybe your organization wants to apply special calendar capabilities such as 13-month? Further, some of your modeling might require a weekly level to be applied to some scenarios while, for others, a monthly or quarterly will be sufficient. Imagine "annual drivers" like price lists that need to be incorporated into weekly sales quantity plans, for example. Scenarios can become complex, and agility can be gained when time requirements are thought of early on.

2. *The right scenario for the right purpose.* Companies tend to enforce scenarios to follow two types of models depending on their needs: generic and assumption-based scenarios.

   ○ Companies would use a generic scenario for standard financial or nonfinancial predictable models. This is a simple model with basic information such as time (January), geography (Germany), products (Jeans) and other generic organizational information. A generic scenario makes it easy to catalog and relate information across the company as it is often restricted to generically understood views.

- A more complex scenario could require "assumption scenario types." How do you accurately forecast across multiple geographies, products and changes in currency values over time? An assumption model type accommodates precisely this situation. Imagine that your company wants to forecast quantities of biking equipment for the next six months. The company results (quantity of bikes and revenue amount) stem from the results of the organization's two subsidiaries in Germany and Switzerland. These two subsidiaries run their business in different currencies and their price lists are different, although they sell the same products. In order to forecast accurately, the corporate office, which reports revenue in U.S. dollars, has to build into its scenario the various assumptions of the local subsidiaries and plan for potential impact of currency fluctuation: what their current and future conversion rates are and what their price list is today and what it might be by the time forecast results are measured. As you can see, there are many different assumptions to take into account and the accuracy of a forecast hinges on the organization's ability to work with these assumptions across the various models.

3. *Scenarios need to understand financial logic.* Built-in financial logic such as consolidation rules and calculations need to be considered when building scenarios. For example, this becomes relevant when minority interest in partial ownership scenarios needs to be calculated and the proper legally consolidated results provided. You can build types that simply assume full ownership of all entities being consolidated but, based on the type of scenario you are building, the proper calculations should be thought through up front as it will become difficult to come back

after the scenarios are built and modify consolidation rules.

4. *Scenarios need to be controlled, owned and flexible.* In finalizing scenarios, it's important to think again about the business behavior behind the model. The model needs to capture the key drivers of results in the business. Some simple questions can be asked to assess whether or not the key drivers are being articulated.

   ○ *Control.* If you look at a scenario, you should be able to trace its control directly to the individuals who are asked to submit the information. Let's say marketing is running a pricing and promotion forecast. They set the price point for the promotion; this is what they control. However, they do have dependencies on both sales and operations. The promotion needs to align with volume, margin and cost of sale considerations. In addition, operational supply will impact the promotional price (i.e., marketing can guarantee a given price point only if at least 50,000 units are produced). These dependencies on other groups are key drivers and they should be taken into account into the marketing plans.

   ○ *Accountability.* If people contributing budget information are willing to tie their performance incentives to the drivers being planned, then the proper drivers need to be with the proper people. In the preceding example, it could be easy for sales to determine the level of the rebate-based cost-of-sale considerations. However, if marketing owns and is accountable for pricing rebates, and if they chose to run a rebate, the level of rebate decision would need to come from the driver of the model. Marketing's pricing promotion is based on competitive pressure. Owners are accountable and own the drivers of given initiatives. In this case, the sales team can't be accountable for the pricing rebate and shouldn't be asked to plan it.

○ *Flexibility.* If something suddenly changes in the business, the model should contain the proper drivers to allow rapid reaction and update to plans. Consider the example of "what-if" scenarios. Remember the example under "assumption scenario types." "What if the dollar plummeted," "What if we reprice our bikes in Germany based on competitive pressure." Driver-based modeling provides the basis for either exercise. Currencies and price lists in this example are the drivers. Scenarios need to contain the proper drivers so they can be modeled with high flexibility to respond to the changing needs of the business.

Agility "Built In"

There are many situations that companies need to anticipate. To build agility into models, a company must not only think about its key business drivers and objectives, but it also needs to think about the way performance is managed up- and downstream.

Beyond building flexible models and scenarios, companies might want to explore plan, budget, and forecast cycles. While most corporations have agreed-upon timelines for reviewing and approving these cycles, many consider moving to more flexible schedules.

Some companies take a unique approach to plans, budgets, and forecasts and go beyond some of the practices highlighted earlier around modeling, consolidations and scenarios. They build in agility based on the following tenets:

• *Change cannot be scheduled.* Most companies follow a strict discipline for developing plans, budgets and forecasts. They often implement rigid cycles (maybe three or four times a year), during which most of the finance department is dedicated to the completion of the strategic planning, budgeting, forecasting and reporting cycles. While discipline in reporting numbers is essential, most companies find themselves quickly unable to adapt to change between cycles. Suppose, for instance, that a major acquisition at a competitor occurs between two of your cycles and you'd like to reorganize your accounts to capitalize on the opportunity. Due to the rigidity of the company's processes, this new opportunity will have to wait for the next planning cycle to occur. Such a limitation makes it difficult for the planning, budgeting and forecasting cycles to provide value to its constituents (i.e., those seeking to capitalize on this opportunity will be forced to wait). These business leaders may make the changes "outside the system" and these changes will be applied only later. This creates a gap between the plans and the execution itself, making it difficult to view the planning, budgeting, and forecasting exercise as an enabler of strategy. Beware of regimented cycles. Discipline is important but flexibility is paramount. Build in short and flexible schedules within planning cycles so changes can be captured continuously. Not only will this provide a more realistic view of the business to management, but budget and plan owners will benefit from serving their stakeholders better, thus having fewer people work "outside the system."

- *Plans, budgets, and forecasts are for everyone.* For many years, plans, budgets, and forecasts have been the domain of Finance only, where experts use specific terminology and tools comprehensible only to them and uninteresting to all other business users. Where planning has been sequestered to the boundaries of Finance groups, most employees are shielded from the results a well-run planning process can bring to the entire organization. This is why, when most employees are asked if they perceive the planning process as useful for their performance, they often say "No." This creates problems for management and the finance function alike. As Finance departments try to become agile, they rarely get understanding from the rest of the organization thus making it difficult to change the paradigm. To this day, many of the solutions have been designed for the "Office of CFO" only and they rarely participate in enabling the entire organization to plan better. Best-practice companies, however, believe that planning, budgeting, and forecasting activities are for everyone. This notion should not be new however as forecasting is done by most employees today, just perhaps not as a part of the formal corporate finance function or systems. In the words of Energizer's Benz:

Everyone is a budget owner! If you have costs and revenues and if you run a team, might it be in operations, sales or any other function, you are accountable to your budget![14]

- *We don't build around the solution, the solution builds around us.* Before you align your processes to available solutions in the market, look at different ways you can improve your processes. There are some benefits to taking advantage of best practices implemented in software solutions, but your company processes are unique. First figure out what your processes should be, and then look for a solution that maps best to them. Packaged solutions might restrict an organization from having agility to adapt to changing conditions (remember, the Heath brothers point about how plans need to be adaptive as "no plan survives contact with the enemy").

- *Play to win; don't play "not to lose."* In *Beyond Budgeting*[15] Jeremy Hope and Robin Fraser explain that less than 20% of companies today change their budgets within the fiscal year. Given the constantly changing dynamics of business, why is that?

○ Either most companies are very good at predicting business conditions or no big changes are required throughout the year.

○ Or budgets and plans are not used to their appropriate value. Available software solutions may have been so inflexible that they limited the company's ability to apply change easily. In these instances, over time plans and budgets have become "plans of record" for financial purposes.

The latter is often the case—most organizations run based on "plans of record" rather than use planning processes as the mechanism to drive agility across the company. The best representations of this case are when groups sandbag results and "use it or lose" behaviors are permitted, even worse ones, such as "hit my quota and stop," are encouraged.

A good planning process makes budgets a tool of innovation, not of protection. If your plans, budgets, and forecasts are set to protect your organization from not achieving minimum results, agility is never attained to its fullest. At that point, the organization is not managing to win because it is managing to "not lose." When you are managing to the number, you can never do better than the target, you have put a cap on your success. Remember, as we said before: "It is good to know what you want, but isn't it better to get the best you can get?"

Hope and Frasier's model is based on taking budgeting from a fixed process to an adaptive model. They address the disconnect between planning cycles and the rest of the activities that happen at the same time across the organization and which contribute to business performance. The most agile companies are able to integrate their planning cycles with their monitoring and analytics activities. Doing so, they not only can respond better to changing business conditions but also can end up with better plans and execution.

Rolling Forecasts

A great example of such agile practices is the use of "rolling forecasts." This technique allows an organization to forecast six months ahead and reforecast for these six months every month.

This technique has two key benefits:

1. It improves the accuracy and predictability of the forecast as the time of forecast gets closer to the month being forecasted (for instance, in May, your forecast for June will be more accurate than it was in January for the same month).

2. It allows the organization to truly use the forecast as a flexible tool to drive better execution. As the organization is continuously in forecasting motion, it constantly reevaluating its execution as it relates to the strategy.

These benefits can be accomplished only when your forecasting processes are efficient. Indeed, your organization needs forecasting to be evaluated continuously; it has to provide flexibility and ease of use, so that the forecasting activity does not have barring implications on your employees' productivity.

Companies like Millipore use rolling forecasts extensively and find that it is a great way to tie planning activities to strategic initiatives such as scorecarding:

> Our rolling forecasts give us visibility 6 months ahead, our financial organization looks at the calendar year, and specifically

the next quarter. Finally our scorecards look at activities for the next six quarters. You have to find a way to align the information and goals between short-term and longer-term objectives so that performance analysis doesn't become overwhelming for management.[16]

ACCOUNTABILITY AND EMPOWERMENT

So far, we have discussed two key components of planning:

1. *Alignment*: This occurs when a company can effectively align its processes and people around the planning exercise and has eliminated overlap and inefficiencies across the company.

2. *Agility*: This happens when a company can run planning processes faster and also more efficiently. It happens when applying change becomes feasible regardless of where the process is—at the strategic planning phase or the target-setting exercise.

One last key component is the ability for organizations to drive better accountability through the planning process. By accountability, we don't mean the implementation of a "command and control" system that transforms planning activities into a blaming process. We mean implementing a culture of performance, which occurs as responsibilities for performance are embraced and accepted and a positive approach to planning execution has been successfully fostered.

Remember Benz's guidance earlier in this chapter when he discussed the importance of a "mental shift":

> In the end, it's about taking advantage of the number one asset you've got: your people. If you believe each of your employees is a difference maker, the job of performance management solutions is to empower these people to make the right decisions for their business. Only empowered people can truly be accountable.[17]

It's about the People

Many types of people are involved in the development of a planning solution. Process owners, planning owners, contributors, and, finally, upper managers are all involved:

- Process owners make sure that the planning process occurs as planned and within the correct time frame. They are typically involved in all planning processes, from strategic planning to forecast.
- Planning owners and contributors are responsible for execution and delivering the numbers. They own the contribution of accurate projections (forward looking) and results (reporting). They are typically involved at the operational levels in budgeting and forecasting exercises.
- Upper managers often work at the corporate office and focus on direction (strategic planning), assessment of progress through reporting, and course correction globally through target setting.

Recognizing each of these roles and establishing a vision for their involvement in your planning process—what they should focus on, what they should not work on—is key to a great performance management solution. Many companies do so by establishing "accountability maps."

Accountability Mapping

An accountability map is a diagram that shows the relationship between each step and each owner involved in the planning process. Accountability maps represent the fiber of your planning processes—they allow your planning process owners to close planning cycles faster. They become very handy when auditing for delays and changes throughout the process and rewarding key people for successes.

Often, reporting checkpoints are implemented in conjunction with accountability maps, so information can continuously be validated as it moves from one owner to the other. Imagine looking at a consolidated forecast and thinking that it had been fully submitted, but discovering later that a few countries had not committed their numbers. You are likely to want to know who is holding up the process, right? That's what accountability mapping allows you to know.

Tremendous benefits can be reaped from good account ability mapping and continuous reporting. Consider the example of Skanska USA. They manage more than 2,000 multiyear construction projects aggressively in order to maintain project profitability. Delays, fees, and other cost increases can quickly eliminate any profit margin from a project, so budget adjustments, monthly forecasts and visibility into other performance data are critical to composing an overall project view.

> At every stage of the process, our ability to accurately project, anticipate and control costs, then anticipate and react to issues is vital.[18]

Skanska relies heavily on the ability of its project managers, its folks in the front line, not only to own the local decisions but to project the success of their project with the highest level of accuracy.

At corporate, Skanska implemented a system of empowerment that matched its goals. They built a common model for execution company-wide and monitored it centrally. However, they recognized that each project was unique and that empowering the employees that are close to the action to accurately respond and forecast based on local demands was the surest way to better performance. "Empowering each employee to make the right decisions and report back continuously on their work was a great way to enable a culture of accountability," says Allen

Emerick, director of IT, applications and integration group, Skanska USA.

At the Service of Your Managers

"Empowering people to make them more accountable" is a very good sound bite, but it is not as easy as just giving your employees more applications or more information. In order to empower your front-line managers to better participate in the planning process, you need to look at two key enabling functions across the organization: your process owners and your upper managers.

In a way, both process owners and upper managers need to be "at the service" of the empowering managers. As we have discussed, managers are the key resources that will influence the planning process.

Build It ... Will They Come?

Often, organizations believe that if they build a set of intuitive and user-friendly solutions for their managers, they will use it. However, adoption and participation with such solutions have been abysmal over the last decade. As *InformationWeek* research discusses in a recent survey, over 75% of companies have not found a way provide intelligence to more than one-fourth of their employees.[19]

This is not due to the lack of innovative applications or interfaces. Software offerings have looked better over the years. Building something that is attractive is not enough. There is something beyond look-and-feel that drives adoption, and a recurrent theme is common to a lot of the best-practice companies we have engaged with over the years. Participation happens when employees feel engaged, when they not only feel they are responsible for driving better performance, but also when they understand that the organization is willing to empower them appropriately.

Wells Fargo is a great example of company that has developed this culture of accountability.

At Wells Fargo, Walter McFarland describes how they instill a "Run It Like You Own It" culture. This direction, easy to remember for all employees, is as much about developing a culture of accountability as it is about helping each employee to make the right decisions for their business on a daily basis. There are several specific ways Wells Fargo communicates broadly the value of this simple six-word mission statement:

- Wells Fargo is one of the last banking companies to have a formalized nine-month-long management program for their relationship managers in which they train their employees to understand information about their customer base and turn into actionable intelligence.
- The company accepts that the "Run It Like You Own It" mantra could have different messages for various roles across the company. For instance, if you are a teller, or a branch manager, the tactics used to run your business like you own it are different. The point is to remind employees that they are in charge.
- Finally, Wells Fargo's mantra is more than just words. Infrastructure and processes have been set up to reinforce individual accountability. As McFarland explains: "We didn't implement the 'Run It Like You Own It' mantra because systems or processes were not efficient. On the contrary, our infrastructure and processes are very efficient. At Wells Fargo, our number one asset is our human capital, and we use the 'Run It Like You Own It' mantra to remind them that *they* are the ones making a difference."[20]

Beyond better interfaces, integrated systems, and great mission statements, your company will need to automate a lot of the processes that create adoption issues today. Indeed, it is one thing to engage employees, but your information system will need to accommodate their requests and the processes they are engaged in, for instance say a budget contribution exercise. Information cycles define the way information is collected from managers throughout the planning process. They are particularly important in putting into practice the concept of employee engagement.

Information Cycles

Clear and specific cycles streamline participation and empower managers to provide their information in a way that is efficient for them.

There are three key criteria for good information cycles:

1. *Cycles enforce compliance.* This means that cycles understand who can view, edit, and add information. In today's environment of increasing rigor around audit and compliance, the ability to clearly understand the flow of information is vital. While it may be a tempting shortcut to administer access to everything, process owners should carefully consider their security needs and assign the proper security privileges to the appropriate manager roles.

2. *Cycles understand roles.* Business roles are the foundation of a good planning solution. It is not individuals but business roles that should be considered when granting access to particular business models. Within those models, cycles need to understand the specific role of each individual. For instance, let's say that a manager is in charge of a manufacturing company. Manufacturing relies on two separate models: an operational model which governs the cost of operating the manufacturing plant and a distribution model which represents the way the manufacturer

manages its relationship with suppliers. While the manufacturing manager has access to the entire information for that plant, he might have different roles across both models. For instance, he might be the "approver" of one model and the "contributor" of another one. Business roles are a key component to factor as they enable your managers to better understand their accountability as it relates to specific business processes and operations.

3. *Cycles understand time.* Finally, once security and business user roles have been well understood and communicated, time frame is critical in driving accountability for the process. In some cases, such as a forecast, it may be appropriate to have a several-week window during which contributors may submit new information or change existing forecast data. However, collecting and consolidating actual information for reporting purposes is generally a process open for only a few days, and submission beyond a certain point in time would compromise the integrity of reporting.

Security, roles, and times are characteristics that need to be well thought out before starting each cycle. They will not only facilitate the management of the cycle itself but will also focus the activities of your managers, streamlining their contribution and allowing for a more accurate and participative performance management process.

Accountability Is Personal, Simple, and Familiar

Once cycles have been established, the best way to drive accountability with your people is to provide them with personal information that is simple to understand and in a familiar context.

- *Personal information.* Many best practices point to the importance of providing information that is pertinent to the end audience's use. If you are trying to complete a bottom-up forecast exercise starting at the country level, for example, you may want to provide a Japanese manager with the information that you need to collect, but also historical information about Japan and other relevant countries or scenarios that would be instructive for the manager to review. Some companies will even prepopulate the numbers of the forecast required from the manager (often referred to as seeding), giving them a sense of the ballpark numbers expected from him or her. A lot can be accommodated to facilitate the contribution of forecast and budgeting information, and much can be automated based on business rules on historical averages, allocation of higher-level targets, and so on. However, there is no substitute for personal information to communicate a better sense of accountability to a manager, whose forecast you are expecting. This will have implications on your information management strategy and cycles.

- *Simple.* Sometimes the information that is required from managers will be run through complex calculations to consolidate information across business units all the way up to corporate models. Calculations may range from simple variance computations (for example actual data compared to budget data) to complex allocations that might be used to spread shared infrastructure costs to individual operating units for accurate profitability analysis. In short, this process can get very complex. However, managers do not always need to know the intricate details of calculations in order to complete their part of the picture. Sure, you can provide them with capabilities to help them consolidate numbers themselves as they are forecasting them. However, we encourage organizations to provide "lean and mean" contribution applications for your managers. Remember that participants are not data rule experts: all they are trying to do is complete their forecast so they can go back to their daily jobs!

- *Familiar context.* As part of the planning processes, managers tend to provide information in any of the following three fashions:

  1. By the time they enter the number in their forecast contribution system (i.e., the system they use to provide their forecast), they have figured out the optimum numbers and the exercise consists of copying and pasting information and submitting the forecast. Why? Because they have figured out, outside of the contribution system, what the best numbers are.

  2. Managers come to the forecasting application with a good sense for what their forecast/budget information should be, but they need to use additional information to firm up their final decisions. Sometimes they may need the forecast application to calculate formulas for them based on information they have in mind or new information they see in the forecast application itself (maybe historical information on performance provided in the forecast application).

  3. Managers have some sense of the numbers they would like to submit but they would like to run their assumptions via the forecast application to test their validity. They might need to simulate scenarios by modifying business drivers, rely on data-mining techniques to forecast outcomes for them, or even combine gut feel numbers.

Most managers go through a combination of the above three examples multiple times throughout the forecast elaboration and submission process. Accommodating all or a combination of the three above examples in an environment that managers themselves already know how to use will increase participation.

Managers almost always first use a different application to get to their optimum number than the forecast application you might have built for them. That other application is one that they personally know how to use—perhaps a familiar spreadsheet program. Once they have come up with their desired outcome, they ask "their people" to enter the number into the final forecasting application.

This is when the process starts breaking. Beyond inefficiencies and error risks associated with such a "workaround," there are risks of transferring accountability for optimizing their numbers to others. Additionally, the true forecast owner becomes disassociated with the number; they become less engaged in the process, and, therefore, less inclined to claim accountability.

Measure and Report Beyond Financial Information

Once your process for collecting information has been established and the accountability has been embraced across the board, you need to measure and report.

Reporting is the activity of presenting information to employees who need it to make decisions, perform actions or communicate to others. On the surface, reporting would seem like a straightforward task. However, in practice, it can prove an extraordinarily difficult task. Information may not be easily accessible, and even when it is, it may have come from different places, making it difficult to put together in a meaningful way. System data and information may not be how business users want to think about the data.

Many companies today have a good understanding of their financial data, but far fewer are able to easily leverage operational data.

Companies should take a holistic approach to reporting on performance. Those companies that fail to do so end up with a distorted view of the business. A recent manufacturing company we talked to equated performance reporting as trying to paint a room where only "one of the walls is ready to be painted." In performance management initiatives, be wary of spending most of the budget and energy gathering and analyzing financial information. Your performance management solution should allow you to accommodate your information needs, both financial and operational.

Don't Just Start with Actuals

Another trend to watch is the tendency that some companies have to build a solution solely on the data that is currently available, or "actuals." While this may seem like a subtle point, it can often determine adoption and effectiveness of a plan. A good example of working with improper data is the case of developing a plan solely from actual data rather than a driver-based plan.

We've talked about the importance of understanding key drivers and using those for input to inform a plan. If we look at a report of actual data, we see items like "Total Sales," "Total Costs," and "Total Expenses." Often, managers will feel safe when taking numbers offline and calculating their own plan based on the numbers alone. However, there are other factors that determine the validity of these numbers. Total sales may be the result of "Quantity Sold" minus "Quantity Returned" multiplied by "Sale Price."

When employees individually develop their own offline plan, they end up creating inconsistent results due to the fact that amounts, when derived in offline models, will have different business logic across the organization. Perhaps in some regions "Total Sales" is captured as above, but it is also entirely possible that other groups ignore "Quantity Returned" and simply compute "Total Sales" as "Quantity" multiplied by "Price."

Now you can see how this approach can expose you to some issues. Neither computation for "Total Sales" is wrong, but by being inconsistent, wrong decisions may be made. Furthermore, these total amounts are static in the process. If, near the end of the budgeting cycle, it is decided that pricing expectations for a given product need to be adjusted for unforeseen competition, all end users must prepare their numbers again and resubmit.

In this driver-based plan example, pricing assumptions could be adjusted and totals recomputed. Contributors may be asked to evaluate the new model and change some quantity expectations based on their own local market characteristics. Through the process, though, the core factors or drivers are where attention is focused. There are clear definitions behind the numbers that appear in plan review reports, and consistency is delivered across the organization.

When preparing your planning solution, the key message is to be as granular as you can in modeling the business. Certainly, you'll start from actual data, but take the time to model the primary factors of those results. Particularly, focus on the drivers that people in the organization can control and can be measured on. A few simple drivers will result in simple calculations and an easy model. A complex business will have many drivers with complicated interactions.

An effective solution makes it possible for those interactions to be centrally defined once and reused. This is far superior to leaving it up to each individual contributor to determine the computations and submit a total result.

Finally, Don't Report Just on Business Performance

Don't measure and report just business performance, but rather measure and report on the actual process of closing your forecast. A couple of trends seem to distinguish the winners in this category:

1. *They deconstruct and manage the planning process.* From strategic planning to forecasting, leading companies in this category analyze each and every step of the planning process. They do so not only to drive better efficiencies but to identify specific areas of accountability within the planning process. Indeed, creating good plans is not the responsibility of a single team. Consider, for example, this manufacturing company that drives planning activities across three teams. The first team works on pricing and promotion models for their goods. The second team uses this information to create sales models based on market demands and available distribution channels. Finally, the third team uses the information from the first two models to draw efficient production plans. Being able to identify timing and responsibility each step of the way is critical in enabling a collaborative and continuous planning process. We encourage companies to establish measurement points for when particular milestones are reached. This will help drive further accountability, and help everyone realize the way in which they contribute. In addition, having clear visibility of the health of the process helps management gain greater confidence in the numbers.

2. *They are transparent.* Creating great plans and executing on them effectively requires a lot of commitment from the management team and the rest of the organization. Planning, when used in isolation, when

mastered by the few in the office of the CFO only, will not be able to reach its full potential. Remember to be transparent not only on what you measure but also on how you measure it. If you have particular checkpoints along the planning process, communicate them. Remember that not everyone in your company is involved in planning activities directly themselves. However, their actions will impact the effectiveness of your plans! In his book *The Performance Management Revolution*, Howard Dresner offers a great definition for a "performance-accountable" organization: "It is the commitment to increasing each person's knowledge and understanding of what drives performance in that organization."[21] Be transparent and win!

In this chapter, we discussed how alignment, agility, and accountability can be attained through planning. Companies that win in planning recognize that planning is only one piece of the puzzle. To plan better, they need to monitor and analyze better. The interaction of all three capabilities contributes to the greater effectiveness of each.

CONCLUSION

In this chapter, we have discussed the role planning, budgeting, and forecasting play in driving business performance. We have highlighted how organizations drive alignment by communicating and collaborating on plans and targets. How models, budgets, and forecasts can help to garner this alignment has been reviewed as well. We've discussed how organizations can become more agile in their consolidations, scenarios and simulations. We've encouraged the use of driver-based plans and rolling financial forecasts, and provided real-world examples and considerations of how to apply these. Finally, we've shown how accountability is increased by incorporating tools like accountability mapping and information cycles.

How to Know If You Have the Ability to Plan

We have discussed the three guiding principles to which an organization must adhere to Plan effectively:

1. *Alignment*: This occurs when a company can effectively align its processes and people around the planning exercise and has eliminated overlap and inefficiencies across the company.
2. *Agility*: This happens when a company can run planning processes faster but also more efficiently. It happens when applying change becomes feasible regardless of where the process is—at the strategic planning phase or the target-setting exercise.
3. *Accountability*: This occurs when the organization can empower more employees to be part of the planning process. Through deeper participation and a broader commitment to performance ownership across the organization, companies rely on better information and ultimately better business performance.

The following test may prove helpful in assessing your organization's Plan capabilities. Think about it as a framework to organize a conversation around the subject of performance management with your teams across divisions and groups within your organization.

Take the Test

Some of the statements below are multifaceted, and you may find you have stronger agreement with some parts of the statement than other parts. Answer "True" if you find that the statement is generally true and "False" if you find the statement is generally false in describing your organization.

1. When our management team starts its long-range planning exercise, they are able to do so by rapidly gaining insight from information about where the business is today, where it has been and where it can be in the future. They also have visibility on competitive benchmarks. The planning process provides management with data they can trust and information that is easy for our teams to produce. Also, it allows them to start to construct a plan around the driving factors of the business.

2. When our company provides top-down guidance, they can set realistic targets based on what the company's objectives are and with a good sense of the performance the various parts of the business can and cannot provide. Business drivers are well understood across the board, and specific targets can be provided to drive the behaviors that maximize results.

3. When budgets are run, most of the process owners' work has been automated and they can define clear time frames to hold every stakeholder accountable to the loop in time. Finally, alignment between local budgets and corporate plans is done easily, allowing the organization to rebudget multiple times throughout the year without having to mobilize an entire team of financial and business analysts.

4. Forecasts are managed and part of a defined process. We don't need to exchange documents and spreadsheets via e-mail to run our forecasts. Our processes are integrated so that corporate and local entities can collaborate and communicate throughout the forecasting process with high efficiency and agility—they can iterate versions of their forecasts without having to delay the forecasting cycle.

5. Our models reflect the true drivers of our activities. They can be communicated in a way that is simple for everyone to understand but sophisticated enough to represent the complexity of our business. For instance, if we have to associate models across two different units, sales and production for example, we have an automated way of dealing with the discrepancies of both without having to "dummy them down" for the sake of simplicity.

6. Our models are not just financial. They encompass operational, sales, marketing, production, and human resource information. When dealing with multiple models across the various parts of our business, we understand and manage their interdependencies.

7. We can quickly obtain high-level views of our business. We can aggregate and consolidate information regardless of our business complexities. We can take care of multiple currencies, allocations of overhead costs to operating units, and eliminations of internal transactions between operating units and handle varying consolidation local regulations, even if they are different from corporate consolidation requirements. When business conditions change (e.g., if we acquire a company and need to restructure our business), we can rectify the rules that govern the way we measure performance across the business without having to overhaul our entire system.

8. Our models help managers contribute to forecasts and budgets faster because they not only provide baseline numbers to start with but also provide the ability to simulate different scenarios. For instance, all contributors can run "what-if" scenarios before they submit their final numbers.

9. Individuals and groups, whether in finance or any other department, are held accountable for closing their plans. We can audit delays and changes throughout the entire planning process, and tie accountability of processes to specific individuals or groups. For instance, if needed, we can report on which group or task is slowing down planning cycles. This allows us to close our planning cycles faster.

10. When running our forecasting and budgeting process, we have automated contribution and consolidation with information management cycles. The cycles not only allow for the process to be run without human intervention, they also manage users and their access rights, and recognize who they are based on their profiles. This allows us to ensure compliance but also make sure that information is personalized to the end audience. Each individual receives information that relates to them and their roles only.

When reviewing your score, note that the score should not be viewed as an outcome ("How did we do?"), but rather as a starting point ("Where are we starting from?"). The purpose of the test is not just to give you a number, but to provide a framework for driving performance excellence.

Add up the number of "True" answers you provided above. If you have answered all of the above "True," the people in your organization are equipped with the ability to plan, and management has its finger on the pulse of the organization. For the rest of us, refer to the following:

0–2 True answers = limited Plan strength; your score is 1.

3–5 True answers = moderate Plan strength; your score is 2.

6–8 True answers — major Plan strength; your score is 3.

9–10 True answers = superior Plan strength; your score is 4.

Note your score, as you will need it to determine your stage in Chapter 6. Further guidance on how to improve your planning skills is also provided below.

Improve Your Results

If you answered "False" to any of the above questions, note the number of the question and review the corresponding suggested remedy below to help move you to a "True" answer—and more importantly, provide your organization with competitive advantage.

1. When teams cannot obtain a clear and accurate picture of the business without having to rely on heavy manual processes, the validity of their planning activities is put in jeopardy. They are slow to understand the rhythm of the business and spend time scrutinizing numbers, rather than relying on a strong foundation to start planning. Developing a scalable way to bring in information from multiple sources (operational and financial) and tying long-range planning activities to more operational processes such as forecasts, allows management to align the organization and all employees to execute on the right things. Look for solutions that allow your company to maintain business models, regardless of their

data sources (internal or external) or cycle length (three months or three years). Although a strategic planning model might last for three years while a forecast might last for three months, your solution should allow you to link both so you are guaranteed to execute in alignment with your organization's long-term roles.

2. When companies cannot set realistic targets they expose themselves to very long forecast cycles and unpredictable results. Time to close forecasts is lengthy because targets become the source of arguments and negotiation meetings. When targets are wrong and accepted without discussion, the business sets itself for failure. Utilize solutions that allow you to embed strong analytical functionality so targets can be established with the highest level of confidence. This will avoid discussions about the target and focus teams on execution strategies to develop to deliver on the target.

3. When budgets are not automated, they are rarely closed on time. Process owners struggle to define clear timeframes; budget owners don't submit projections on time. Sometimes, budget contribution is "delegated" to local finance employees as a way for business owners to "delegate" responsibility of budgets until later. This delays accurate revenue and cost projections and jeopardizes execution of strategy. By incorporating calendaring and automation abilities you can rely less on manual intervention to get the budgets closed. Automate the alignment between corporate models and local budget models so that rebudgeting can be done with high flexibility.

4. When an organization exchanges documents and spreadsheets via email to run its forecasts, it exposes itself to potential errors. Manual intervention

throughout the process prevents a fast close and inconsistency abounds. In addition, contributors and analysts find the forecast process so tedious and unnerving that they become less inclined to use it as a performance management tool but rather just complete it because they have to. Organizations should automate forecast development and contribution. The forecast process is iterative and collaborative, so you will need a solution that allows individuals to submit multiple forecast versions but also one that facilitates the contribution and approval process. Finally, solutions that provide functionality such as seeding (populating forecast numbers for contributors ahead of time) and have integrated analysis and monitoring capabilities will help forecast owners use the forecast solution to better run their business.

5. When models don't reflect the true drivers of a business activity, forecasts and budgets aren't valid. Corporate offices and business units struggle to run the business efficiently at a macro as well as a detailed level. Moreover, projections are inaccurate and successes and failures cannot easily be explained logically. Models are at the heart of your performance management solution and as such, they should allow your organization to best describe how the business is run. Organizations should develop the ability to easily describe the details of their activity without requiring IT administrators to code a lot of information. Models should ideally be managed by business analysts and they should accommodate the granularity needed to describe key business drivers, calculations, and rules (consolidations, eliminations, foreign exchange, and others). Strong models can enable better driver-based planning and thus help the organization become more agile.

6. When models describe only financial information, they fail to represent most of the business activity. The best models include not only operational, sales, marketing, production and human resource information and drivers, but they also have an automated way of dealing with the relationship across these multiple models. For instance, if a sales model has assumptions and rules that affect production, the best modeling solutions will not only relate both models but it will also provide the ability to customize the particular assumptions and rules that run that relationship. Doing so allows organizations to not only orchestrate forecasts and budgets more efficiently, but also obtain much clearer visibility on the true drivers of their activities.

7. When organizations cannot easily consolidate information across their business, they lose flexibility. Business changes, such as acquisitions and reorganizations, might require systems overhaul and slow the business down. Consider the multiple currencies, various allocations, eliminations, and consolidation rules that are required in order to properly run your business as part of your modeling requirements. Business conditions change and other events that will cause your teams to modify the rules and calculations constantly. With strong consolidation capabilities, your analysts will be able to react to business changes with great agility and continue to deliver accurate forecasts and budgets.

8. When scenarios and simulations cannot be run by every forecast or budget contributor, the organization does not get the best results they can get. Their contributors either submit the "safe" numbers or they take time to contribute because they had to work out the best contribution numbers outside of their

budgeting and forecasting application. Remember the plumbing and faucet analogy. With strong baseline information provided by consolidation and other rules (the plumbing), employees should be able to adjust and simulate budgets and forecasts in their environment (the faucet). Solid scenarios and simulation abilities help employee better contribute because they allow them to run "what-if" scenarios before they submit their final numbers. This functionality also needs to be intuitive. Organizations should allow all employees to simulate forecasts and budgets in a familiar environment so they can focus on business results rather than learning complex calculations and simulations functions.

9. When an organization is unable to identify clear owners throughout the planning process, bottlenecks cannot be identified quickly enough to close cycles on time. As a consequence, forecasts and budgets can be submitted late and the organization doesn't become leaner. Mapping accountability of the planning process is enabled when the planning solution can log and store all aspects of the budget and forecast steps centrally. With a central database governing the planning activity, delays and changes can be audited and accountability of processes tied to specific individuals or groups. Implement solutions that not only allow your organization to run world-class planning processes but that also provide you with the entire information set behind the process: users, rules, contribution schedules, approval checks, and other key process items should be logged and stored in a format that can be easily reported against. Consider solutions that provide out-of-box reporting capabilities so your analysts and administrators do not have to figure out process management audits by themselves.

10. Information cycles govern how information flows across models, plans, budgets and forecasts. When information cycles are mismanaged, the organization cannot automate the contribution of forecasts, budgets, and plans. Remember the key attributes of cycles: Cycles need to enforce compliance, and they need to understand user roles and time. Today's environment of increasing rigor around audit and compliance requires the ability to clearly understand the flow of information—information cycles should be easily auditable. However, do not simply minister full access to everyone; part of your information cycle functionality should include the ability to assign the proper security privileges to the appropriate manager roles. Finally, information cycles govern contribution time. As such, they should be flexible and allow to set and communicate clear timeframes and timetables for given processes. In the event of a forecast, for instance, it may be appropriate to have a several-week window during which contributors may submit new information or change existing forecast data. However, collecting and consolidating actual information for reporting purposes is generally a process open only for a few days and submission beyond a certain point in time would compromise the integrity of reporting.

NOTES

1. Jack Welch and Suzy Welch, *Winning* (New York: Harper Collins, 2005).

2. Interview with Randy Benz, Energizer, September 2007. Video available at www.cultureofperformance.com.

3. Discussion with Christophe Couturier, December 2007.

4. Discussion with Ron Van Zanten, Premier Bankcard, November 2007.

5. Leaders of Europe's BW50 http://images.businessweek.com/ss/
   05/06/0526eubw50/6.htm.

6. Jean Paul Votron (Brussels, Investor Day: March 2007)

7. Conversation with Jean-François Gigot, Global Project Manager,
   Fortis—December 2007.

8. Discussion with Jeremy Hope, December 2007

9. Chip and Dan Heath, *Made to Stick* (New York: Random House,
   2007).

10. Discussion with Christophe Couturier, December 2007.

11. *Ibid.*

12. Conversation with Jean-François Gigot, Global Project Manager,
    Fortis—December 2007.

13. Ulf Hilton, Group Finance Manager, Oticon A/S.

14. Discussion with Randy Benz, Energizer, September 2007.

15. Beyond Budgeting Web site, www.beyondbudgetingplus.com.

16. Discussion with Christophe Couturier, December 2007.

17. Discussion with Randy Benz, Energizer, September 2007.

18. Discussion with Andy Hough, Director, IT Managed Services,
    Skanska USA.

19. Mary Hayes Weier, "Business Objects, Microsoft Promise Pervasive
    Business Intelligence–Again," *InformationWeek*, (May 3, 2007),
    http://www.informationweek.com/story/showArticle.jhtml?article
    ID=199203494.

20. Discussion with Walter McFarland, Vice President of Strategy at
    Wells Fargo, December 2007.

21. Howard Dresner, *The Performance Management Revolution* (Hoboken,
    NJ: John Wiley & Sons, 2008), p. 49.

∼ 6 ∼

Pull it All Together

What's Your Organization's Stage?

Retain faith that you will prevail in the end, regardless of the difficulties AND at the same time
confront the most brutal facts of your current reality, whatever they might be.

Jim Collins[1]

IN THIS CHAPTER

Now that we have detailed the three capabilities required
to drive business performance, we can discuss how these
three capabilities enable you to experience the six stages of
performance management value.

In this chapter, we will:

- Explain how the three capabilities deliver the six stages
  of performance management value.
- Identify your organization's monitor, analyze, and plan
  scores.
- Enable you to determine your company's stage.

251

- Provide guidance for how to move closer to a culture of performance.
- Provide examples of how leading companies demonstrate the interaction of monitor, analyze, and plan capabilities to deliver each stage.

HOW THE THREE CAPABILITIES DELIVER THE SIX STAGES OF PERFORMANCE MANAGEMENT VALUE

As discussed in Chapter 1, organizations begin a performance improvement initiative to solve a business problem. They are trying to attain one or more of the six stages of performance management value. Whether they are increasing visibility to understand how the organization is performing, planning for success to better model their business and forecast future performance, or incorporating external benchmarks to attain the power to compete, they begin their performance improvement initiatives with one (or more) of these six stages in mind.

So, once organizations know what they want to get out of performance management, what do they do next? They begin to develop monitoring, analyzing and planning capabilities so they can attain the benefits they are seeking.

Capability Strength Is Relative to Stages

Depending on what organizations are trying to accomplish, a varying degree of the three Monitor, Analyze, and Plan capabilities is required. For instance, if you're trying to move beyond gut feel, you need to develop a really strong analytical muscle. If you are trying to plan for success, the ability to plan will be critical to your success.

More importantly, the key point to note is that no matter what type of value the organization is seeking to attain, it is *never* just one capability that delivers the benefits they are seeking, but rather it is *always* a combination of the three capabilities that is required.

To be very clear, there are three concepts to understand in order to see how capabilities deliver the six stages of success:

1. *Three capabilities are required.* Organizations must be able to monitor, analyze, and plan to achieve any of the six stages.
2. *They are required together.* Organizations must be able to Monitor *and* Analyze *and* Plan.
3. *They are required at different strength depending on what you are trying to accomplish.* How much of your monitoring, analyzing, and planning muscles you need to flex is relative to the requirements of a given stage. Sometimes you need more monitoring, sometimes more analyzing or more planning.

Understanding the Stages

Figure 6.1 shows three things:

1. *The six stages of performance management value in circles at the top.* This answers the question, "What are we seeking to accomplish with our performance management efforts?"
2. *The three capabilities (Monitor, Analyze, Plan [MAP]).* This answers the question, "What combination of capabilities will we need to develop to attain the value we seek?"
3. *The guiding principles, skills, and assets that are needed to develop the capability.* These answer the question,

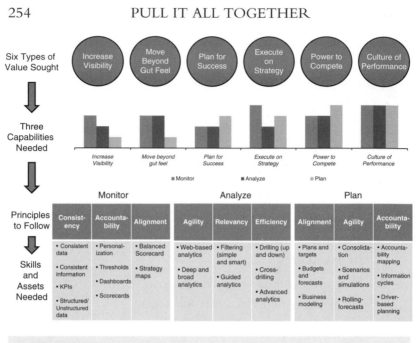

FIGURE 6.1 The Culture of Performance Methodology

"What skills and assets do we need to develop each capability?"

Let's now take a look at the stages in more detail to understand the relative strength of the capabilities, including the specific skills and assets, needed to deliver each.

Review the stage scores in Figure 6.2 and read the brief descriptions below to understand how the capabilities deliver each stage. Understanding these stages in more detail will help you understand your score, your stage, and the recommendations we will provide on what stages you should target.

Increase Visibility The Increase Visibility stage is represented by a MAP score of at least 3 for Monitor, 2 for Analyze, and 1 for Plan (3, 2, 1) (see Figure 6.3):

- *Monitor (3 or better)*: Companies in this stage are particularly strong in monitoring, which establishes "one

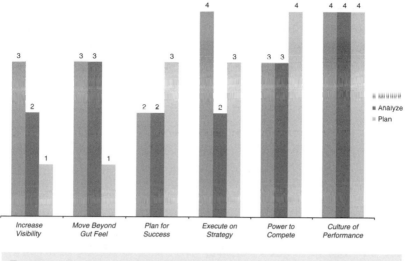

FIGURE 6.2 Stages and Capabilities

version of the truth." Without consistency, organizations are unable to have a clear understanding of performance. Specifically, consistency is embodied by the creation of KPIs, thresholds, reports, and dashboards. Companies in this stage increase their organizational awareness and broaden their monitoring ability. When goals have been clearly defined and communicated and are understood broadly, ownership and accountability are better internalized. Organizations in this

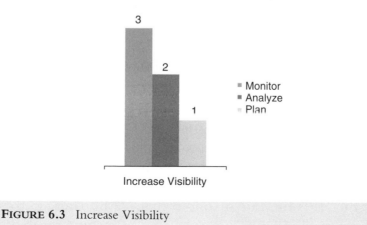

FIGURE 6.3 Increase Visibility

stage may follow methodologies such as the Balanced Scorecard to guide their approach to measuring and managing performance. They are often trying to "get off the reporting treadmill" by streamlining reporting processes so they can more quickly deliver the information people need when they need it.

- *Analyze (2 or better)*: Analytics play a supporting role in increasing visibility, as the ability to query information is needed to understand the factors impacting the business. Companies in this stage start to move from "flat" reports that they cannot investigate to more interactive dashboards that allow inquiry. They begin to connect their reports and dashboards by drilling to details to get answers to the question "Why?"

- *Plan (1 or better)*: While not as core to visibility as monitoring, the Plan capability increases visibility as employees collaborate around the budgets and forecasts and become more aware and involved in planning processes. While companies at this stage may have business modeling, planning and forecasting processes, these are often restricted in their scope and utilized by a limited audience.

Move Beyond Gut Feel   The Move Beyond Gut Feel stage is represented by a MAP score of at least (3, 3, 1) (see Figure 6.4):

- *Monitor (3 or better)*: The Monitor capability is a major capability area in allowing organizations to make fact-based, data-driven decisions. As organizations develop their monitoring skills and assets, employees are able to trust their data and know their information is consistent with their business intentions and goals. Data and information consistency allow employees to trust the KPIs they are seeing in their dashboards, so they can trust insights (derived from the analytic capability,

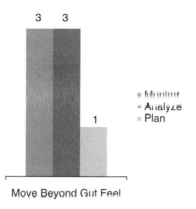

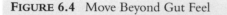

FIGURE 6.4   Move Beyond Gut Feel

which also plays a major role in the Move Beyond Gut Feel stage) and decisions.

- *Analyze (3 or better)*: The Analyze capability plays a major role in enabling the organization to move beyond gut feel. Analytic assets such as filtering and drilling (up, down, and across) enable employees to uncover the answers to why things are happening. When investigating a hunch, employees understand complex information faster, thus making the organization more agile. They also have the facts about what the organizational priorities are—context for what is important and how to weigh the findings in light of organizational objectives (leveraging the strength of the Monitor capability).

- *Plan (1 or better)*: With increased analytical capability, organizations at this stage may begin to better analyze forecasts, budgets, and plans to optimize for more reliable results. These companies might be able to produce multiple scenarios, which delivers increased predictability and allows them to anticipate results with better accuracy.

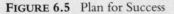

FIGURE 6.5 Plan for Success

Plan for Success   The Plan for Success stage is represented by a MAP score of at least (2, 2, 3) (see Figure 6.5):

- *Monitor (2 or better)*: In order to effectively forecast and plan, an organization needs the knowledge of how its business has performed historically and is currently performing. Monitoring skills and assets such as KPIs and reports inform the strategic decisions that need to be made to build better plans. Consistency of information and access to structured and unstructured data are important as the organization attempts to get a complete picture of performance to date.

- *Analyze (2 or better)*: The focus of the analytic capability in this stage is to better inform the planning process. Companies often utilize deep and broad analytics, drilling and filtering to understand why factors have impacted, are impacting, or will impact business.

- *Plan (3 or better)*: The ability to plan plays a critical role in planning for success. At this stage, the focus is around automating the planning process to improve organizational agility (e.g., to react faster to changing market conditions, take advantage of new business opportunities, respond to competitive pressure, etc.).

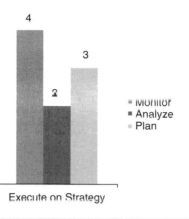

FIGURE 6.6   Execute on Strategy

These companies can build models that are aligned to corporate strategy. They have set up processes that streamline the management of information as it is consolidated throughout the organization. These companies might also be experimenting with rolling forecasts or driver-based planning.

Execute on Strategy   The Execute on Strategy stage is represented by a MAP score of at least (4, 2, 3) (see Figure 6.6):

- *Monitor (4)*: The Monitor capability provides the critical skills needed to execute strategy effectively. In environments where plans are communicated and strategies are aligned, the impact is amplified—more people are accountable to work effectively toward aligned and complementary goals. KPIs, scorecards, and strategy maps are central to enabling this coordinated execution. Strategy maps help ensure that strategies are effectively formulated, documented, communicated, and owned across the organizations.

- *Analyze (2 or better)*: At this stage, the focus of the analytic capability is to refine your execution. Companies at this stage care not only about having picked the right metrics, but also that the right metrics are consistently and currently being utilized to better execute strategy. They use their analytical capabilities to identify specific KPIs and trends and refine metrics (e.g., modifying thresholds) or even recycle KPIs (e.g., selecting new metrics).

- *Plan (3 or better)*: The Plan capability plays a major role in executing strategy because at this stage there is an explicit tie between the planning and monitoring capabilities. A good example of this linkage may be how the results of long-term planning are represented and communicated across the organization in strategy maps. At the Execute on Strategy stage, companies become much more dynamic—with strong planning capabilities and superior monitoring capabilities—so that when plans change, the organization can adapt quickly.

Power to Compete   The Power to Compete stage is represented by a MAP score of at least (3, 3, 4) (see Figure 6.7):

- *Monitor (3 or better)*: The Monitor capability plays a major role in providing the Power to Compete.

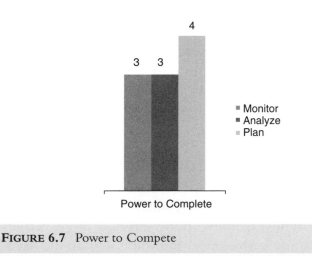

FIGURE 6.7 Power to Compete

The Power to Compete requires an understanding of how to benchmark the organization against the competition and plan for future conditions. Before a company can really focus on external factors such as competition and forecast future state of the plan option, it must first know itself internally and in its present condition.

- *Analyze (3 or better)*: The Analyze capability plays a major role in delivering the Power to Compete. Companies at this stage not only gain access to external information, but more importantly are now able to analyze external benchmarks and relate them to the way they measure their own execution. They are also able to analyze characteristics common to different teams or groups to better understand the effectiveness of internal competition and contribution to organizational goals.

- *Plan (4)*: Superior planning capabilities help to deliver the Power to Compete. Companies at this stage have already automated their planning processes and realized the benefits of enhanced agility. At this stage, companies can take advantage of this agility implement creative approaches to planning to further their competitive advantage. The use of rolling forecasts, driver-based planning, accountability maps, and methodologies like Beyond Budgeting are great examples of planning skills used at this stage.

Culture of Performance   The Culture of Performance stage is represented by a MAP score of (4, 4, 4) (see Figure 6.8):

- *Monitor (4)*: Within a Culture of Performance, organizations monitor their business as a part of their daily execution—working against known, complementary, and aligned objectives with a sense of accountability and the context for how their actions impact the

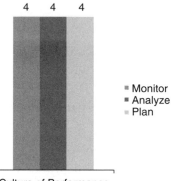

4   4   4

- Monitor
- Analyze
- Plan

Culture of Performance

FIGURE 6.8 Culture of Performance

greater organization. Their culture is such that they speak in terms of "reds, yellows, and greens." Access to consistent and relevant information is not a discrete task, but instead a part of their everyday environment.

- *Analyze (4)*: Within a Culture of Performance, analysis is not the domain of only a few employees. Rather than being entitled to know, people across the organization are empowered and expected to know the factors impacting their business. Their analytics are predictive and guide them to the answers they seek. They provide rapid focus and understanding through advanced analytical capabilities like performance maps, decomposition trees, and other advanced performance visualization tools.

- *Plan (4)*: Companies at the Culture of Performance stage are able to use the planning processes to drive better organizational performance. Front-line people who want to modify their forecasts and plans of budgets don't have to wait for a particular time of year, or for a particular process to begin to make changes. They can make adjustments when it is most relevant to their business activity, and are empowered as "agents of change" to move the organization from centralized and regimented planning processes to continuous business improvement.

UNDERSTANDING THE CULTURE OF PERFORMANCE MODEL

As you review your scores keep the following points in mind:

- *The model proposes a balance of the Monitor, Analyze, and Plan capabilities.* In order to develop a Culture of Performance, superior Monitor *and* Analyze *and* Plan capabilities are required, so it is best to start to supplement your weaknesses early. Even superior capabilities, if only in a single area, yield limited impact. Broaden your strengths across MAP to increase your impact and competitive advantage.

- *You may not necessarily start at the Increase Visibility stage.* Depending on how your organization has developed performance management capabilities, you may enter at different stages.

- *The respective MAP capabilities do not individually increase from stage to stage; the combined MAP strength does.* Notice that the scores are cumulatively increasing, but the combination of MAP strengths in each stage is different. Each Monitor, Analyze, and Plan capability does not necessarily progress linearly from Increase Visibility to Culture of Performance. For some stages, the Monitor capability needs to be particularly strong; for others, Analyze plays a major role in realizing the targeted value; for others, it's planning that needs to do the heavy lifting.

While the respective MAP capabilities may not individually increase from stage to stage, the combined strength does. From Increase Visibility to Culture of Performance, the combined score totals 6, 7, 7, 9, 10, and 12, respectively.

So, why isn't there an increase from Move Beyond Gut Feel to Plan for Success (both total 7)? This reflects the transition in the capability strength needed to move from just managing the past and present to developing the Plan capability to look ahead and manage the future.

- *The greater the cumulative MAP capability strength, the greater the impact.* The more capabilities you can develop to a strong (3) or superior (4) level, the more your overall impact increases. Organizations that have:

  ○ One MAP strength (Monitor or Analyze or Plan score of 3 or 4) can only execute at two possible stages: Increase Visibility (if Monitor is the strength) or Plan for Success (if Plan is the strength).

  ○ Two MAP strengths doubles the impact to four possible stages available.

  ○ Three MAP strengths triples the impact to six possible stages, including the Power to Compete and the Culture of Performance stages.

- *Backfill stages before progressing.* As noted above, depending on how you have developed skills and assets within your organization, you may enter the Culture of Performance model at different stages. However, given the foundational roles of the Increase Visibility stage in particular, we suggest developing capabilities to backfill stages. This strengthens your foundation upon which to build.

For instance, if you have invested very heavily in planning capabilities, but have done so for only a few people and not yet developed monitoring and analyzing capabilities, you are likely to have a score of (1, 1, 3) or (1, 1, 4). Your first step will be to increase your monitoring and analyzing skills enough to Plan for Success—and in so doing, you will develop the foundational Increase Visibility and Move Beyond Gut Feel stages. You will also have better-quality data and information on which to plan and more collaborative processes as additional groups and teams are included in the performance management processes. Both of these improvements will provide you with more reliable plans, budgets, and forecasts.

Increase Visibility and Move Beyond Gut Feel are foundational stages and, even if you come in at a more advanced stage, go back and fill in gaps in capability strength to achieve these stages before trying to progress higher.

- *No stage does not mean no hope.* If your company's score does not qualify for a stage, there's no reason to panic. If you are just starting to develop your performance management capabilities, you now have a framework to follow. You are more likely to take a balanced approach to performance management and are armed with an understanding of how the MAP capabilities deliver the competitive advantage you seek. You should be able to avoid much of the costly expense and time otherwise lost on mistakes trying to figure it out as you go.

If you already have been developing performance management capabilities and have not yet landed on a stage, the first step may simply be to increase the breadth of your capabilities. It may mean that you have developed too few skills and assets, but may also mean that you have developed capabilities but just delivered these to too few people across the organization.

WHAT ARE YOUR COMPANY'S SCORES?

Let's now determine where your organization lands on the six stages. You may recall that we provided a way for you to determine the strength of your MAP capabilities at the end of Chapters 3, 4, and 5, respectively.

Now you can use each of those capability scores to identify your stage. If you haven't done so already, compute your organization's respective MAP scores based on the number of "True" responses to determine whether you are limited (1), moderate (2), strong (3), or superior (4) in each:[2]

- Page 111 for your Monitor score
- Page 180 for your Analyze score
- Page 243 for your Plan score

Write down your score in Monitor, Analyze, and Plan order, so your Monitor score goes first, then your Analyze score, then your Plan score (e.g., 1, 2, 3). Now, let's review the model and better understand the stages so you can identify where your company fits.

Companies with whom we have worked commonly refer to their performance management initiatives as a journey rather than a destination. When reviewing your score, note that the score should not be viewed as an outcome ("How did we do?"), but rather as a starting point ("Where are we starting from?"). One of the companies we worked with aptly describes the philosophy of the self-assessment:

> In general, these questions reflect an "ideal" company and the level of performance management and discipline we are striving to achieve. Answering TRUE to every question would mean we have accomplished our vision and strategy. I would answer many of these differently a year from now.[3]

WHAT SCENARIO DESCRIBES YOUR ORGANIZATION?

Review your MAP score to determine which of the following three scenarios your company fits in. Your company might be.

1. Limited to moderate in all three capabilities— Monitor, Analyze, and Plan. This is reflected by MAP scores of 2 or 1 in each.
2. Strong to superior in *one of the capabilities*—Monitor *or* Analyze *or* Plan. This is reflected by scores of 3 or 4 in any *one* of the three capabilities.
3. Strong to superior in *two of the capabilities*—Monitor and Analyze, or Monitor and Plan, or Analyze and Plan, or Plan and Monitor. This is reflected by scores of 3 or 4 in any *two* of the three capabilities.
4. Strong to superior in *all three capabilities*—Monitor *and* Analyze *and* Plan. This is reflected by scores of 3 or 4 in all *three* of the three capabilities.

Let's now look at each of the three scenarios to determine your company's current stage and which stages you should be targeting based on your relative capability strengths.

Limited to Moderate in All Three Capabilities—Monitor, Analyze, and Plan

Companies with limited to moderate scores across all three capabilities are identified with MAP scores of 2 or below in each area (i.e., they do not have a score of 3 in any of the capabilities).

Stage These companies have scores such as (1, 1, 1); (2, 1, 1); (1, 1, 2); and so on. In the best-case scenario, these companies may have MAP scores of 2, 2, 2. These companies are just chartering their performance management initiatives and have not yet attained any of the Culture of Performance stages.

Situation For these companies, we recommend reviewing Chapter 3 to develop a strong monitoring capability to learn about the concepts of consistent data and consistent information. Recall our earlier guidance; Increase Visibility and Move Beyond Gut Feel are foundational stages. Even if organizations come in at a more advanced stage, if they lack the requisite scores for these stages we recommend that they go back and fill in gaps in capability strength to achieve these stages.

Recommendations

- Focus on driving consistency throughout the organization. Without consistency, nothing else matters. KPIs, reports, or dashboards will be irrelevant if you can't trust your data and agree on data definitions. Review the guidance on the three types of trust and the foundational role that trustworthy data plays (Chapter 2, "Trust Your Data").
- Focus your efforts on the skills and assets required for the Increase Visibility stage (3, 3, 1) where a lot of emphasis is put on understanding what is happening and what drives your business. Start looking into the development of your planning capability as it will become important when you use past and present information to impact the future.

Stage Guidance In reviewing Figure 6.2, notice that with a limited (score of 1) Monitor or Analyze capability, you

have not yet attained any of the six stages. These companies should target the Increase Visibility stage. Companies
with a score of (2, 2, 2) may also aspire to increase visibility, but may choose to develop their planning capabilities
to attain the Plan for Success stage, depending on organizational needs and short term priorities. Just remember the
overall guidance on backfilling first —which makes Increase
Visibility a general recommended priority.

Strong to Superior in One of the Capabilities—Monitor *or* Analyze *or* Plan

Companies with strength in one of the capabilities are identified with at least one MAP score of 3 (strong) or 4 (superior).

Stage Companies that have strength in one capability have
scores such as (3, 2, 1); (1, 3, 2); (1, 1, 3); (2, 4, 1); (4, 1,
1); and so on. These companies are moderate or limited in
their other two capabilities.

Situation Companies in this scenario are not new to performance management, as they have developed one capability to at least a strong and sometimes even to a superior
degree. However, they have not taken a balanced approach
and remain weak in two of their three capability areas. We
recommend reviewing the "Improve Your Results" section
at the end of the chapters in which your weaker capabilities are discussed (Chapter 3 for Monitor, Chapter 4 for
Analyze, and Chapter 5 for Plan).

The number one issue for companies in this scenario is
to figure out how to best leverage their one strong capability
and develop their other two. We provide recommendations
below, based on their one area of strength, whether it is
Monitor, Analyze or Plan.

Recommendations

- *Monitoring is your strong/superior capability.* With a strong Monitor capability, you are likely to have consistent information, KPIs, and dashboards already in use (see Figure 6.1). More importantly, the organization has moved beyond the need to drive consistency and is now using its monitoring capability to drive accountability and alignment.

  If you are in this scenario, you might have graduated from the Increase Visibility stage and are now looking at expanding your skills and assets to attain other stages.

  Do not rush into the Execute on Strategy stage without incorporating your planning skills. You might not be ready to evolve from simple ways to understand business conditions (dashboards and reports) to using monitoring capabilities as a tool to drive your organization toward the execution of agreed corporate objectives. The planning skills will become predominant here in helping your company use good dashboard capability to implement sane scorecards and strategy maps, for example.

- *Analyze is your strong/superior capability.* Companies with strong analytic capabilities may be agile and efficient because their employees can analyze with high efficiency: They can look at reports, drill up and down, sometimes even cross-drill or use advanced visualizations. In this case, use your analytical capability to increase visibility. Your tendency will naturally lead you to gravitate toward the Move Beyond Gut Feel stage (because it relies heavily on a superior analytic capability). However, you should attempt to use analytics to improve your dashboards and, more specifically, your KPIs. By developing better KPIs, the rest of the organization will benefit from your insights,

and you will be able to mature dashboards into scorecards, thus enabling the organization to move toward
the Execute on Strategy stage.

- *Plan is your strong/superior capability.* Companies with
  this strength can drive better accountability and operational excellence around planning, budgeting, and
  forecasting processes. With superior planning skills,
  you are able to Plan for Success. Use your understanding of your company's business drivers to drive
  better KPIs and ultimately build out your monitoring
  skills. When done well, this will lead the organization to the Increase Visibility stage and ultimately to
  the Execute on Strategy stage as KPIs, dashboards,
  scorecards, and reports become better connected to
  planning processes.

Stage Guidance   In reviewing Figure 6.2, we can immediately see that organizations with only one strong capability
may be at the Increase Visibility stage or the Plan for Success stage. (Notice the other stages require at least two scores
of 3.)

If your strength is in monitoring, you may be at the
Increase Visibility stage. If your strength is in planning,
you may be able to plan for success. However, if your only
strength is in analyzing, you are not yet able to attain a stage
in the Culture of Performance model. Why is that? While it
is valuable to have strong analytical capabilities, tying them
to your monitoring and planning capabilities is more important. If you are strong in analytics alone, the scope of your
impact is limited. The insights your analytics deliver cannot
be recognized broadly through scorecards or dashboards because the monitoring capability is not yet developed. Nor
can your analytics impact your plans (using predictive analysis to improve forecasts, for instance). If your Analyze capability is your strong capability, focus on developing your
Monitor capabilities to be able to increase visibility.

Strong to Superior in Two of the Capabilities—Monitor and Analyze, *or* Monitor and Plan, *or* Analyze and Plan

Companies with strength in two of the capabilities are identified with two MAP scores of 3 (strong) or 4 (superior).

Stage   Companies that have strength in two capabilities have scores of 3 or 4 in two of their capabilities, such as (4, 2, 3); (3, 3, 1); (2, 3, 4); and so on. These companies have a score of 1 or 2 in their other capability.

Situation   Companies in this scenario have developed two of their capabilities and they have started their journey to a Culture of Performance. While they have taken a more balanced approach than those with one strong capability, one of their capabilities has not been developed, and this limits their impact. We recommend reviewing the "Improve Your Results" section at the end of the chapter in which your weakest capability is discussed (Chapter 3 for Monitor, Chapter 4 for Analyze, Chapter 5 for Plan).

Generally, companies in this scenario should strive to develop their one weak capability in order to increase the overall impact of their performance.

Recommendations

- *Monitoring and analytics have primarily been developed.* Companies with strong monitoring and analytics capabilities are either executing at the Increase Visibility or Move Beyond Gut Feel stage because a strong plan capability is needed to execute at any of the other stages (score of 3 or above). These companies are focused on what is currently impacting their business and may not have a clear sense of future direction. These companies have not yet taken advantage of their strong monitor and analyze assets to operationalize their performance management practices. Their analytical insights derived from their strong analyze capabilities do not inform their plans. While planning may occur in an isolated fashion, it has not yet been developed or communicated broadly, thus preventing all employees from focusing on future outcomes.

- *Monitoring and planning have primarily been developed.*

  Companies with strong Monitor and Plan capabilities have underdeveloped Analyze capabilities, which impacts their efficiency and agility. For instance, their scorecards may be related to plans, but they have no efficient way to understand business drivers or investigate root causes of particular business issues. If your analytic capabilities are limited (score of 1), you have not yet realized a stage despite your monitoring and planning strength.

  Companies fitting this description should focus on developing their analytic skills. Even if they are limited in this area today, by developing their Analyze capability even to a moderate level, this will allow them to increase visibility, plan for success, *and* even execute on strategy (if their Monitor strength is superior). Only a modest improvement in Analyze yields great impact, thanks to the strength of their existing Monitor and Plan capabilities.

  Your company might be executing the Execute on Strategy stage. However, your ability to question information doesn't happen with the agility it should. You find that your teams struggle when you ask to better understand the "why" of particular trends or KPIs. In this stage, developing analytical capabilities becomes extremely important, especially if you want to move up to the Power to Compete stage. Without a flexible way to incorporate external metrics and analyze information with high efficiency, you could compromise your company's ability to respond to unexpected events. Agility might be in danger here.

These companies should target the Plan for Success stage next. This will require that you develop and better integrate your planning capabilities.

- *Analytics and planning have primarily been developed.*

    If you have developed Analyze and Plan capabilities, you have great insight into the drivers of your business and may also be able to predict your results. These strong capabilities may have contributed to developing strong KPIs for your company. However, your weak monitoring capability prevents you from making these KPIs broadly available through reports, scorecards, dashboards, or strategy maps. As a consequence, employees have limited visibility and lack a clear "line of sight" to the strategy. This prevents your company from having full control of the strategy. You may have a strong strategy but lack the ability to communicate it broadly. Developing scorecards and dashboards will allow you to move from strategy formulation to strategy execution.

Stage Guidance In reviewing Figure 6.2, note that most stages require at least two strong capabilities; only two don't—Increase Visibility and Plan for Success. For this reason, companies with two strengths often have already achieved these two stages.

However, with limited Monitor or Analyze capabilities (scores of 1), you have not yet achieved a stage and need to focus on developing these foundational capabilities.

Depending on which capability is weak, we offer different stage guidance:

- If your Monitor score is 2, you are executing at the Planning for Success stage (due to the strength of your

Analyze and Plan capabilities). We recommend developing your monitoring skills, which will allow you to increase visibility and move beyond gut feel (as you already have strong Analyze and Plan capabilities)

- If your Analyze score is 2, you are executing at the Increase Visibility and Plan for Success stages (due to the strength of your Monitor and Plan capabilities), and may even be executing on strategy. We recommend developing your analytical skills to get to the Move Beyond Gut Feel stage.

- If your Plan score is 2, you are already executing at the Increase Visibility and Move Beyond Gut Feel stages (due to the strength of your Monitor and Analyze capabilities and the fact that these two stages only require a score of 1 for Plan). We recommend developing your analytic skills to be able to Plan for Success.

Strong to Superior in All Three Capabilities—Monitor *and* Analyze *and* Plan

Companies with strength in all three capabilities are identified with scores of 3 (strong) or 4 (superior) across Monitor *and* Analyze *and* Plan.

Stage   Companies that have strength in all three capabilities have scores such as (3, 3, 3); (4, 3, 3); (3, 4, 3); (3, 3, 4); (4, 4, 3); and so on.

Situation   Companies in this scenario have world–class performance management capabilities, as they have developed their capabilities to at least a strong and sometimes even to a superior degree. They set examples of performance excellence and are often the benchmark to which others compare themselves. While most companies may only experience this excellence in one department, these organizations have it everywhere. These companies may not be household names as you may think, as sometimes smaller organizations are able to develop these capabilities across the enterprise faster.

Recommendations   The guidance for companies with strong MAP capabilities is to develop superiority to further their competitive advantage. For those with a superior capability already, we offer the following guidance:

- *Superiority in Monitor.* Your capabilities already allow you to execute on strategy, and your internal management is strong. Turn your attention to increased competitive advantage by incorporating external benchmarks in your day-to-day operations.

- *Superiority in Analyze.* Your analytic capabilities can be leveraged to enhance your monitoring and planning capabilities. Look to improve integration between your analytics and your monitoring, so when employees see a dashboard they can easily investigate cause and effect. Also, by better integrating analytics and planning capabilities, your employees will be able to produce more accurate plans —your enhanced analytical capabilities allow employees to better predict business results and also anticipate market changes rather than reacting to them.

- *Superiority in Plan.* With superior planning capabilities, you have attained the Power to Compete. We now recommend that you increase your Monitor capabilities to communicate plans, budgets, and forecasts more broadly through strategy maps and scorecards. On the planning side, look at driver-based planning to increase efficiencies of the planning process. Driver-based planning should further the adoption of your planning capabilities throughout the company as, implemented well, it should simplify contributions.

Stage Guidance In reviewing Figure 6.2, notice that only two stages require scores of strong across all three capabilities—the Power to Compete and the Culture of Performance.

Companies that are strong across all three capabilities but superior in none (3, 3, 3), should first develop out their Monitor capability to the Execute on Strategy stage requirements. The same guidance is provided for companies with superior analytic capabilities. Companies that already have superior monitoring skills should focus on developing their planning capabilities to achieve the Power to Compete. Organizations that have already achieved superior planning skills, however, should target the Execute on Strategy stage to better leverage their existing planning skills.

CONCLUSION

As we noted in the Preface, we wrote this book with three particular messages in mind:

1. People drive performance — enabling more people across the enterprise can increase competitive advantage
2. There are 3 capabilities to effectively manage performance: Monitor, Analyze and Plan
3. Organizations with these capabilities can experience Six Stages of Performance Management Value

We have shared the details of the Culture of Performance model (Figure 6.1), describing the six stages and explaining the combination of MAP capabilities needed to achieve each. We have also discussed the guiding principles organizations follow to attain these capabilities, as well as detailed the specific skills and assets organizations need to develop.

We hope you now have a frame of reference to understand where you are on your journey to a Culture of Performance, and a framework for developing your capabilities to get there faster.

As a companion website to this book, the authors have created *www.cultureofperformance.com,* a home for individuals and organizations seeking to develop competitive advantage with the Culture of Performance methodology. There you will find resources and tools for developing a Culture of Performance, including best practices from a community of leading practitioners.

NOTES

1. Jim Collins, *Good to Great: Why Some Companies Make the Leap . . . and Others Don't* (New York: Harper Collins, 2001).
2. Also available online at www.cultureofperformance.com.
3. Anonymous.

Index